AF477707

Post-Communist Economies and
Western Trade Discrimination

Political Evolution and Institutional Change

Bo Rothstein and Sven Steinmo, editors

Exploring the dynamic relationships among political institutions, attitudes, behaviors, and outcomes, this series is problem-driven and pluralistic in methodology. It examines the evolution of governance, public policy, and political economy in different national and historical contexts.

It will explore social dilemmas, such as collective action problems, and enhance understanding of how political outcomes result from the interaction among political ideas—including values, beliefs or social norms-institutions, and interests. It will promote cutting-edge work in historical institutionalism, rational choice and game theory, and the processes of institutional change and/or evolutionary models of political history.

Post-Communist Economies and Western Trade Discrimination: Are NMEs Our Enemies?

Cynthia M. Horne

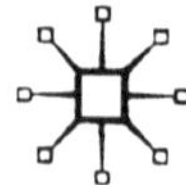

First published in 2006 by
PALGRAVE MACMILLAN™
175 Fifth Avenue, New York, N.Y. 10010 and
Houndmills, Basingstoke, Hampshire, England RG21 6XS
Companies and representatives throughout the world.

PALGRAVE MACMILLAN is the global academic imprint of the Palgrave Macmillan division of St. Martin's Press, LLC and of Palgrave Macmillan Ltd. Macmillan® is a registered trademark in the United States, United Kingdom and other countries. Palgrave is a registered trademark in the European Union and other countries.

ISBN-13: 978–1–4039–7451–8
ISBN-10: 1–4039–7451–9

Library of Congress Cataloging-in-Publication Data is available from the Library of Congress.

A catalogue record for this book is available from the British Library.

Design by Newgen Imaging Systems (P) Ltd., Chennai, India.

First edition: November 2006

10 9 8 7 6 5 4 3 2 1

Printed in the United States of America.

CONTENTS

LIST OF TABLES

LIST OF FIGURES

ACKNOWLEDGMENTS

The idea for this book started more than ten years ago. At that time the entire world was transfixed by the start of the political and economic transitions in the former Soviet bloc, and I was no exception. I was intrigued by trade as a vehicle for international development, and perplexed about any impediments that the former Soviet bloc faced achieving this goal. As such, I was captured by the urge to participate in the international policy community's efforts to facilitate the economic transformations in Eastern Europe and the former Soviet Union. So I put this project on a shelf, and returned to it only several years later. After dusting off the initial idea and presenting it in an incredibly passionate yet completely undisciplined form, I was encouraged to take my puzzle—about the cause of continuing Western trade protection against post-Communist economies—and systematically investigate it. I owe a tremendous intellectual debt to Margaret Levi not only for helping me to develop the analytical and theoretical tools to investigate my puzzle, but for also ensuring that I actually used those tools in an intellectually rigorous way. Both her encouragement as well as her corrections challenged me to work harder. I have not figured out a way to thank her appropriately for all her untold personal and intellectual support.

I am especially grateful to James Caporaso for his skepticism at critical stages in the drafting of the initial manuscript. Jim's simple but precise questions—"but what is the puzzle?" and "how can you measure that?"—sent me back to the drawing board more than once. The project is much better as a result. Anthony Gill walked me through countless permutations of variable conceptualization and operationalization. His tutelage, advice, and patience were invaluable in the initial project design and implementation. Bryan Jones unlocked a new theoretical door for me. For introducing me to the beauty and frustration of evolutionary psychology and the behavioral theory of organizations, I am quite indebted.

I have been very grateful to have colleagues and friends agree to read parts of the manuscript at different points in time. I am so thankful that they have been willing to suspend their disbelief that anti-dumping trade remedy laws were *in fact* fabulously interesting, and actually share my interest if not my passion for this issue. I am especially thankful to Dave Brockington, Deborah Elms, Mary Alice Haddad, Joseph Jupille, and Jason Brayden for their generous comments and encouragement. On the final stages of this project I was lucky enough to meet a new colleague who lent a fresh eye and thoughtful perspective. I would like to thank Eric Smith for his practical advice and indulgent ear. I have presented various incarnations of this project at conferences, including the American Political Science Association conference and the International Studies Association Conference, as well as several retreats organized by the *Society for Comparative Research/Center for Comparative Social Analysis* under the guidance of Ivan Szelenyi. I am most appreciative for the thoughtful comments and criticisms I have gotten from colleagues in these various fora. Despite all the feedback and assistance from others, I am well aware of the flaws in this project. I accept full responsibility for any and all errors that remain.

I benefited from fellowships and grants that supported different phases of the research for this project. The University of Washington's research support helped fund part of the fieldwork in Washington, DC. I am most grateful for the resident research fellowship support provided by the Max-Planck-Institut für Gesellschaftsforschung in Köln during the European research component of this project. Fritz Scharpf's helpful advice was particularly appreciated. Most recently the summer research grant from Seton Hall University helped me to update and improve the final manuscript.

There is one person who has been with me from the initial idea through the arduous, disappointing, thrilling, exhausting, enlightening, frustrating, and self-actualizing journey that was this book. Your support has meant everything to me. You know who you are. Thank you.

CHAPTER ONE

Introduction: Transitions and Trade

Pity the unpopular Russians. In July [2000], Mexico elects its first president from outside the ruling party; The Economist magazine labels it a "real democracy." Russia elects a president from the political opposition in 1991, then holds no fewer than five competitive generally free national elections in the following years; The Economist calls it a "phony democracy." Colombia has a problem with organized crime, and Washington gives its government $1.3 billion to help fight the drug lords. Russia also has a problem with organized crime, and American politicians sternly lecture Moscow not to expect any more aid until it cleans up its act. An undercover U.S. operation finds several Mexican banks laundering drug money in the United States, and Washington apologizes to the Mexicans for conducting sting operations on their territory. An American bank allegedly launders money for Russian organized criminals, and a leading senator accuses the Russian government of being "the worlds most virulent kleptocracy." When the Asian crisis scares investors away from the Brazilian market and the real collapses, commentators declare it a bump in the road. When the Asian crisis scared foreign investors away from the Russian market and the ruble collapses, commentators declare the crash proof of the failure of liberal economic reform in Russia. . . . As readers of the Western press know, there are no business men in Russia only mafiosi; no democrats, only corrupt politicians; no citizens, only an impoverished, nationalistic mass. Members of the Russian middle class are often discouraged to learn, upon picking up Western papers, that they do not yet exist.
    —Daniel Treisman, 2000. "Blaming Russia First."
Foreign Affairs, 79:6, pp. 146–7.

Introduction

Trade is critical to the success of the economic and political reforms in post-Communist economies. "Free trade" with the West is vital as both a source of revenue and a conduit of market discipline to former centrally planned industries. The U.S. Department of Commerce has stated that "international trade helps ensure political stability in foreign nations, promotes better international understanding and higher standards of living, and improves bilateral relations through the interchange of products, ideas, and culture" (U.S. Department of Commerce 2000a). Capitalist and democratic institutions are assumed to be mutually reinforcing. The West's promotion of economic development and international trade in transitional economies is therefore presumed to have positive spillover effects on their political systems, thereby aiding in the process of democratization (Haggard and Kaufman 1995; Lipset 1994; Przeworski 1985, 1991; Rueschmeyer, Stephens, and Stephens 1992). Moreover, the ability of post-Communist countries to participate in the international political economy is a good indicator of the depth and scope of their transitions.

Official American and European Union (EU) policies have stressed an explicit role for trade in supporting the political and economic reform efforts in Central and Eastern Europe, the former Soviet Union, and China. Starting in the early 1990s, the normalization of economic and trade relations with non-market economies has been a recurrent theme in American foreign policy (Bush 1990; Clinton 1995; U.S. Department of Commerce 2000b). While Vice President, Al Gore proclaimed, "Trade not aid [is] the ultimate guarantor of economic growth in the former Soviet Union" (Gore 1995). As the European Union's Chief Trade Negotiator, Sir Leon Brittan, stated, "Global integration through trade and investment are [*sic*] essential to achieving increased prosperity, sustainable economic growth and social security in the form of job creation . . . A liberal trade regime is a fundamental element in the creation of a cooperative, inclusive society both within Russia, and in Russia's relations with the rest of the world" (Brittan 1997a). The West understands that post-Communist societies rely on open trade with the international system in order to support their domestic reform efforts.

Unfortunately for post-Communist countries, access to Western markets has not been unfettered. Trade is one of those issue areas in which perceptions about the other affect the nature of the exchange relationship. Beliefs about the nature of the trading partner influence the way trade is framed, beneficial or harmful, and can affect the level and intensity of trade protection. For example, Russia and other economies in transition are not simply developing countries according to the West, but former Communist developing countries. The Communist institutional legacy, with all its economic, strategic, social, and political connotations, has continued to affect the way these countries have been perceived by others. The epigraph of this chapter illustrates several issue areas in which Russian actions or conditions have been framed more negatively than the same actions or conditions in other developing countries. This includes the implementation of Western trade policy toward post-Communist societies in the post–cold war period, specifically through the period of this study 2004.

During the cold war, the United States and the countries of the European Union presumed that Communist countries or so called non-market economies (NMEs) posed an economic threat, and devised special trade rules to address this perceived threat (see table 1.1). The term non-market economy is both a political and an economic designation reflecting the cold war beliefs behind it. The official U.S. definition refers to "any foreign country that the administering authority determines does not operate on market principles of cost or pricing structures, so that sales of merchandise in such a country do not reflect the fair value of the merchandise" (U.S. Department of Commerce 1988). However, in practice NME refers only to countries that were or are Communist. Moreover it only refers to countries that were actively part of Soviet or Chinese alliance structures.[1]

The special NME designation allowed the United States and EU to apply different trade rules to Poland, Russia, and China than to developing countries like Bangladesh, Hong Kong, or Brazil. While designed for cold war trade, the NME designation and different rules continued into the post–cold war period. These different rules, primarily anti-dumping trade remedy laws, resulted in more restrictive treatment of non-market economy exports than those from other countries. I argue that this "special" or differential treatment resulted in trade

Table 1.1 Traditional List of Non-Market Economies

Albania	Bulgaria	China	Czech Republic	Hungary
Poland	Romania	Slovakia	Armenia	Azerbaijan
Belarus	Estonia	Georgia	Latvia	Lithuania
Kazakhstan	Kyrgyzstan	Moldova	Russia	Tajikistan
Turkmenistan	Ukraine	Uzbekistan	Vietnam	

Note: In 1991, the Soviet Union was removed and its 15 member states were added. Starting in 1993, changes were made to this list.

discrimination. The title of this project asks are NMEs (non-market economies) our enemies? According to the words and deeds of both the U.S. Department of Commerce and the European Commission's Trade Policy Directorate with respect to trade policy, the answer has been yes.[2]

This book questions why the U.S. and EU have continued to differentiate trade with NMEs from trade with other developing countries, resulting in not only differential but discriminatory treatment. Differential treatment during the cold war might be predicted and expected, but not in the post–cold war period necessarily. The manner in which the United States and European Union have continued to implement their trade laws toward these countries is puzzling. Since the end of the cold war, the United States and European Union have each made substantive changes to their anti-dumping laws in order to make the treatment of imports from non-market economies more "fair." In several key areas, the formal laws have changed but they have been administered in such as way as to negate or circumvent the changes. In essence, there has been outcome stasis in the face of institutional change, resulting in a continuation of high levels of trade protection. In other cases there have been fledgling attempts to change not only the formal laws but the manner in which they were implemented. Therefore the second order question this book poses is why have changes to the formal trade rules as applied to NMEs been implemented in some but not most cases? Specifically, what caused outcome stasis in terms of the implementation of trade rules, despite the formal rule changes and improvements to the trade laws?

To address these questions, I establish a causal role for cold war beliefs in the implementation of Western trade policies toward NMEs over the period 1980–2004. I present a model of belief stasis and belief change in order to understand how beliefs matter and under what conditions they change. First, I demonstrate how beliefs function as information discounters. By discounting new information that is contrary to the original cold war belief, beliefs minimize or obviate changes in policy outcomes. The information discounting effect of beliefs helps to explain why formal trade rules can change, but the policy outcomes might remain the same.

Second, I address how and under what conditions beliefs are likely to change, resulting in commensurate changes in policy outcomes. While belief stasis may impede the actual implementation of formal rule change for some time, anachronistic beliefs cannot impede policy change indefinitely. I examine under what conditions institutional safeguards, iterated exchanges between actors, and information flows affect belief change.

To understand the mechanism by which beliefs discount new information, I consider the certainty with which the belief is held. Beliefs held with greater certainty will discount more information than beliefs held with less certainty. Beliefs held with less certainty will be the first to change, given changes in information and evidence. As such, introducing the concept of belief certainty into discussions about belief stasis and belief change helps to present a unifying logic between the two. Additionally, introducing belief certainty into models of how beliefs affect decision making and policy outcomes helps to explain why the United States and EU have self-initiated formal rule changes to their trade remedy laws, yet failed to implement them in practice.

Anti-Dumping Laws and Free Trade

To examine patterns of Western trade protection against post-Communist economies, one must investigate anti-dumping trade remedy laws. They are the only trade remedy law, outside of tariffs, that can be applied to non-market economies. Anti-dumping laws are trade remedy regulations, both sanctioned and monitored by the World Trade Organization (WTO), which are designed to redress trade at less than fair value or "normal value." According to Article 2.1 of the World Trade Organization (WTO) Anti-Dumping Agreement (Article VI, Section 1 of the General Agreement on Tariffs and Trade (GATT)) dumping is defined as:

> A product is considered as being dumped, i.e. introduced into the commerce of another country at less than its normal value, if the export price of the product exported from one country to another is less than the comparable price, in the ordinary course of trade, for the like product when destined for consumption in the exporting country." (World Trade Organization 1994)[3]

This law legally empowers countries to apply dumping duties (a type of tariff or tax) to imports that are selling at "less than normal value" in order to protect domestic firms from unfair pricing practices. Anti-dumping laws are quasi-legal procedures, with strict rules and guidelines specifying the economic calculations of normal value. However, there are some differences in the way each country has chosen to interpret the GATT definition of dumping and apply the trade regulations. Hence, this project compares the United States and European Union's application of anti-dumping laws in order to draw out differences and similarities in their treatment of NMEs.

Dumping determinations rest on what is considered fair value. The method of calculating fair value is taken up in some detail later in the book, but a brief summary of how fair value determinations are made highlights the different treatment of non-market economies from other countries. In a typical U.S. anti-dumping case, such as pencils from India, the United States would compare the import price of pencils with the average price for pencils sold in the domestic Indian market. If the price of pencils coming into the United States was substantially lower than the price of pencils sold in India, then the Indian firm(s) could be investigated for dumping.

In a case involving pencils from China, or any other NME, the United States would not use the average price of pencils sold in the Chinese market as a point of comparison. Since prices in Communist countries are assumed to be centrally planned and therefore not reflective of the forces of supply and demand, the United States would disregard the Chinese price information. Instead the United States would determine the factor inputs used in the construction of pencils: wood, lead, eraser, metal, labor, energy, etc. It would value these factor inputs in a comparable market economy, in the case of China this might be India, Indonesia, or Thailand. It would then sum up the average price for each of the factor inputs, add a profit margin on top, and compare this constructed price to the price of pencils imported into the United States from China. If the constructed price was more than the imported price, China could be accused of dumping. It should come as little surprise that the constructed value almost always results in dumping.[4]

Anti-dumping cases are interesting to examine for a number of reasons. First, they are one of the most, if not the most, important and widely used trade remedy law in the international system (O'Grady 2004; Economist 1999; Europe Information Service 2000c; Sanger 1998). Developing countries, like India, Brazil, and Taiwan, have literally taken a page from developed countries' books by copying their anti-dumping laws and liberally applying them (O'Grady 2004, 50; Economist 2000; Tharakan 1999). Anti-dumping laws have been called the "cruise missiles of protection, that by flying low to the ground have escaped detection as protection by the conventional radar systems" (Staiger and Wolak 1994a, 104). The impact of anti-dumping cases on economic welfare is great. In 1995, the U.S. International Trade Commission estimated that removing anti-dumping orders would produce an economy-wide welfare gain of $1.6 billion (U.S. International

Trade Commission 1995). An EU study calculated that trade protection, anti-dumping being the most widely used variety, costs the European Union 6–7 percent of its gross domestic product per year (Messerlin 2001).

Second, anti-dumping cases are the least likely trade cases to find systematic international political patterns of trade protection (Finger, Hall, and Nelson 1982). Anti-dumping rules have been regularized, legalized, and formalized in such a way as to remove most opportunity for political manipulation. They are quasi-judicial in their highly legalistic structures, with strict rules and guidelines that conform to WTO standards. In the United States, the agencies charged with administering the anti-dumping laws were intentionally insulated from the pressures of Congress and special interest groups in order to depoliticize their application (Anderson 1993; Moore 1992). Even the U.S. President cannot legally override anti-dumping duties on policy grounds (Winters, Rubin, and Bond 1998). In the European Union, anti-dumping laws and practices constitute a form of "secondary legislation" confirmed by European Court of Justice decisions. Speaking on behalf of the European Commission's Directorate General for Trade, Patrick Laurent explained, "EU legislation on anti-dumping is a strict legal system which does not give very much room for discretion by the Commission when judging the various aspects of the cases" (Laurent 1996).

The strict domestic rules and guidelines combined with the standards imposed by the WTO Agreement on anti-dumping have removed much of the room for political considerations in anti-dumping determinations. This "depoliticized" legal structure of anti-dumping laws affords them a sense of legitimacy not enjoyed by other more politically malleable trade policies, like Section 301, Super 301 legislation, tariffs, and the escape clause. Other authors have confirmed that political factors cannot explain anti-dumping use (Lott 1995). Finger argues that international political influences do not show up as significant and are "most soundly rejected" (Finger, Hall, and Nelson 1982, 459). Therefore, anti-dumping laws are the least likely form of trade protection for international political considerations, such as hostile beliefs about the intentions of post-Communist countries, to systematically affect the interpretation and implementation of trade laws.

Third, anti-dumping laws have been liberally applied to trade with non-market economies. They have a substantial trade deterrent effect as well, and have risen to the level of "high politics" in negotiations between former Communist economies and the West. There has been a generalized feeling of discontent among trade officials in Central and Eastern Europe, the former Soviet Union, and China at what they perceived as the undermining of their export performance by anti-dumping actions and "discriminatory trade policies" (Chernomyrdin 1997; Organisation for Economic Co-operation and Development 1994, 1996).[5] These countries have been particularly upset at their continued differential labeling, marking them as special trade threats (BBC Worldwide Monitoring 2004; Cheng 2004b; China Daily 1999; ITAR-TASS 2000; Moscow News 2001; Russian Economic News 1999a; Russian Economic News 1999b).

Non-market economies have also been upset about the volume of cases filed against them. Cases span a range of products and sectors, including low, medium, and high value-added commodities. The NME label has made the countries easy targets for anti-dumping suits because of the near guaranteed success of obtaining trade protection. "Some 25 years after it launched market oriented reforms, China has become the world's largest anti-dumping target—largely because it has been labeled a non-market economy" (Financial Times Information 2004). One in every seven anti-dumping cases initiated world wide is against China (Agence France Presse 2004). As of June 2000, Ukraine was the subject of more than 100 anti-dumping investigations across 26 commodity groups (Interfax News Agency 2001b). This is a substantial number of cases. To put it in perspective, between 1980–1999 Japan was the subject of a total of 85 U.S. anti-dumping trade cases (U.S. International Trade Commission 2000). The number of active cases pending against Ukraine in one year, albeit from several countries, sharply demonstrates the level of trade protection faced by NMEs in general.

The volume of trade cases has not gone unrecognized by international institutions. In Spring 2001, the European Bank for Reconstruction and Development explicitly condemned the United States and European Union's use of anti-dumping protection against Russian products, charging them with unfair methods of administering the laws (Moscow Times 2001). Anti-dumping has become such a politically charged issue that it was carefully excluded from the Association Agreements signed between the EU and several East European countries, and from China's World Trade Organization membership negotiations. Anti-dumping laws have diplomatic as well as trade implications, and are of importance to both the West and the former Communist bloc.

Fourth, the value of foregone trade to NMEs as a result of anti-dumping cases has been large. It was estimated that anti-dumping duties cost Russia between $500 million and $1.3 billion annually (Clark 2002a; Granik 2002). Between 1998 and 2000, Russian steel producers incurred industry losses in excess of $1.5 billion due to the more than

50 anti-dumping investigations launched against them by various countries (Interfax News Agency 2001a). In addition, the duties resulting from Chinese anti-dumping investigations have regularly exceeded 100 percent of the value of imports from China (Santos and Vakerics 1994). As of October 2003, it was estimated that anti-dumping measures had cost China a cumulated total of $16 billion (Bezlova 2004). Ukraine estimated a $300 million negative impact on businesses as a result of anti-dumping measures using the differential NME treatment (Financial Times, Information 2006).

These figures underestimate the actual cost to NMEs in terms of dumping duties and deterred trade. Anti-dumping laws have a "harassment effect" (Finger and Murray 1990; Prusa 1992; Staiger and Wolak 1994b). The mere filing of a case is often enough to scare foreign firms into cutting exports or raising prices. Many non-market economies have limited the quantity or composition of their exports to the West because they feared dumping accusations and the ensuing trade reprisals. As a result, there is no way to calculate the total cost of anti-dumping laws to non-market economies because it is difficult to put a dollar amount on the trade deterring effects. Given the debt burdens of these countries, this forgone trade revenue has substantial economic effects.

Fifth, membership in international organizations like the World Trade Organization did not alter the treatment of these countries as non-market economies under Western anti-dumping laws. In what appears to be a violation of WTO statutes, membership in the WTO has not precluded the continued use of special NME treatment. Although China (2001), Moldova (2001), Kyrgyzstan (1998), Georgia (2000), and Armenia (2003) were WTO members, all were still classified as non-market economies and treated as such under Western anti-dumping laws (World Trade Organization 2004). To become a member of the WTO one has to be a "market economy." Moreover, once any WTO member country treats another country (member or non-member) as a market economy in an anti-dumping investigation, then that country must be treated as a market economy by all countries. India intentionally reclassified Russia as a market economy, and Singapore, Malaysia, Thailand, and New Zealand recognized China as a market economy in order to force the issue of market/non-market status for the implementation of anti-dumping laws (Asia Pulse 2003, 2004). In violation of this statute, the United States and the European Union continued to treat these countries as NMEs. International institutional affiliations are supposed to improve the fairness of the application of trade remedy laws; however this does not appear to hold consistently in the case of NMEs.

In sum, anti-dumping laws have important policy implications for the West and non-market economies. They have posed substantial impediments to the integration of non-market economies into the international political economy, and entailed sizable economic costs. They are also the least likely case for political manipulation and therefore provide a particularly rigorous test of a hypothesis looking at a causal impact of beliefs on trade policy.

Difference Results in Discrimination

One cannot summarily conclude discrimination from differential treatment. If non-market economies have been discriminated against by the United States and European Union, this must be demonstrated. A 1998 World Bank study reviewing the application of U.S. and EU unfair trade laws to NMEs concluded that their treatment was fair, albeit different from other types of developing countries (Ehrenhaft et al. 1997). However, I prove this difference amounts to discrimination. The difference in adjudication of non-market economies' anti-dumping cases resulted in more onerous information requirements, less transparency, and more disregard for the market conditions operating in these economies than in cases involving similarly situated developing countries. This different treatment resulted in higher levels of trade protection against non-market economies.

Some figures will illustrate the magnitude of the trade protection. From 1980 to 2004 the United States initiated more than 200 cases and the European Union initiated more than 350 anti-dumping cases against imports from NMEs or former NMEs.[6] This is a substantial volume of cases in both relative and absolute terms. For example, this constituted approximately 40 percent of all European Union anti-dumping cases and approximately 25 percent of all U.S. anti-dumping cases. These figures are especially high considering that NME imports accounted for an average of 5 percent of total U.S. imports and approximately $5\frac{1}{2}$ percent of total EU imports. Looking at the post–cold war period, alone, NMEs comprised 40 percent of EU anti-dumping cases but an average of 6.8 percent of imports. For the United States, NMEs comprised 25 percent of anti-dumping cases and 8 percent of imports. While imports from NMEs to the West have been steadily rising, during this period there was no apparent relationship between change in import volume and anti-dumping cases, as evidenced in figure 1.1 (United States) and figure 1.2 (EU).[7]

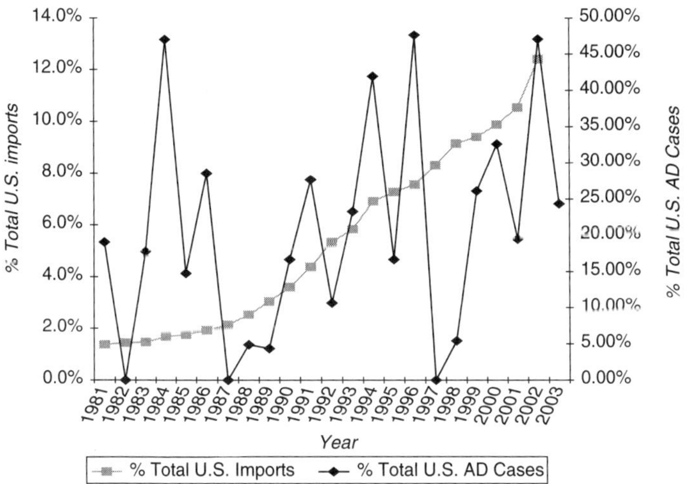

Figure 1.1   U.S. Imports Compared to Anti-dumping Cases, Non-Market Economies, 1981–2003

Note: 1980 data is omitted because NMEs accounted for 100% of cases in that year. Including 1980 skews the perspective of the graph.

Sources: International Monetary Fund, *IMF Direction of Trade Statistics Yearbook*, 1980–2003; and U.S. Department of Commerce, Import Administration, *Anti-dumping and Countervailing Duty Petitions Filed Since January 1, 1980*, <www.ita.dov.gov/import_admin/records/stats/>.

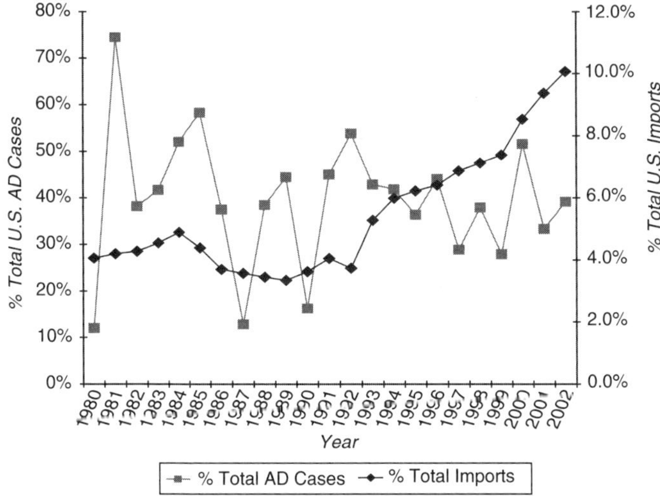

Figure 1.2   EU Imports Compared to Anti-dumping Cases, Non-Market Economies, 1980–2002

Sources: International Monetary Fund, *IMF Direction of Trade Statistics Yearbook*, 1980–2003; and European Commission, *Annual Report from the Commission to the European Parliament on the Community's Anti-Dumping and Anti-Subsidy Activities*, 1983–2005.

The relationship between NME trade volume and levels of trade protection is puzzling when compared to the relative patterns of trade volume and trade protection against other countries. Traditional trade theories roughly predict a direct positive relationship between trade volume and trade protection. As country A exports more goods to country B, the probability of country B using trade protection against country A increases. Graphed together, import volumes and import protection should demonstrate upward sloping regression lines.

The United Stated and EU have grouped their trading partners into country aggregates: such as Big Emerging Markets, Asian Newly Industrialized Countries, Other Asian Countries, European Countries, South American countries, to name a few.[8] This allows for a comparison of import volumes and levels of protection across the regional aggregates. Figures 1.3 and 1.4 demonstrate that for both the EU and the United States, there is a direct positive relationship between import volume and import protection. As predicted, as the percentage of total imports from country group A increases, the percentage of anti-dumping cases initiated against country group A also increases. This is the case for all country groupings except NMEs. In both figures, the linear regression lines plotting the ratio of percentage total anti-dumping cases to percentage total imports are slightly negative sloping for non-market economies. This unusual trade pattern is puzzling. It is especially puzzling given that both the United States and the EU evidenced the same unusual pattern of trade protection against non-market economies alone.

Not only is the pattern of trade protection against a non-market economies unusual relative to import volumes, but it is also unusual in terms of the shear magnitude of the trade protection. Figures 1.5 and 1.6 compare the percentage total of anti-dumping cases initiated against a certain country or country groupings over the past 20 years. NMEs have been consistently subjected to more anti-dumping cases than other countries, and the average percentage of anti-dumping cases against NMEs has been greater than the percentage of cases initiated against other countries for most years.

NMEs export a variety of products to the United States and European Union. Export profiles included low value-added products, such as lumber and minerals, medium value-added products, such as leather purses and iron pipe, and high value-added products, such as color TVs and microwave ovens. Non-market economies did not have an unusual concentration in a single sector or a few sectors, which might account for the especially high levels of trade protection. For example, figure 1.7 presents a visual breakdown by sector of all EU anti-dumping cases over a 12-year period. Figure 1.8 presents only EU imports from NMEs by

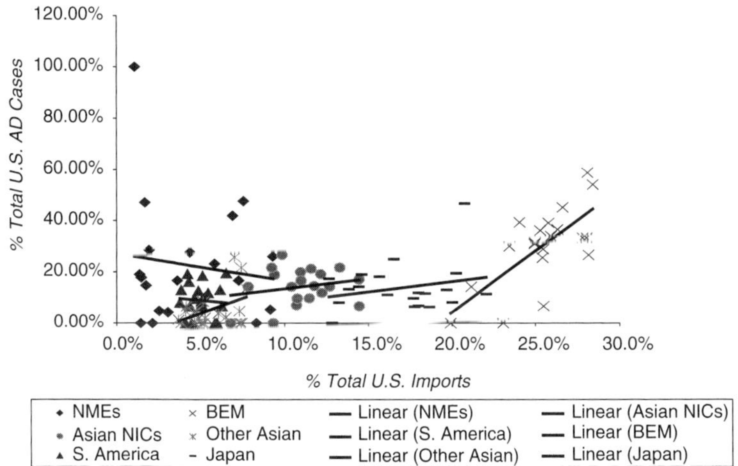

Figure 1.3 Ratio of Imports to AD Cases—Cross Regional Comparison, U.S. Trade Data, 1980–2002

Sources: International Monetary Fund, *IMF Direction of Trade Statistics Yearbook*, 1980–2003; and U.S. Department of Commerce. International Trade Administration, Anti-Dumping and Countervailing Duty Petitions Filed Since January 1, 1980, <www.ita.doc.gov/import_admin/records/stats/>.

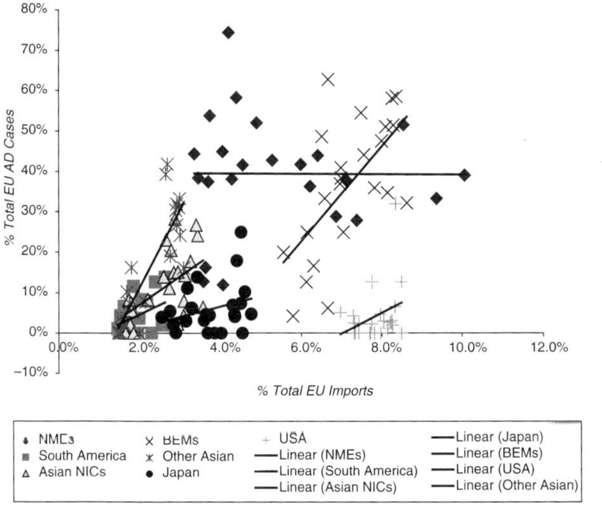

Figure 1.4 Ratio of Imports to AD Cases—Cross Regional Comparison, EU Trade Data 1980–2002

Sources: International Monetary Fund, IMF Direction of Trade Statistics Yearbook, 1980–2005; and European Commission, *Annual Report from the Commission to the European Parliament on the Community's Anti-Dumping and Anti-Subsidy Activities*, 1983–2005.

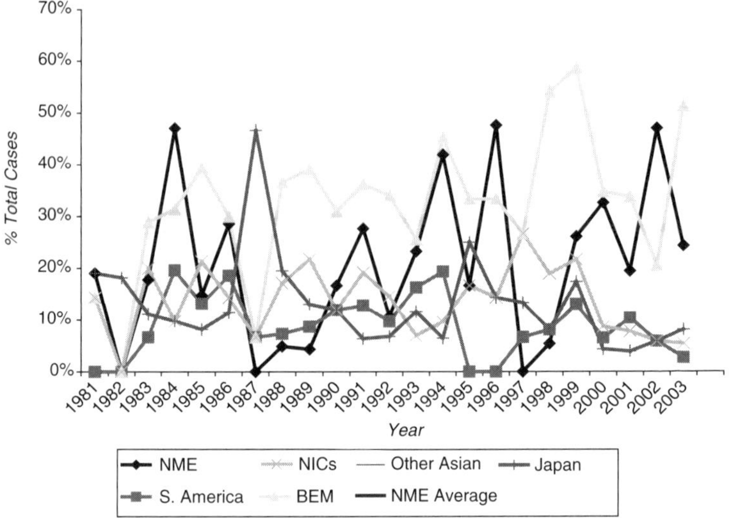

Figure 1.5 Cross Group Comparison of U.S. Anti-dumping Cases, 1981–2003

Note: 1980 data is omitted because NMEs accounted for 100% of cases in that year. This skews the scale of the graph, minimizing variation across time.

Sources: U.S. Department of Commerce, International Trade Administration, Anti-dumping and Countervailing Duty Cases Initiated since January 1, 1900. <www.ia.ita.doc.gov/stats/pdf-init.html>, and *Federal Register*, 1981–2004

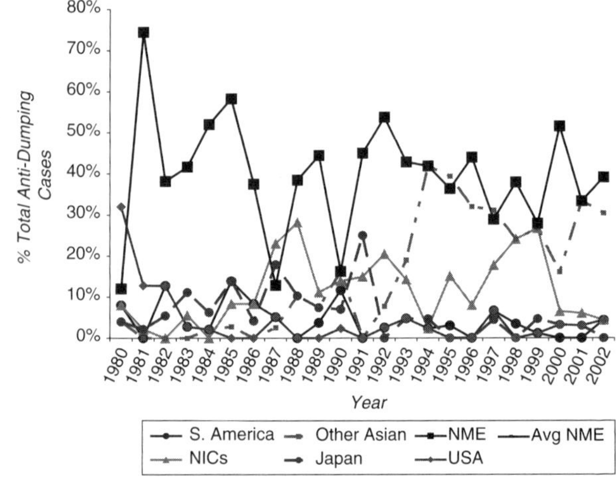

Figure 1.6 Cross Group Comparison of EU Anti-dumping Cases, 1980–2002

Sources: European Commission, Annual Report from the Commission to the European Parliament on the Community's Anti-dumping and Anti-subsidy Activities, 1983–2005.

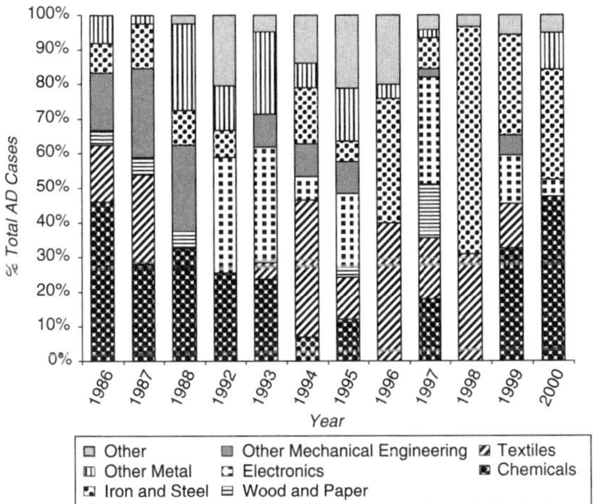

Figure 1.7   EU Anti-dumping and Anti-subsidy Cases Initiated by Sector

Note: European Commission places cases in respective categories.

Sources: The European Commission, 1983–2001. *Annual Report from the Commission to the European Parliament on the Community's Anti-dumping and Anti-subsidy Activities*. Brussels: European Commission.

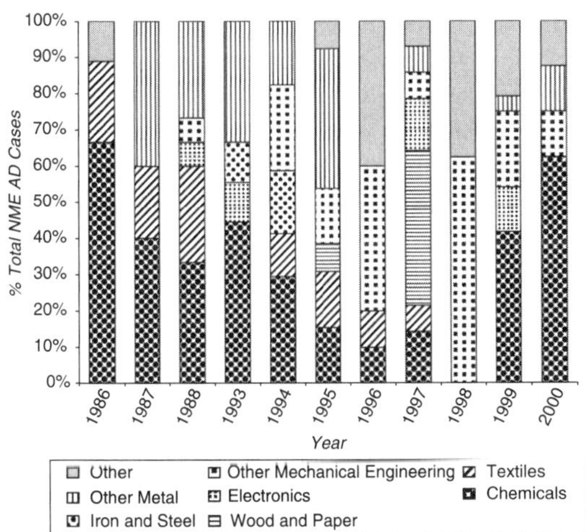

Figure 1.8   EU Anti-dumping Cases against NMEs by Sector

Note: Author placed cases in respective categories.

Sources: The European Commission, 1983–2001. *Annual Report from the Commission to the European* Parliament on the Community's Anti-dumping and Anti-subsidy Activities. Brussels: European Commission.

sector. A comparison of the two figures shows that the sector composition of NME trade was not unusual, and certainly not different enough from the general EU sector distribution of trade to explain the unusual pattern of trade protection against NMEs. This will be more rigorously tested using U.S. anti-dumping cases in chapter three.

In sum, anti-dumping use against NMEs over the period 1980–2004 in both relative and absolute terms is puzzling. This preliminary evidence suggests that the treatment of NMEs was not just different, it was also discriminatory. To prove discrimination, one has to investigate the method by which the anti-dumping cases were administered. This is explored in later chapters. For now, the question remains, what explains the West's different pattern of trade protection against non-market economies? And why has the pattern been so different and so penalizing to NME exports as to manifest itself as trade discrimination?

Overview of the Book

To understand the continued use of discriminatory methods of administering anti-dumping laws to post-Communist economies, I examine how the relevant trade agencies in the United States and European Union actually interpreted and implemented the laws. In the case of the United States, this means an examination of the United States International Trade Administration within the Department of Commerce, and in the case of the European Union, the Directorate General in charge of Trade Policy (external economic relations) in the European Commission. If I am going to argue that lingering cold war beliefs have continued to impact trade policy in the post–cold war period, I must examine the trade agencies that held and reproduced these beliefs. These organizations are also in charge of policy assessment, initiate all rule changes, and are singularly tasked with implementation of the trade laws. Therefore, they are the primary agents in this project.

I review the use of anti-dumping laws against non-market economies by these trade agencies over more than 20 years (1980–2004), with an emphasis on the changes to the law since the end of the cold war. I examine the universe of anti-dumping cases against non-market economies in order to process trace the evolution of the laws and their changing application.[9]

The United States and European Union are two of the most frequent users of anti-dumping protection, and therefore provide substantial variation in terms of commodities and countries against which cases were initiated. In addition, showing that beliefs affected both the U.S. and EU's application of anti-dumping laws obviates the possibility that the lingering cold war beliefs were simply a function of isolated bureaucratic idiosyncrasy.

The various rule changes to the anti-dumping trade laws provide a direct comparison of outcome stasis in the face of policy change. I examine five such cases of formal rule change to the anti-dumping laws, comparing how the United States and EU have chosen to self initiate, interpret and implement each of these modifications. In different but consistent ways, these cases demonstrate the lingering effects of cold war beliefs on policy interpretation, as well as the manner in which beliefs about NMEs have begun to change.

By combining interviews, process tracing of legal cases, archival research of unpublished memoranda and correspondence, and observation of court hearings, I am able to elucidate how beliefs affected policy implementation and test how beliefs have started to change. Demonstrating a connection between the beliefs held by individual agents and the agency in which they worked involves examining both individual and agency level data sources. At the individual level, I use a combination of official and unofficial letters and policy memos from the trade agents, as well as interviews with policymakers. At the organizational level, I use the formal trade cases, the case law, the official trade law, and agency generated policy statements. Therefore, there will be a blending of the individual and organizational levels of analysis in order to demonstrate that the individuals were socialized to hold and implement the beliefs espoused by the agencies themselves. As such, I am able to triangulate the examination of beliefs using a variety of methods in order to show how ideational factors have affected the interpretation and implementation of trade remedy laws.

There are many alternative hypotheses possible when explaining or predicting patterns of trade protection. Therefore, before one can present a discursive argument about how and why beliefs about NMEs affected patterns of trade protection, one must address robust alternative theories of trade protection. As such, I review and test various traditional explanations of trade protection, such as interest group accounts, sector based explanations focused on the composition of export commodities, sensitive sector theories, and international economic explanations looking at changes in import volume and import penetration. Using an original large-N dataset, I quantitatively demonstrate that these traditional political economy explanations are inadequate to explain patterns of trade protection against non-market economies.

The remainder of this book is structured as follows. Chapter Two is the theoretical core of the project. In this chapter I develop a theory about belief stasis and belief change to explain Western patterns of trade protection against NMEs. Testable hypotheses are elucidated, to be applied later in the case study chapters. Chapter Three reviews traditional political economy explanations of trade protection, and derives and tests alternative hypotheses. Chapter Four provides an overview of anti-dumping laws, and reviews the structure and function of the agencies charged with administering the laws.

Chapters Five, Six, and Seven constitute the case study core of the book. In these chapters the five formal rule changes are examined. In each chapter the U.S. policy approach to NMEs is compared to the EU policy approach. In this way I am able to present a structured, focused comparison of Western trade policy toward non-market economies, illustrating both outcome stasis in the face of belief stasis, and outcome change in connection with fledgling belief change.

In the conclusion, I draw out some of the policy implications and theoretical implications of this study. Theoretically speaking, presenting a model in which informal constraints, such as beliefs, trump formal institutions, and rule changes, is an important contribution to the work being done by new institutionalists. Moreover, introducing belief certainty into decision making calculations permits more variation in the discussion of the causal role of beliefs. Thinking about the impact of ideational factors on decision making is important not only for trade policy, but might also provide more theoretical leverage over a host of domestic and international issues. Finally, in policy terms one needs to consider how Western trade practices might have affected the reform efforts of transitional economies. If creating economically self-sufficient, politically stable, internationally integrated post-Communist societies is the goal, the West must address if its policies have in fact been supporting or hindering this common objective.

A Logic of Belief Stasis and Belief Change

The great rule of conduct for use in regard to foreign nations is in extending our commercial relations to have with them as little *political* connections as possible . . . Harmony, liberal intercourse with all nations are recommended by policy, humanity, and interest. But even our commercial policy should hold an equal and impartial hand, neither seeking nor granting exclusive favors or preferences.

—George Washington (in Cooper 1987, 320).

Introduction

This chapter lays out a coherent logic of both belief stasis and belief change. It specifies the conditions under which static beliefs could become more dynamic. It also presents testable hypotheses with respect to how U.S. and EU beliefs regarding NMEs have affected the implementation of trade remedy laws. Traditional neoclassical economic accounts of trade policy focus on material interests, loosely defined, and ignore the role of ideas and beliefs (Caves, Frankel, and Jones 1990). These ideationally impoverished accounts of trade policy rob us of both predictive and explanatory capacity. I suggest that turning our attention to the role of beliefs and ideas may open up new ways of thinking about patterns of trade protection. In accordance with this goal, I present a belief based hypothesis both as a foil and a complement to more traditional political economy theories, reflecting the complex reality of trade policy.

What is a Belief?

Barner-Barry defines a belief as "an understanding about ourselves or the environment we regard as fact" (Barner-Barry 1990, 205). Modifying this definition slightly, I define beliefs as probabilistic understandings about something or someone that we regard as fact. Beliefs are supported by "what the holder of the belief considers is relevant or valid knowledge," which may include expectations and anticipations reflecting prevailing values and common understandings (Barner-Barry 1990, 205).[1]

This definition of beliefs differs from Converse's understanding of generalized world belief systems (Converse 1964). I am examining specific beliefs held by specialized agents in a given issue area. I focus on a belief that party A holds about party B in issue X. The belief could carry over into issues Y and Z, but does not necessarily have to. This definition is derived from the trust literature. For example, Hardin, Levi, and others examine relationships in which agent A (dis)trusts agent B to do X (something) (Hardin 1998; Levi 1998). Trust is fundamentally cognitive; it is a belief. "To trust or to distrust others is to have some *presumption* of knowledge about them" (Hardin 1998, 11, emphasis added). Therefore I draw heavily on the trust/distrust literature in developing my thoughts regarding the effect beliefs have on exchange relations.

In determining whether to believe someone with respect to issue X, I assume that the parties make rational calculations, given both information limitations and their own cognitive limitations (Simon 1955, 1985). Rational does not mean perfect information updating, or errorless judgments. As Simon has demonstrated, humans have cognitive limitations and are imperfect processors of information. Humans are prone to satisficing, not maximizing. This does not suggest irrational behavior on the part of decision makers though. Parties assess available information, knowing that there may be limitations to the veracity or scope of information, and make probabilistic assumptions about the nature of someone or something.

The belief is probabilistic because party A can hold the belief with greater or lesser certainty. This is similar to the trust literature's view of the probabilistic nature of trusting relations. In determining whether one will trust or not, one makes a probabilistic assessment about the interests, incentives, and capabilities of the other and decides whether to make oneself vulnerable (Coleman 1988; Gambetta 1988). Certainty levels vary based on assessments of factors related to the other. Party A can strongly believe that party B is trustworthy, can moderately believe that party B is trustworthy, or can weakly believe or doubt that party B is trustworthy with respect to issue X. The certainty or strength of the belief affects the nature of the relationships between the parties in the given issue area. In this project, I examine the role of beliefs in trade policy so the issue remains constant while the parties vary and therefore the intensity with which the belief is held vis-à-vis parties varies. In order to ascertain degrees of belief certainty between different actors, one must conceptualize beliefs in probabilistic terms.

My definition and use of beliefs in this project combines the notion of principled and causal beliefs.[2] Principled beliefs are normative criteria for distinguishing right from wrong, and serve as doctrinal guidelines for action (Goldstein and Keohane 1993, 9). Causal beliefs are beliefs about cause and effect relationships, consensually agreed upon and recognized by elites (10). Within the context of this project, Party A, in this case the West, believed that party B, in this case the Communist Bloc, was antagonistic and harmful. The assessment of the Communist Bloc by the West had an overt normative component. Communism was bad, and capitalism was good. Communist countries, and the Soviet Union specifically, constituted "the evil empire." The belief was causal as well. The West believed that exchange relations with Communist countries would disproportionately benefit Communist countries. Exchange would cause Communist countries to prosper and would cause harm to the West. The two presumptions are necessary in order to understand the mechanism by which the belief originated and was perpetuated. This is discussed in detail later in this chapter.

Logic of Belief Stasis

Once beliefs are formed, they are sticky, and somewhat resistant to direct change. "Beliefs are not easily altered through reasoned, dispassionate discussion of evidence" (Gerber and Green 1999, 191). There are various reasons that beliefs remain sticky. First, decision makers are not natural Bayesians, that is, they do not engage in timely information updating in order to change their responses to situations (Simon 1978, 9: Tetlock 1999). Second, people use rules of thumb, and other cognitive heuristics to help them make decisions in the face of complex and voluminous amounts of information (Barner-Barry 1990, 204; Stone and Schaffner 1988, Chapter 7). Relying on cognitive shortcuts and heuristics, such as preformed beliefs and decision making shortcuts, may involve ignoring contradictory information and therefore perpetuating belief stickiness (Tversky and Kahneman 1974). This does not mean that beliefs are irrational, or that they are affect driven. The origin of beliefs can be highly rational, based on the best possible maximization of options, given information limitations. Yet the rational origin of the belief might belie its somewhat anachronistic continued use, even after the empirical conditions that initially engendered it have changed.

Belief perseverance theory focuses on how the stickiness of beliefs can cause decision makers to systematically disregard new, contradictory information, in rendering policy decisions. Beliefs can be sticky if they are institutionalized into formal rules and procedures (Goldstein and Keohane 1993, 12). For example, Larson has used this to explain how foreign policy makers can maintain consistent belief structures even if they have to ignore or misinterpret new, relevant information to do so (Larson 1985, 40). Jervis used the concept of belief perseverance to explain why decision makers maintain hostile images of their adversaries in spite of contrary information (Jervis 1976, 68). "Cognitive mechanisms such as selective attention and biased assimilation of contradictory evidence buffer beliefs from refutation," thereby perpetuating the bad faith model of one's opponents (Tetlock 1998, 880). One assumes the worst of one's enemy and has difficulty changing beliefs and perceptions about him even when the enemy changes. This book on trade policy toward non-market economies evidences this propensity to maintain an adversarial image of the enemy and his intentions despite disconfirming information. However, it is different from the aforementioned studies because it does not take beliefs as static variables; it allows for some dynamism in the way beliefs affect outcomes.

Bryan Jones gets us closer to a dynamic understanding of the role of beliefs in the decision making process. He argues that both individuals and organizations engage in "disproportionate information processing" (Jones 2001, 9). By this he means that objective information or empirical "facts" might only be selectively assimilated due to the environmental constraints and cognitive limitations of the decision making organization. According to Jones,

> This [disproportionate information processing] implies that objective information is transformed in the process of thought. It involves the tendency of people to react differently to identical information depending on the context in which the information is presented. What is essentially identical information provokes different responses in situations that are similar in all major respects except the interpretation that decision makers have placed on the information. In one context, a bit of information is ignored. In another, it becomes meaningful and stimulates action. (Jones 2001, 9)

Jones does two things. First, he shows how disproportionate processing behaviors hold true for both individuals and organizations. Second, he is able to theorize and demonstrate that while beliefs may be sticky, they are not completely impervious to change. Jones has argued for the "episodic and disjointed manner" of belief change due to human's inherent adaptive tendencies (Jones 2001, 21). Others have also demonstrated how belief change tends to appear in punctuated or disjointed steps, rather than incrementally (George 1983; Nisbett and Ross 1980; North 2005). Thinking about belief change in terms of fits and starts is consistent with an understanding of the sticky nature of beliefs, while also allowing a possibility of dynamism.

Under what conditions do beliefs change? In this project I adapt Goldstein's notion of "layering" to understand the conditions under which beliefs will change (1993, 2).[3] I argue that institutionalized beliefs may impede the actual implementation of formal rule change for some time because of the discounting effect they have on new information. This discounting of new information does not mean that individuals or agencies are blinded from seeing or understanding the new information. Disconfirming evidence exists and is recognized, although it is discounted. The degree to which the new information will be discounted declines over time as additional disconfirming evidence amasses. The mounting disconfirming evidence as well as the declining certainty with which a belief is held will in fact cause an unsustainable tension between empirical reality and belief structures. At some critical tipping point, the layering of formal rule changes on top of a foundation of beliefs that are inconsistent with those formal rule changes will result in policy change, albeit incomplete policy change. Eventually a shift in the underlying belief structure will also be required. The nature of that change will be punctuated or episodic.

What causes a change in formal rules if beliefs discount new information? Given that disproportionate information processing has been defined as a tendency of individuals to react differently to identical information depending on the context, it is possible for individuals to initiate formal rule changes that may remain unimplemented by the organization in which the individual is a member. Different propensities to adapt to new information, different frames of reference, and different cognitive heuristics may cause some individuals to initiate innovative formal rule changes. Individual innovation is always possible, since one would not predict individuals would process all information the same way at the same rate. Individuals are not blinded by beliefs. Beliefs are filters through which some information is assimilated and other information is ignored. Different individual information discounting rates opens up the possibility of formal rule innovation in the face of overarching discordant organizational beliefs.

There is also a critical need to disaggregate the process of rule change from rule implementation. The initiation or even the enactment of a formal rule change is not synonymous with the acceptance of new, possibly belief disconfirming information. To signal the acceptance or adoption of a new set of principles or beliefs for action, rule change must be consistent with rule implementation. Therefore, in this book the two processes of rule change and rule implementation are separated in order to understand how beliefs affect the two processes differently. Rule implementation indicates a deeper level of belief change than that required for rule change.

Logic of Belief Change

The degree to which beliefs resist change or are amenable to change is partially a function of the certainty with which the belief is held, and partially a function of changes in information. In this way, degree of certainty acts as a discounting agent, with higher belief certainty minimizing the impact of information changes more than lower belief certainty. This section explores some of the ways that information processed by organizations can change, as well as some of the factors affecting organizational level assessments of belief certainty.[4]

First, in order to conceptualize belief certainty in predictable ways, I argue that certainty is an assessment that Party A makes about Party B with respect to issue area X. This means that belief certainty is specifically tied to two parties and an issue, not a generalized belief or value system. Belief certainty is a function of Party A's evaluation of the interests, incentives, and capabilities of Party B with respect to issue X. The belief certainty is not completely subjective, as it is objectively grounded in an assessment of the other's interests, incentives, and capabilities.

Belief certainty is probabilistic. It is a discount rate on a continuum from total certainty to total uncertainty, essentially a number between 0 and 1. Therefore the degree of belief certainty can be derived by examining the underlying factors affecting A's perception of B. If a belief is held with greater certainty, it will discount changes in information more than if it is held with lesser certainty. Strongly held beliefs will discount information changes and impede belief change. Therefore high belief certainty can result in policy stasis in the face of information changes.

Weakly held beliefs will still discount some information but will be less likely to impede belief change or outcome change. The belief change could be positive or negative. Party A's beliefs about Party B could improve or worsen based on changes to the empirical reality or information.

Taking a multidimensional concept like belief certainty and mapping it on a unidimensional continuum from high to low belief certainty implies that the parties are able to assign weights to the attributes and rank them accordingly. The ends of the continuum will be easier to map than the middle of the spectrum. However, the mid-range will be somewhat more difficult to map along a single dimension, and therefore may be more sensitive to changes in the weighting of the attributes, the framing of the issue, or the institutional context. I address this issue later in the chapter when I attempt to map NMEs' empirical dimensions on a single issue continuum.

Second, information changes can affect beliefs. Of course, new facts or changes in empirical conditions are primary causes of changes information. However, there are a number of factors that can change information, besides the addition of new facts. Exogenous shocks, institutions and institutional safeguards, iterated interaction, and a change in issue attentiveness are all possible sources of information change. I briefly touch upon these four sources of information change, highlighting the ones I pay particular attention to in this project.

First, exogenous shocks can shake the foundations of an idea and prompt belief change. During periods of crisis or change, novel if not always new ideas might become particularly salient (Hall 1989). For example, Goldstein discusses how people are most receptive to new information and ideas during periods of crisis when old methods are no longer working (Goldstein 1993, 13). Second, iterated interactions can help to change beliefs over time (Axelrod 1984; Axelrod and Keohane 1986, 230–238; Larson 1997, 240–247). Experimental economics has shown that beliefs can be changed if the actors engage in repeated play with rapid, unequivocal feedback regarding actions (Goldgeier and Tetlock 2001, 76).

Third, the creation of new institutions can promote belief change. By fostering credible commitments and enforcement mechanisms, institutions can facilitate information flows and promote interactions (Bates 1998; Greif 1998; Levi 1997; North 1990; Ostrom 1990). Institutions also lower transaction costs and decrease uncertainty, thereby facilitating more information flows (Keohane 1984, 89–95). By altering information flows, the beliefs of the parties involved can change.

Fourth, the attention an issue receives can affect information flows. Shifts in attentiveness to different underlying aspects of preferences can change the choices made by a decision maker, without actually changing his preferences (Simon 1978, 13; Simon 1985, 302). Because decision makers tend to process information serially, changing focus can alter information flows (Jones 1994, especially Chapter 3).

In sum, information changes are not only about changes in facts but also about changes in framing, attentiveness, and perception of facts. These information changes are discounted by the certainty of beliefs. A real change in beliefs and a concomitant change in policy will result when there is a change in belief certainty and/or a sufficiently large change in information. Thinking about beliefs in terms of degree of certainty offers insight into the unifying logic of belief stasis and belief change. Information changes might still result in belief stasis when there are high levels of belief certainty. With lower levels of belief certainty or higher levels of information change, belief change is possible. How beliefs persist and how they change can be reconciled under a unifying logic when one considers the size of the discounting factor of belief certainty.

Belief certainty is a new variable, not previously emphasized in comparative or international political economy literature. This project supports the ideational research agenda in international relations and comparative politics, and expands it by suggesting that while beliefs are sticky they do have an internal logic of change. It also contributes to the institutionalist research agenda by demonstrating the limitations of institutions to foster exchange relations in the face of informal constraints, such as beliefs and ideas.

Origins of the Cold War Belief System

The beliefs held by the Department of Commerce and the European Commission toward non-market economies with respect to trade policy were derived from the broader cold war belief system held by the West. The West's cold war belief system was grounded in strategic, institutional, and ideological reasons (Gaddis 1972; Paterson 1973; Rees 1967; Schlesinger 1967). First, the West looked upon Communist expansion as a direct threat to capitalism. The military capabilities and expansionary interests of the Sino-Soviet bloc, combined with a zero sum conceptualization of the international system, all worked to create a sense of a Communist strategic threat. Therefore on a strategic basis, it was rational for the West to develop a belief about antagonistic Communist interests.

Second, the Communist bloc had domestic economic and political institutions that appeared to threaten the West. Economically, a centrally planned economy was a threat to Western capitalism due to its ability to absorb short-term or sectoral losses for the overall good of the economy (Wilczynski 1969, 178–186). Competition from centrally planned firms might drive Western market oriented firms out of business. It was assumed that centrally planned economies enjoyed numerous unfair trade advantages, including: a Ministry of Foreign Trade that helped support and direct trade and exercised a monopoly on foreign trade; multiple exchange rates; domestic price controls; and government credit facilities (Gregory and Stuart 1990, Chapters 7–8, 163–250; Kornai 1992, 262–292 and 333–351; Murrell 1990, Chapter 3, 25–42). The domestic structure of the economy not only gave NMEs a purported unfair trade advantage but also gave them an incentive to dump goods in order to disrupt Western markets (Holzman 1987a).

Moreover, it was widely believed that NMEs had incentives to dump exports in order to unload occasional surpluses in stock, to overcome market entry handicaps, to absorb discriminatory tariff and nontariff barriers, to fulfill state dictated export plans, and to meet shortages of foreign exchange (Marer 1984, 129). During the debt crisis of the 1970s and 1980s, Eastern Europe and the Soviet Union dumped exports to quickly raise hard currency reserves and temporarily ameliorate balance of payments deficits (Neuberger and Lara 1977, 29–30). These actions were interpreted by the West as proof of the inherent threat that Communist exports generally posed to the competitiveness of Western industries.

From a normative perspective, the West viscerally disagreed with Communist political institutions that legitimized the violation of individual liberties, freedom of expression and assembly, and political choice. The West also feared the organizational capacity of a highly centralized authoritarian government. As such, both economic and political institutions in centrally planned economies created a belief in the West about the harmful nature of interactions with Communist countries. Looking at the domestic institutions in NMEs, the West derived a belief about the threatening nature of interactions with Communist countries.

Third, the cold war was an ideological confrontation as much, if not more so, than a security confrontation. The attempt by each ideological orientation to demonstrate its moral supremacy fueled cold war conflict

(Kennan 1947). Marxist-Leninism predicted the inevitable downfall of capitalism. (Lenin 1932; Marx and Engels 1978, 19–20). An ideology premised on the demise of capitalism would appear threatening to the liberal, democratic West.

Ideological differences, institutional differences, and strategic differences all combined to create a generalized cold war belief system in which neither the West nor the East trusted the institutional incentives or interests of the other side. Trade policy with its strategic, economic, and ideological components, proved to be yet another venue for the struggle between communism and capitalism. Western trade agencies perceived and operationalized these generalized cold war beliefs into specific trade laws and practices.

In applying the cold war beliefs to trade policy, these agencies developed very specific principled and causal beliefs about the impact of trade with NMEs. The beliefs were principled in that they involved an interpretation of what constituted a "proper" political and economic system, namely capitalist democracies. They were causal in the sense that they embodied a belief about what would happen to the West should it open itself to trade freely with Communist countries. These normative and causal assumptions influenced the laws developed by Western trade institutions.

Specifically, the West developed a belief that non-market economies had an interest in dumping in order to hurt Western industries. "In the West, dumping by Socialist countries [was] often viewed as a deliberate conspiracy to disrupt Capitalist markets and discredit free enterprise" (Wilczynski 1969, 138). Dumping was an important element of the strategic and ideological warfare between the East and the West. The Department of Commerce and the European Commission designed a set of special anti-dumping trade rules to protect the West from the perceived extraordinary threat posed by trade with NMEs.

The belief that NMEs were inherently antagonistic to the West was based on a rational appraisal of the capabilities, interests, and incentives of NMEs during the cold war. These institutionalized beliefs have continued to affect the administration of trade laws in the post–cold war period. Although the beliefs are anachronistic in the post–cold war period, that does not mean they are irrational. The rules were rationally derived based on calculations of the material and ideological conditions of Communist countries. While they may become outdated, one cannot conclude they are irrational. The previous discussion regarding cognitive limitations to change preconceived beliefs demonstrates that discordance between beliefs and facts is not definitionally irrational.

Testing an Explanatory Role for Beliefs

Given the West's generally antagonistic beliefs about the nature of Communism and the potential threat posed to Western trade interests, I have developed a series of hypotheses to examine the linkages between belief certainty, information shifts, and rule changes. I use the administration of U.S. and European Union anti-dumping legislation as evidence to explore the connections between beliefs and outcomes. Different observable patterns of behavior would be predicted by ideational variables and interest based or institution based variables, both in terms of outcomes and processes. This section highlights what trade policy evidence would look like, if beliefs have affected the interpretation and implementation of Western trade practices.

First, a belief based hypothesis would predict that NMEs would be treated worse than similarly situated developing country. There would be a disconnect between the economic and political conditions in NMEs and the manner in which they have been treated under Western trade law. Interest or institution based theories would predict that countries at similar levels of economic development, with similar levels of economic openness or political liberalization would be treated similarly under Western trade policy. Belief based explanations would predict different treatment despite the similar institutional structures of the groups. If beliefs about the antagonistic nature of NMEs and their threatening trade capacity affected the application of trade policies, one would predict that economic and political institutions would not determine trade policy implementation. *If cold war beliefs about NMEs affected trade policy, in the post–cold war period non-market economies would have been treated worse than other developing countries at similar levels of economic development and with similar institutional structures.*

Second, if cold war beliefs about NMEs have affected current trade policy, the economic and political reforms in these countries would not be translated directly into policy. The United States and EU might enact formal rule changes, but there would be a substantial lag between policy change and actual policy implementation. This is not an institutional lag, because the institutions themselves are changing. One should observe a lag in policy implementation, manifesting itself in the circumvention of formal rule changes or actions designed to obviate the formal rule change. If institution based accounts hold true, one would predict that a change in institutions or rules would change trade policy outcomes. *If cold war beliefs about NMEs affected recent trade policy, formal rules and institutions would not effect commensurate changes in the process of administering trade cases or the outcome of those cases.*

It is also possible to derive more specific predictions about belief stasis and belief change with respect to U.S. and European trade policy in the post–cold war period by drawing on our understandings of information changes and belief certainty. If beliefs are probabilistic assessments of the capabilities, interests, and incentives of NMEs during the cold war, then one can derive a continuum of degree of belief certainty from an assessment of underlying interests, incentives, and capabilities. One can then predict that belief change should most likely happen first toward countries for which the initial assessment of incentives and interests was least antagonistic and last in countries for which the initial assessment of incentives and interests was the most antagonistic.

All the countries of Central and Eastern Europe, the former Soviet Union, and China were Communist. So according to the cold war belief system that equated Communist with enemy, all the countries were by definition antagonistic and potentially threatening. Nonetheless, there were gradations within the Communist bloc, with some being more threatening than others. Differentiating degree of belief certainty among the group of NMEs requires an evaluation of incentives and interest differences within the group. I derive interests from international level factors and institutional incentives from domestic level factors in order to provide some variation in terms of level of Western belief certainty about the threat posed by each country.

At the international level, I group NMEs into satellite states and core states. Western perceptions of NME interests are derived from the international structure, core being more threatening than periphery. Since core states would be viewed as the most threatening to the West, beliefs about their antagonistic intentions would be held with the greatest certainty. In contrast, satellite states would be seen as lesser threats than core states, and presumably beliefs about their antagonistic intentions would be held with less certainty. In dividing up the Communistic bloc, it is generally understood that the Soviet Union and China represented the core. These two countries were responsible for the propagation of Communist ideology, and shouldered the security burden for the other countries. The Soviet Union and China were also the nuclear powers who called the ideological and political shots for the other Communist countries.

Eastern Europe and Vietnam constituted the satellite states. They followed the ideological direction of the core countries. In the case of Eastern Europe, they followed the economic direction of the Soviet Union under the Council for Mutual Economic Assistance (Comecom), and were directly influenced by the overt political control of the Soviet

Union (Brown 1988, especially Chapter 4).[5] The Warsaw Treaty Organization (Warsaw Pact) ensured that Eastern Europe's foreign security policies were directed by the Soviet Union (Brown 1988, especially Chapter 2; Simons 1991). Substantial economic and military aid to Vietnam from the Soviet Union helped to keep Vietnam within the Soviet sphere of influence.

At the domestic level, I divide non-market economies in terms of the orthodoxy of their adherence to Communist style economic and political institutions. While all non-market economies were by definition centrally planned, Communist systems, some NME were more orthodox and some more deviant than others. It is possible to roughly divide NMEs on this criterion, by examining the nature of their economic and political institutions, and therefore differentiate among the domestic institutional incentive structures of the NMEs. Economically and politically orthodox countries had centrally planned economic systems without devolution of power. Orthodox countries had strong one party Communist rule. Orthodox countries did not stage revolutions, or experience social movements designed to undermine the Communist institutions.

By contrast, deviant Communist countries had modified traditional Communist economic and political institutions. Countries that decentralized production decisions, or refused to collectivize agriculture, or focused on the production of consumer products at the expense of industrial production would all be considered economically deviant. Reforms designed to devolve economic power from the state would be considered deviant, since they deviated from the essential precepts of orthodox Communist economics, as epitomized by Russia and China. Additionally, countries that experienced social revolutions designed to modify or dismantle communism would be considered politically deviant. Countries that experienced mini-revolutions against the regime or countries experimenting with multiparty elections would be classified as politically deviant as well.

Therefore, I expect that Western cold war beliefs about the threatening or antagonistic nature of NMEs would be affected by signals about the orthodoxy or deviance of the countries with respect to their domestic institutionally determined incentives. Countries that did not embrace Communist incentive structures would be less threatening than countries that did. Countries with modified economic systems would not enjoy the same purported unfair trade advantages as fully centralized economic systems. Governments with a more tenuous hold on political power would also be less threatening than countries with a single party monopoly of political power. Of course all NMEs had Communist institutions. They all had some variation of centrally planned, one party Communist systems. Therefore the degree to which these countries were deviant or orthodox is relative to the other NMEs, not relative to the universe of countries in the international system.

Along these two dimensions, international interests and domestic institutions, belief about satellites should change before beliefs about core countries. Beliefs about deviant countries should change before beliefs about orthodox countries. These types of broadly defined international and domestic level factors would be observable from the West during and after the cold war. For example, a revolution or a major economic reform program would have been substantial enough to be recognized by Western governments. Actual capabilities of these countries would be harder to ascertain because of the closed nature of information flows coming out of NMEs. Therefore, I focus on deriving interests and incentives in order to develop a proxy for degree of belief certainty. In this way a two by two matrix can be designed along the satellite/core dimension and the domestically deviant/domestically orthodox dimension.

In order to map this two by two onto a single issue space, I assign a relative preference ordering to internationally determined interests and domestically determined incentives (see table 2.1). How this maps onto a single issue space continuum of belief certainty is partially a function of which variable the West chose to emphasize during the cold war. Both dimensions of the issue are important, but the timing, issue framing, and ability to grapple with complex information affect which dimension will be preferred (Jones 1994, 75; Jones 1996).[6] In this case, internationally determined interests were the first order concern, and domestically determined institutional incentives were the second order, albeit an important, one. The distinction between satellite and core was particularly salient within the context of the cold war, and was cognitively easier to discern. Therefore, this factor should have been more important in assessing belief certainty than domestic institutional factors within the context of the cold war.

Table 2.1   Belief Certainly: Matrix of Interests and Incentives

Internationally Determined Interests (Satellite/Core)	*Domestically Determined Institutional Incentives (Deviant/Orthodox)*	
	Deviant Satellite Country	Orthodox Satellite Country
	Deviant Core Country	Orthodox Core Country

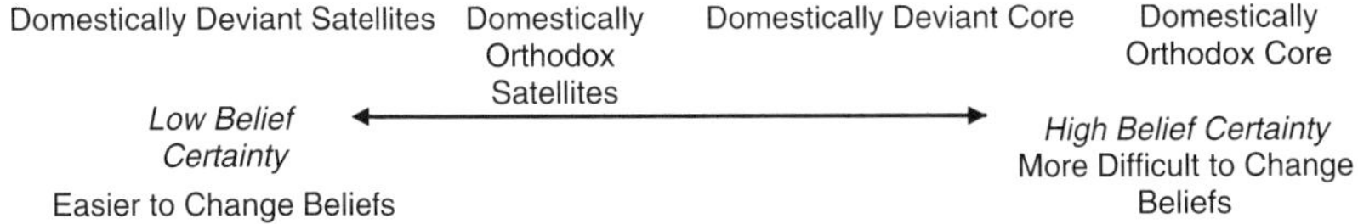

Figure 2.1   Continuum of Certainty Levels by Group: Predicting Belief Change

Figure 2.1 summarizes the hypothesized direction of belief change among the four categories and across the country types. Beliefs held by the West with the lowest level of certainty should change first, because they should function as the weakest information discounters. Beliefs held with the highest level of certainty should be most resistant to change, because they function as the strongest information discounters. Beliefs in the middle of the continuum are affected by the preferencing of issue dimensions by the trade agencies, as discussed. Based on this continuum I predict: *Countries for which the West held antagonistic beliefs with the least certainty should experience an improvement in Western policy first.*

In order to derive testable predictions, I place the NMEs into the two by two matrix and then map them onto the single continuum. To ascertain country placements, one needs to know a little about the domestic institutions, both political and economic, that were in place during the cold war. The following section briefly reviews the domestically determined institutional incentives of various NMEs.

Domestically Deviant Satellites

Czechoslovakia, Hungary, Poland, and the German Democratic Republic were satellites of the Soviet Union, and all were domestically deviant in one way or another. Czechoslovakia attempted to break free from Communist style institutions in 1968. The government drew up a plan to implement political pluralism, remove political censorship, and institute economic reforms devolving economic control from the state (Janos 2000, 314–320). Although these economic and political reforms were crushed by the Soviet army in the Prague Spring of 1968, Czechoslovakia continued to protest Soviet rule and Communist institutions through acts of student and intellectual protest, such as Charter 77 (Brown 1991, 166–175; Ramet 1995, 122–134). As such, Czechoslovakia was signaling to the West that it was not as orthodox as the Soviet Union in its adherence to communism.

Hungary experienced both political revolution (1956) and economic reform. Under Kadar's rule in Hungary, the New Economic

Mechanism (NEM) was instituted in 1968. This economic reform program devolved control over production decisions to factories and industries and away from the central government (Brown 1988, 200–229). Hungary's relatively insubordinate attitudes within the Eastern Bloc were generally recognized by the West (Janos 2000, 307).

The GDR also attempted to implement a New Economic System (1963) to decentralize the economy, maintained preferential relations with West Germany, continued to buy products including advanced machinery from the West, and was even a de facto associate member of the Common Market (Janos 2000, 307–314). In spite of Soviet involvement in the government of the GDR, the country was not economically or politically orthodox relative to the other NMEs.

Poland was the only NME that did not collectivize agriculture. Collectivization of agriculture was crucial to the function of an orthodox centrally planned economy.[7] Poland also had a history of worker opposition to the Communist regime starting with the Polish Workers' Revolt in 1970 and culminating in the Solidarity Movement. Ramet even goes as far as to say a "parallel society" existed in Poland, working to undermine the regime (Ramet 1995, especially Chapter 4). Polish economic and political opposition to Communist institutions attests to its relative institutional deviation from the Communist norm (Brown 1988, 158–199)

In sum, each of these countries was able to signal to the West that they were not "true believers."[8] Their domestic institutions were both politically and economically deviant from the Soviet or Chinese ideal. As such, the West should have held beliefs about the inherently antagonistic and threatening nature of these countries with the least amount of certainty.

Domestically Orthodox Satellites

Bulgaria, Romania, Albania, and Vietnam fall into the category of domestically orthodox satellites. Each of these countries maintained and perpetuated strong Communist political and economic institutions, sometimes even without the assistance of the core. For example, although Albania was not aligned with the Soviet Union, it embraced a dogmatic brand of neo-Stalinism and was true to Marxist–Leninist understandings of economic and political institutions. The leader of Albania, Enver Hoxha, went even farther than Chinese leadership in ensuring both the collectivization of agriculture and a dogmatic adherence to state controlled production decisions (Brown 1988, 374).

Bulgaria remained closely allied with the Soviet Union. Bulgaria was ideologically orthodox and did not deviate from the Soviet/Communist design of its political and economic institutions (Janos 2000, 322). It was not until right before the fall of the Berlin Wall in 1989 that any social dissent began to surface in Bulgaria (Brown 1991, 190–192; Ramet 1995, 279–287).

Romania chose to rebel against Soviet domination, so at first glance it might appear to have been domestically deviant. Romania withdrew from Soviet economic control in 1964, and denounced the Soviet invasion of Czechoslovakia in 1968 (Brown 1991, 200). However, after gaining some independence from the direct control of the Soviet Union, Romania proceeded to institutionalize a one party monopoly of Communist power and a centrally planned economic system. Romania went farther than many countries in "systematizing" the country, or rendering everything homogeneous so as to squelch unrest (204). Romania's brand of orthodox communism was intertwined with nationalism, but its domestic and economic institutions still looked very similar to those in the USSR. Compared to other NMEs, its highly centralized economic system and tightly controlled political system appeared true to the Communist ideal.

Similar to Romania, Vietnam embraced a mixture of communism and nationalism. Like Romania it also constructed orthodox Communist economic and political institutions, including the collectivization of agriculture, a focus on heavy industry, central planning of economic activity, and one party rule. Signaling Vietnam's close affiliation with Communist orthodoxy, it remained one of the USSR's most important client states up until the break up of the Soviet Union (Duncan and Ekedahl 1990, 154; Graziani 1990).

In sum, the countries in this category were satellites, therefore one would predict that beliefs about them would change before beliefs about the core. However, each retained tightly centralized economic and political systems. Each country adhered to the precepts of Marxist-Leninism, regardless of its allegiances with the Soviet Union or China. If the West held antagonistic beliefs about Communist countries due to their domestic institutions, then the West should have been fairly certain of its beliefs regarding these countries. Therefore although these countries should experience belief change before core countries, beliefs about them should not change as fast as deviant satellites. Domestically orthodox satellites would be the second category to experience belief change.

Domestically Deviant Core

Technically part of the Soviet Union, the three Baltic nations, Latvia, Lithuania, and Estonia, were never at peace with this arrangement. The Baltics were invaded and annexed by the Soviet Union during World War II, and continued to resist Soviet rule until September 1991, when the Soviet Union recognized the independence of all three states (Simons 1991, 47). During the cold war there were numerous riots and rebellions against Soviet rule, including riots in Lithuania in 1956, 1960, and 1972, in Estonia in 1972, 1976, and 1977, and in Latvia in 1977 (Plakans 1995; Raun 1991). In August 1979, 45 Baltic activists issued a declaration calling for the restoration of Baltic Independence. The Baltics even addressed the United Nations Secretary General in 1980, appealing to Western powers to recognize the unjust Soviet occupation of the countries (Institute of Baltic Studies: Arts and Humanities 2001).

These examples of repeated, sustained politically unorthodox behavior were signals to the West of the lack of commitment that the Baltics had to Communist political and economic institutions. Therefore, although part of the Soviet core, the West should have been relatively uncertain about the degree to which these countries were inherently antagonistic and threatening to the West. However, these countries did not effect any economic reforms. They were firmly under Soviet control. Therefore assuming that the West constructed its beliefs based on an assessment of the incentives and interests of the countries, the West should hold beliefs about the antagonistic tendencies of these countries with more certainty than satellite countries but with less certainty than the orthodox core category. As a result, one would predict these countries would be the third group of countries about whom Western beliefs would change.

Domestically Orthodox Core

If belief certainty is a function of an assessment of interests and incentives, this group of countries left the least room for Western doubt about their antagonistic nature. The domestically orthodox core countries set the example for all the other NMEs. Institutionally orthodox countries that are part of the strategic core should be the last group of countries for which Western beliefs will change. Beliefs about the threatening nature of these countries will linger the longest in the face of contrary information, and function as the greatest information discounters.

This is not to deny that reform efforts did take place in the two primary core countries. Russia and China each experimented with slight institutional modifications to Marxist-Leninism, yet remained

Table 2.2   Predicting Levels of Belief Certainty

	Domestically deviant	*Domestically orthodox*
Satellites	Czech Republic, GDR, Hungary, Poland, Slovakia	Albania, Bulgaria, Romania, Vietnam
Core	Estonia, Latvia, Lithuania	China, Belarus, Kazakhstan, Russia, Ukraine

steadfast supporters of and adherents to central planning and a one party Communist monopoly of political power. Social dissent was summarily suppressed, and economic reforms were cautiously designed to enhance but not disrupt the centralization of the means of production. Any economic reforms that were too deviant were reversed. For example, economic decentralization was toyed with during China's Great Leap Forward (1958–1960) but this was subsequently remanded (Fairbanks 1986, 296–315). Similarly, Khrushchev attempted some devolution of economic control to *Sovnarkhozy* (Council of the National Economy), and a shuffling of party positions giving ordinary citizens more say in political decisions (Hosking 1990, 344–347). Each of these reforms was met with resistance, and once Khrushchev was removed from power they were reversed. In essence, the core, institutionally orthodox countries remained true to the image of a centrally planned, Communist totalitarian regime.[9]

In sum, table 2.2 places these four categories into the two by two matrix. Mapping these specific country classifications onto a single issue space, one arrives at predictions along the belief certainty continuum.

Beliefs about deviant satellites should change first, and beliefs about orthodox core countries should change last. Within the middle of the continuum, beliefs about orthodox satellites should change before beliefs about deviant core countries.

European and American Differences

There are differences in belief certainty and information sources between the United States and EU that should differentiate their behavior toward NMEs. Both changes in information and different levels of belief certainty should affect belief change. Therefore, comparing the United States and EU adds another dimension for testing if and how beliefs affect policy outcomes.

The United States was the archenemy of the Soviet Union during the cold war, and dogmatically anti-Communist. The United States developed the concept of the global containment of communism, and was the muscle behind enforcing it. In contrast, Europe did not exhibit the same virulent anti-Communism. European governments allowed Communist parties to participate in government. As Gaddis explains with regard to the policy of containment, "the [U.S.] administration had done little publicly to explain that all Communists were not equally dangerous" (Gaddis 1982, 102). Europe was more aware of differences between NMEs, and was able to differentiate its policies toward Eastern Europe from those toward the Soviet Union. As a result, ideologically speaking one would have predicted that the United States would hold beliefs about the antagonistic interests and threatening nature of trade with NMEs with more certainty than the European Union.

However, differing intensities of belief certainty are only one factor differentiating the European Union from the United States. Each also received different information about NMEs, as a result of differences in institutional safeguards, iterated interactions, and issue attentiveness. These differences in information are not simply differences in news or facts about NMEs, but also about differences in perceptions of information coming from NMEs. By this measure, the EU generally received more new information than the United States. Europe continued to have multilevel interactions with Eastern Europe, and West Germany, in particular, maintained close ties with East Germany. Europe traded more with Eastern Europe than the United States, thereby maintaining regular interactions with these countries. Additionally, geographic proximity should factor into the EU's beliefs about NMEs. Geographic proximity increases issue saliency and attentiveness, because of the real potential for spillover effects. Moreover, geographic proximity encourages interactions and information exchanges. Frequency of interactions and the establishment of institutions to facilitate exchange promoted by geographic proximity would be hypothesized to reduce degree of belief certainty. This yields the prediction: *The European Union should improve its treatment of imports from nonmarket economies before the United States, because they were less certain of the inherent danger of trade with Communist countries than the Americans.*

In sum, due to both overall belief certainty and information flows, I predict differences in the durability and intensity of trade related cold war beliefs between the United States and European Union. The EU should hold beliefs about the threatening nature of trade with Communist countries with less general certainty than the United States. Areas of difference should be most apparent over the treatment of Eastern Europe. If certainty of beliefs affects the timing of belief change, I predict that U.S. negative beliefs about NMEs should linger longer than EU beliefs.

Conclusion

John Hall provides some cautionary advice for demonstrating a causal role for beliefs in any explanation. When trying to assess the effects of ideas, the best way

> is to recognize the lags that occur between institutional and ideational change. As long as the fit between idea and circumstance remains tight . . . it is impossible to specify an independent ideational impact. But those occasions when circumstance changes and response remains culturally bound do allow us to study ideas as an independent variable. (Hall 1993, 46)

If institutions and interests predict and explain most of the treatment of NMEs by the West, then there is no room for beliefs in this analysis. However, if interest based explanations, or institutions-driven explanations are inadequate, then there is room to consider an ideational explanation. First, one must show that robust alternative explanations, such as more traditional trade theories cannot explain the way NMEs have been treated in the international political economy. Refuting materialist alternatives is a necessary but not a sufficient condition to demonstrate a belief based hypothesis. Second, one must provide a compelling, coherent narrative demonstrating how beliefs can explain behavior across countries and across time. It is in the "lag between institutional and ideational change" that one can observe the impact of beliefs.

The previous discussion has yielded five testable, falsifiable predictions about how and why beliefs affected the implementation of Western trade policy toward NMEs. By examining the process of applying anti-dumping laws to non-market economies, we can test some of the claims made in these hypotheses. Looking at the way in which cases are administered, not simply the outcome (i.e., protectionism or no protectionism), yields clues about how beliefs are perpetuated, and what might prompt belief change. For example, if information provided by non-market economies has been systematically ignored or rejected and trade agencies chose instead to rely on presumptions, one can infer that beliefs were affecting policymaking. If NMEs were held to impossible standards because trade agencies were wary of them, one can infer a role for beliefs.

This must be supplemented with policy documents, speeches, memos, and interview material, all suggesting that perceptions, assumptions, and beliefs about NMEs have affected policy.

Demonstrating the inadequacy of interest based explanations is not enough. There also needs to be evidence of beliefs at work. Interviewees should comment on their beliefs and presumptions about NMEs and how this impacts decision making. Trade cases should justify discrimination against NMEs based on presumptions about the different and threatening nature of trade with NME type institutions. Qualitative evidence related to perceptions and presumptions about NMEs must also point to a causal role for beliefs. While proving a causal role for beliefs is challenging, sufficient information exists to demonstrate an independent role for beliefs in the administration of trade policy.

Even with additional factors considered in a belief based hypothesis, there are explanatory and predictive limitations. Ideational factors cannot explain all trade policy related research puzzles. Because beliefs do not vary much, they do not directly affect trade volumes, nor can they explain upward or downward trends in patterns of trade protection. However, beliefs can explain larger trade patterns, and in this way beliefs complement interest based accounts of trade protection; they do not supplant interest based accounts. There is a material interest component to trade policy; however, pure interest based accounts cannot explain larger patterns of trade protection against NMEs.

The following chapter presents a variety of international political economy or "materialist" theories to explain patterns of trade protection against NMEs. The hypotheses generated from this literature are then tested in order to demonstrate that these interest based and institution based explanations are insufficient. I have also proffered testable predications about how beliefs affect the structure and implementation of Western trade with NMEs, which are tested in later chapters in order to demonstrate a causal role for beliefs. It is only through a refutation of the alternatives that one can begin to believe a narrative about a causal role for beliefs. I take up this refutation in the following statistical chapter.

CHAPTER THREE

Crawfish, Sparklers, and Rebar: Testing Theories of Trade Protection

Introduction

If institution or interest based factors can explain patterns of trade protection against non-market economies, there is little to be gained by also looking at beliefs. Beliefs might augment a narrative, but not have independent causal weight. However, if traditional explanations fall short in accounting for trade protection against NMEs, that is, if there is a disconnect between institutional or interest changes and policy response as John Hall pointed out, then there is theoretical room to explore ideational factors. As such, in this chapter I briefly review the literature examining the various alternative explanations of trade protection. To derive testable implications from a subset of these theories, I examine selected domestic, international, political, and economic variables. In this way I am able to test likely alternative hypotheses to determine their relative efficacy in explaining patterns of trade protection against NMEs and comparable developing countries.

Theories of Trade Protection

Traditional international political economy literature has generated a host of reasons, sources, and motives for the initiation or continuation of trade protection. These alternative hypotheses are potential explanations for why the United States and EU both initiated and continued their high levels of trade protection against imports from NMEs in the post–cold

Table 3.1   Matrix of Theories Explaining Patterns of Trade Protection

	Economic	*Political*
Domestic	• Sensitive sector theories • Declining macroeconomic conditions	• Interest group theories • Congressional dominance model • Size/strength of the industry
International	• Change in import penetration • Change in import volume	• Political beliefs about trading partner • Trade as tool of foreign policy

war period. Proving a belief based hypothesis requires refuting some of the most robust alternatives before one can suspend disbelief that interests or institutions cannot do most of the explanatory heavy lifting. Table 3.1 presents domestic economic, domestic political, international economic, and international political theories of trade protection. A brief literature review will elucidate what is meant by these general categories.

International Political Causes of Trade Protection

This literature focuses on the strategic nature of trade, the use of trade as a tool of foreign policy, and the importance of trade as a means of maximizing a state's interests (Baldwin 1985a, 1985b; Hirschman 1945). In keeping with the realist school of thought, because the structure of international trade is determined by the interests and power of states, trade policy becomes foreign policy (Cooper 1973; Gilpin 1987, 180–190; Grieco 1993; Krasner 1976). How much is traded or not traded, what is traded, and with whom trade is conducted are all important foreign policy considerations.

As a tool of foreign policy, trade is used to hinder or promote the development of states. Relative economic gains matter, and they are more important with regard to some states than others due to overarching international political considerations (Mastanduno 1993; Prestowitz 1990; Snidal 1993). From this perspective, it matters from whom the United States or European Union is importing. For example, the United States has intentionally used trade or trade protection to promote the development of allies and hinder the development of enemies. During periods of the cold war the United States went as far as to configure trade policy according to criteria of "economic warfare" in order to hinder the economic development of its enemies by denying them gains from trade (Mastanduno 1992, 13). Trade has also been used by the United States to bolster strategically the economies of the Asian Newly Industrializing Countries (NICs), and Europe during the cold war (Gilpin 1987, 131–151; Haggard 1990; Kindleberger 1981). Keeping markets open to trade with some is just as strategic as keeping markets closed to others.

This body of literature can readily explain why the West erected trade barriers to NMEs during the cold war. Strategic concerns are parsimonious and can trump other more complicated explanations of patterns of trade protection (Baldwin 1985a; Gowa 1994; Lake 1988a). However, this body of literature tends to be either too general or too narrow to explain continued Western patterns of trade with NMEs in the post–cold war period. For example, Lott argues that there is no politically motivated anti-dumping discrimination against countries like Poland and Romania because they are not a security threat to the United States (Lott 1995). However, the empirical evidence demonstrates trade discrimination. If the reason is not based on security threats, then there must be other factors involved. Security threats are rather blunt instruments to explain or predict patterns of trade protection. If security considerations explain trade protection against China, what explains trade protection against Kazakhstan and Latvia? I argue misleading conclusions about patterns of trade protection can result from such a highly generalized approach to trade as a function of security alone. Moreover, they provide little guidance in addressing post–cold war trade relations with transitional economies.

However, one cannot simply dismiss international political or strategic considerations as a result of these approaches. New studies taking a more nuanced approach to international political considerations have demonstrated how cultural biases act as trade barriers (Economist 2005b).[1] Linking trust of trading partner with trade patterns might yield new understandings of patterns of trade protection. In this vein, I take a first cut at international political factors, by testing whether region of origin of the good traded matters in explaining incidence and intensity of trade protection. I compare the incidences of protection across country composites used by the U.S. Department of Commerce and the European Commission: South America, Big Emerging Markets, Europe (EU), Non-Market Economies, Asian Newly Industrialized Countries (NICs), and Other Asian countries (see table 3.2). Region of origin is operationalized as a series of dummy variables.[2] Although this is a crude measure of international political factors, it is only a first attempt to test whether country of origin matters. Understanding why country or region of origin might matter, including trust issues associated with various trading partners, is addressed later based on the preliminary findings.

More specifically, if beliefs matter, region of origin will be statistically significant. If beliefs do not matter, then the NME origin for imports will not be a significant factor in explaining patterns of trade protection. This is not proof that beliefs explain trade protection. However, it does lend support for the hypothesis that beliefs about the trading partner affect patterns of trade protection.

Table 3.2   Comparative Groups

(U.S. Department of Commerce Constructed Aggregates)

Asian Newly Industrialized Countries (NICs) (4 countries)
Hong Kong, Singapore, South Korea, Taiwan
Big Emerging Markets (BEMs) (15 countries)
(developing countries)
Argentina, Brazil, Brunei, Hong Kong, India, Indonesia, Malaysia, Mexico, Philippines,
Singapore, South Korea, South Africa, Taiwan, Thailand, Turkey
Europe (15 countries)
Austria, Belgium, Denmark, Finland, France, Germany, Ireland,
Italy, Netherlands, Norway, Portugal, Spain, Sweden, Switzerland, UK
Non-Market Economies (25 countries)*
(former Communist countries)
Albania, Armenia, Azerbaijan, Belarus, Bulgaria, China, Czech Republic, East Germany,
Estonia, Georgia, Hungary, Kazakhstan, Kyrgyzstan, Latvia, Lithuania, Moldova,
Poland, Romania, Russia, Slovak Republic, Tajikistan, Turkmenistan, Ukraine,
Uzbekistan, Vietnam
Other Asian Countries (18 countries)
Afghanistan, Bangladesh, Bhutan, Brunei, Burma, Cambodia, India, Indonesia, Laos,
Macao, Malaysia, Maldive Islands, Mongolia, Nepal, Pakistan, Philippines,
Sri Lanka, Thailand
South America (10 countries)
Argentina, Bolivia, Brazil, Chile, Colombia, Ecuador, Paraguay, Peru, Uruguay,
Venezuela

* Prior to 1991, the list did not separate the republics of the former Soviet Union. The Union of Soviet Socialist Republics (USSR) was the only designation for the 15 republics. Note, Yugoslavia was never included in this group. Cases against the USSR prior to 1991 are counted as one case, and after 1991 the cases are counted against the individual republics. This is in keeping with the classifications and accounting system used by the U.S. Department of Commerce.
Source: United States International Trade Administration. *United States Foreign Trade Highlights*. At <http: www.ita.doc.gov/industry/otea/usfth/method.html.>

International Economic Causes of Trade Protection

International economic explanations relegate politics to a minor role, if any, in accounting for patterns of trade protection. These theories focus on import penetration, import volume, and sudden changes in imports to explain changes in patterns of trade protection (Finger and Murray 1990; Goldstein 1993; Krugman and Baldwin 1990). In these theories, there is a direct, positive relationship between incidences of trade protection and increases in imports (Ehrenhaft et al. 1997; Vandenbussche 1996). Increases in import volume should trigger trade protection, especially under the anti-dumping laws. Finger has demonstrated a positive relationship between changes in import volume and trade protection, specifically anti-dumping trade protection (Finger 1981). Trefler and others have demonstrated that high levels of protection are found in industries with significant import penetration (1993, 130).

These theories would predict that trade protection against non-market economies can be explained by looking at the volume of NME exports to the West. These theories predict that NMEs are the subject of an unusual number of dumping cases because of their high export volumes to the West, and the high import penetration levels of their exports. If international economic explanations can account for patterns of trade protection against NMEs, there is no reason to think beliefs about non-market economies affect trade policy.

These theories predict not only a positive relationship, but a rough proportionality between trade and trade protection. For example, it has been shown that for both developing countries and developed countries as groups, the proportion of anti-dumping cases is about the same as the relative proportion of U.S. imports (Finger 1981, 272; Finger 1991, 1). While I have already demonstrated that this rough proportionality holds true for most countries, it does not hold true for non-market economies (see figures 1.1 and 1.2). However, this level of aggregation might mask a relationship between industry level import changes and trade protection. Therefore in this chapter I probe this relationship a bit more, examining if change in imports at the industry level instead of country level can explain patterns of trade protection.

There are two ways of measuring the import threat posed by foreign imports, namely changes in import volume and levels of import penetration. Import penetration is a static measure, and change in import volume and/or change in import penetration are dynamic. Each tells us something different about the nature of foreign competition. The literature predicts that sectors with high levels of import penetration will be more likely to seek protection than sectors with low levels of import penetration. Theoretically speaking, changes in import volume should be a good predictor of when an anti-dumping case is likely to be initiated, since a rapid increase in imports is part of the very definition of dumping. To capture both types of potential import threats, the two measures of import activity are included. In both cases one would expect direct, positive relationships between trade protection and import levels and penetration. *Industries with high import penetration will be awarded higher levels of trade protection than industries with low import penetration. As the import volume of goods in an industry increases, that industry will receive more trade protection.*

Domestic Economic Causes of Trade Protection

Domestic economic factors are potentially powerful explanations for patterns of trade protection against NMEs. The focus of these theories is on the economic vulnerability or competitiveness of a sector as an explanation for incidences of trade protection (Frieden 1988). As economic vulnerability goes up, trade protection levels also go up. Vulnerable sectors, meaning those routinely in economic distress and recipients of trade protection, have been labeled "sensitive sectors." "Sensitive" connotes low firm profitability, declining employment and domestic shipments, and decreasing domestic wages. Examples of such sectors traditionally include agriculture, textiles, steel, chemicals, and footwear (Banks 1993; Organisation for Economic Co-operation and Development 1994). It is argued that the reason NMEs are more prone to anti-dumping trade protection than other types of countries is they tend to be producers of price sensitive, labor intensive, low value-added primary exports that directly compete with declining industries in advanced industrialized economies (Brenton and Mauro 1998; Ehrenhaft et. al. 1997; Eichengreen and Kohl 1998; Winters, Rubin, and Bond 1998). Domestic economic theories would explain the high levels of trade protection against NMEs as a function of the composition of NME exports.

The value-added level of the industry is often used as a proxy for determining the degree of sensitivity of the industry, with low value-added firms being more vulnerable than high value-added firms.[3] Low value-added industries are labor intensive, produce fungible goods, and employ basic technology; therefore they are the most vulnerable to competition from cheap imports from abroad (see table 3.3 for examples). One predicts an inverse relationship between value-added per employee levels and trade protection.

In addition, to capture the economic vitality of the industry, I examine the profitability of the industry, by constructing a lagged profitability variable taking industry value-added less wages over industry shipments [(valadd-wages)/ind shipments]. Using this relative profitability scale of 0–1, I am able to compare the relative profitability of a broad range of industries, from supercomputer to hairbrush manufacturers. There is a hypothesized inverse relationship between profitability and trade protection. As the profitability of an industry goes down, the trade protection awarded should go up. In sum, if value-added level and industry profitability can explain trade protection against NMEs, this is a strong indication that non-market economies bear the brunt of trade protection due to the nature of their export commodities not antagonistic beliefs about them. This would be evidence against a belief based hypothesis. *Low value-added industries are more likely to win trade protection than high value-added industries because they are more price sensitive. As the profitability of an industry declines, it will be more likely to win trade protection.*

Finally, domestic economic theories suggest that the macroeconomic conditions of the importing country affect whether an industry is granted trade protection. During periods of economic slowdown, industries will be more vulnerable to import competition. Declining real Gross Domestic Product (GDP) or rising rates of unemployment will

Table 3.3 Sample of High, Medium, and Low Value-Added Sectors

High Value-added			
Oil	Aspirin	Semiconductors	Dry photo film
Eproms	Nitrocellulose	Sulfanilic acid	Saccharin
Medium Value-added			
Tin products	Cooking ware	Wire rod	Paper products
Batteries	Picture tubes	Cold rolled steel	Rubber products
Low Value-added			
Paintbrushes	Bauxite	Foam	Ethanol
Fertilizer	Uranium	Bicycles	Raspberries

Source: Author's calculation based on sample of anti-dumping cases used in chapter 3. Value-added figures from *Annual Survey of Manufactures: Statistics for Industry Groups and Industries, 1980–1998, Mining-Industry Series: Economic Census, 1992 and 1997; NBER-CES Manufacturing Industry Database, 1958–1996* and Department of Commerce, GDP: Implicit Price Deflator.

exacerbate the effects of increased import competition. Therefore, macroeconomic conditions should have an interactive effect with some of the other variables. Macroeconomic conditions have an overt political component as well. Politicians or trade representatives may be more likely to award an industry trade protection during an economic slowdown than during a period of relative prosperity. If the macroeconomic conditions of the United States or the EU explain patterns of trade protection against NMEs, this would undermine the explanatory power of a hypothesis based on beliefs. Therefore, I look at both changes in real GDP and changes in unemployment rates to ascertain changes in a country's macroeconomic conditions. As GDP declines, trade protection should increase. As unemployment increases, trade protection should increase. *During periods of macroeconomic decline, industries will be more likely to receive trade protection.*

Domestic Political Causes of Trade Protection

Many theorists argue that trade protection is a function of the political power of domestic interest groups. Domestic political explanations are closely linked with domestic economic explanations. This literature contends that trade protection is awarded to those interests that wield political clout and are able to translate this influence into favorable trade policies. Various studies have demonstrated the relative strength of interest groups in determining tariff levels (Findlay and Wellisz 1982; Schattschneider 1935). Some have demonstrated the importance of interest group constituencies to politicians (Bailey, Goldstein, and Weingast 1997; Baldwin and Magee 2000; Magee, Brock, and Young 1989). Others have focused on the distributional issues related to trade that divide and motivate interest groups (Milner 1987; Rogowski 1989). All have theorized that interest groups affect patterns of trade protection.

There are two schools of thought regarding the manner in which interest groups affect levels of trade protection: "capture theories" and "congressional dominance theories" (Hansen 1990). Capture theories argue that interest groups compete and form coalitions among themselves in an attempt to "capture" politicians and policymakers who will then enact policies to support the interests of the winning group (Gourevitch 1986; Olson 1965; Stigler 1971). For example, Messerlin describes the potential power of interest groups to capture agencies and win protection by examining the influence of agricultural lobbies on agricultural bureaus (Messerlin 1981). Tharakan has even argued that there is a link between lobbying activity and the tenacity of anti-dumping practices, albeit not for NMEs (Tharakan 1999).

The congressional dominance school of thought examines how the institutional structure of Congress and its relations with other agencies affect the making of trade policy. As a result of lobbying efforts, Congress directly influences policy outcomes of trade related agencies by flexing its influence over agency budgets and appointments (O'Halloran 1994; Shepsle and Weingast 1987). More specifically, Congressmen take positions on committees that are relevant to their special interests, sanctioning or rewarding agencies based on their personal interests (Weingast and Moran 1983, 768–769).

There are several problems with interest group theories in general, and with their ability to explain NME patterns of trade protection in particular. First, this approach lacks a priori predictive strength. Interest group theory "tends to lack theoretical rigor and predictive value, largely because it lacks an independent measure of group power" (Ikenberry, Lake, and Mastanduno 1988, 8). An interest group is only powerful after it has achieved a specific outcome, therefore there is no objective measure of power apart from influence over outcomes. Second, many scholars have shown that special interest models have limited explanatory capability when subjected to empirical testing (Anderson 1993; Goldstein 1988; Lake 1988b; Trefler 1993). Third, there is also confusion about the results of interest group studies. For example, studies of Political Action Committees (PACs) have yielded conflicting results showing that PACs do not really use their leverage to sway votes (Magelby and Nelson 1990), that PACs have negligible capacity to influence voting outcomes (Baldwin and Magee 2000), and alternatively that PACs have a substantial impact on Congressional voting patterns (Stratmann 1991). The inconsistent evidence calls into question the generalizability of theories based on the impact of interest groups, and highlights their susceptibility to measurement problems.

With respect to congressional dominance models, it is hard to show direct congressional control over trade policy implementation because neither Congress nor elected officials administer trade policy. Anti-dumping laws are a case in point. The International Trade Commission and International Trade Administration were specially insulated from Congressional influence. Even studies which have shown congressional influence over certain agencies are not generalizable because Congress does not exert the same type or intensity of influence over all agencies or over all tools of trade protection (Weingast and Moran 1983).

In spite of the criticism, interest group theories remain important and robust political economy theories. With regard to trade protection against NME imports, these theories would suggest that NMEs export goods that compete directly with those domestic industries that wield substantial political power. Again the nature of the export composition of NMEs explains patterns of trade protection, not beliefs about non-market economies. According to these theories, one should expect that steel from China and Russia should face the same levels of trade protection as steel from India and Britain. It is the nature of the commodity, not the nature of the country that matters.

There are numerous hypothesized domestic political variables proffered in the literature in order to test the importance of interest group explanations of trade protection. Some include the size (measured in employees and revenue), concentration, degree of unionization, and skill level of the industry. First, it is hypothesized that as the number of workers increases, the amount of trade protection awarded increases. Larger industries have more money for political lobbying and more voting constituents, thereby increasing their political clout. There is a hypothesized positive relationship between industry size and protection.

Second, the skill level of workers in an industry affects the probability of trade protection, with low skill labor favoring higher trade protection I also test whether low value-added industries are more likely to win trade protection. Low value-added industries employ unskilled or semiskilled workers in labor intensive industries in historically important sectors. These "bread and butter" industries, like agriculture, steel, and textiles, are also hypothesized to win more trade protection than other industries because they are politically sensitive. There is a predicted inverse relationship between value-added per employee and trade protection.

Third, high industry concentration and high degrees of unionization are thought to increase the chances of trade protection, because workers will be better able to overcome collective action problems and unite in their call for trade protection.[4] However, there is disagreement regarding the proposed relationships between these factors and trade protection. Kreuger and Trefler have separately demonstrated that the degree of protection afforded to an industry is not correlated with lobbying variables such as unionization (Krueger 1996; Trefler 1993). Finger has demonstrated that the size of an industry but not its concentration has an effect on trade protection (1981; Finger, Hall, and Nelson 1982). Taking these findings into consideration, I examine the size of the industry (in terms of employees and voting power) and its value-added per employee, as a proxy for the skill level of the industry. It is possible that

Table 3.4 Summary of Independent Variables

Independent Variables	Relationship to Incidence and Intensity of Trade Protection
Size of Industry (Employment)	+
Value-Added by Industry Per Employee	−
Profitability	−
Import Penetration	+
Change in Imports	+
Change in Real GDP	−
Change in Unemployment	+
County Type (NME/Other)	+

both/either of these variables can explain patterns of protection against non-market imports. *The larger the industry, the greater the chances for trade protection because it will exert more influence in money and voting terms over congress. Low value-added industries will be more likely to win trade protection than high value-added industries because they are more politically sensitive.*

In sum, international political, international economic, domestic economic, and domestic political explanations of trade protection make specific predications regarding the factors that increase the incidence and intensity of trade protection. I have taken these theoretical predictions and operationalized them, consistent with traditional literature on this topic. The independent variables and their hypothesized relationships to the dependent variable are summarized in table 3.4. These variables will be tested in the following section.

Testing the Hypotheses: Data and Tradeoffs

In order to test the aforementioned hypotheses, I designed a dataset covering the universe of anti-dumping cases initiated by the U.S. Department of Commerce between 1985 and 1999.[5] The independent variables, or factors expected to affect levels of trade protection, were outlined earlier. The dependent variable is trade protection, operational-ized as the outcome of an anti-dumping case. This is the presence or absence of protection in some models, and the size of the protection in other models. Each case in the model is one anti-dumping case initiated against one country for a single commodity in any given year. During an anti-dumping investigation, the Department of Commerce examines information from the last two to four most recently completed fiscal quarters prior to the date of the filing of an investigation.[6] For example, a case filed in mid-1999 would use 1998–1999 economic information. Therefore, I have used one year lagged variables where appropriate.[7] Table 3.5 provides a sample of cases, countries, and years, to illustrate the diversity of both products and countries involved in anti-dumping investigations.

This study uses 4-digit SIC industry level data to test the hypotheses across time and industry. It is important to examine the influence of interest groups at a mid-range level of detail such as this. Many studies aggregate industry level data so they are examining entire sectors, such as the steel sector or the agricultural sector writ large. This results in grand

Table 3.5   Sample of U.S. Anti-dumping Cases (1985–1999)

Country	Product	Year	Country	Product	Year
Saudi Arab	Oil	1999	Italy	Instrument Pads	1992
Russia	Fertilizer	1999	Hungary	Ball Bearings	1991
China	Apple juice	1999	India	Ibuprofen	1991
Indonesia	Polyester resin	1999	Japan	Microwaves	1991
Japan	Masks	1999	Venezuela	Cement	1991
India	Steel plate	1999	Bangladesh	Shop Towels	1991
Kazakhstan	Uranium	1999	Yugoslavia	Cherry Juice	1991
Canada	Cattle	1998	Austria	Paper	1990
Taiwan	Semiconductors	1998	Singapore	Word Processors	1990
India	Rubber tape	1998	Argentina	Steel Wire Rod	1990
Indonesia	Rubber thread	1998	Taiwan	Lug Nuts	1990
Italy	Steel plate	1998	China	Sparklers	1990
Spain	Steel wire	1998	Brazil	Digital Counters	1990
Denmark	Cookies	1998	Israel	Cephalexin	1989
Chile	Mushrooms	1998	Mexico	Steel Pails	1989
Germany	Stainless steel	1997	Korea	12 v Batteries	1989
Trinidad	Steel wire rope	1997	Sweden	Aluminum Sulfate	1989
Chile	Salmon	1997	Taiwan	Telephone Sys	1988
Taiwan	RA memory	1997	Brazil	Shock Absorb	1988
Korea	Nails	1996	Australia	Bauxite	1988
China	Crawfish	1996	Malaysia	Thermostats	1988
Austria	Rayon yarn	1996	UK	Industrial Belts	1988
Turkey	Rebar	1996	Japan	Forklift Trucks	1987
China	Brake drums	1996	Netherlands	Brass Sheet	1987
Indonesia	Dinnerware	1996	Canada	Picture Tubes	1986
UK	Foam	1995	Turkey	Aspirin	1986
Germany	Printing press	1995	Germany	Crankshafts	1986
Italy	Pasta	1995	Iran	Pistachios	1986
China	Bicycles	1995	Brazil	Orange juice	1986
Russia	Magnesium	1994	Belgium	Mirrors	1986
Taiwan	Wheel inserts	1994	E Germany	Urea	1986
Argentina	Tubular goods	1994	Mexico	Cooking Ware	1985

generalizations about these sectors, when in actuality there is great divergence within sectors. For example, a small steel mini-mill producing specialized steel plate is not the same as a large, unspecialized steel mill producing large quantities of cold-rolled steel. One needs to unpack the sectors to figure out what about the sector or product triggers trade protection. For this reason the strength of PACs is generally not used because this data is not available at the subindustry level across time, and therefore requires too high a level of aggregation.[8] Using such a high level of aggregation costs the analysis meaningful variation within the overarching industry, and renders the analysis unable to explain which industry subsectors do or do not receive protection. Moreover, such a high level of abstraction fails to address directly the puzzle regarding trade protection against NMEs.

Analysis I: Which Factors Explain When an Industry Is Granted Trade Protection?

The first set of models tests which factors affect when an industry will receive trade protection. The analysis examines all anti-dumping cases (N = 608) initiated by the United States from 1985 to 1999.[9] The dependent variable is trade protection, whether the domestic industry initiating the anti-dumping case did or did not (1/0) receive trade protection. Trade protection constitutes a final affirmative anti-dumping duty, or the negotiation of a suspension agreement that either limits the foreign industry's allowable export quantities or sets a lowest allowable price. In either case, the domestic industry wins trade protection.

All three of the models test the traditional political economy hypotheses derived from the previous literature review. They also test whether region of origin is a useful predictor of incidence of trade protection. Model 3 incorporates a cold war interactive variable. With respect to non-market economies, if trade protection against NMEs is a function of the composition of their export commodities, then industry level data should account for most of the trade protection during all the time periods. If trade protection against NMEs is a function of cold war geostrategic considerations, one would expect it to be less strong in the period after the cold war. Or, if NME political and economic institutions account for the patterns of trade protection, there should be less need for this type of trade protection in the post–cold war period. However, if beliefs do affect current trade policy, country of origin (NME) should continue to affect trade outcomes irrespective of the cold war or post–cold war time period.

Table 3.6 Which Factors Explain Industry Level Incidence of Trade Protection? Analysis 1—Parameter Values for Logit Model

Dependent Variable: Trade Protection	Model 1 1985–1999	Model 2 1985–1999	Model 3 1985–1999
Size of Industry	−0.14	−0.16	−0.14
(Employment)	(0.12)	(0.12)	(0.12)
Profitability of Industry	−0.69**	−0.70**	−0.70**
	(0.27)	(0.27)	(0.27)
Value Added Per	0.48**	0.50**	0.51**
Employee (Lagged)	(0.19)	(0.19)	(0.19)
Import Penetration	−0.18**	−0.18**	−0.18**
(Lagged)	(0.08)	(0.08)	(0.08)
Import Change	−0.08	−0.1	−0.06
	(0.17)	(0.17)	(0.17)
Change in Real GDP	8.90*	—	8.12*
	(4.41)		(4.48)
Change in Unemployment Rate	—	−1.71**	—
		(0.71)	
cold war (pre/post)	—	—	−0.53
(cold war * NME)			(0.56)
NME	1.91***	1.90***	2.31***
	(0.36)	(0.36)	(0.56)
South America	0.24	0.26	0.24
	[illegible]	[illegible]	[illegible]
Europe	0.57*	0.58*	−0.57*
	(0.33)	(0.33)	(0.33)
Japan	1.80***	1.79***	1.79***
	(0.39)	(0.39)	(0.39)
Asian NICs	0.42	0.41	0.43
	(0.37)	(0.37)	(0.37)
Big Emerging Markets	0.91**	0.91**	0.91**
	(0.35)	(0.35)	(0.35)
Other Asian Countries	0.76*	0.76*	0.77*
	(0.46)	(0.46)	(0.46)
Constant	−41.05*	8.23**	−37.36*
	(20.40)	(3.63)	(20.78)
Pseudo R2 (Cox & Snell)	0.12	0.12	0.12
% Correctly Classified	64.60%	64.80%	64.10%
Sample Size	608	608	608

Note: 1. Natural logs taken for: Value added, employ, import change, profit, and import penetration in order to better approximate a normal distribution. No outliers removed.

2. Coefficients are unstandardized linear regression coefficients; standard errors in parentheses.

3. *p < .05, **p < .01; and ***p < .001, and two-tailed t-test.

Models 1 and 2: 1985–1999

In Model 1, profitability, value-added per employee and import penetration were all statistically significant (see table 3.6). Less profitable industries were more likely to win trade protection, as predicted. But there was a positive relationship between value-added and trade protection, and a negative relationship between import penetration and trade protection. Low import penetration industries were more likely to receive trade protection, contrary to the standard trade literature. This suggests that industries with already low import penetration levels are the ones receiving protection, not industries facing high levels of import penetration. Value-added was positively related to trade protection, contrary to the hypothesized relationship. This suggests that low value-added industries, in traditional blue collar sectors, are not necessarily more likely to receive trade protection. In fact, the positive relationship suggests that high value-added industries, like semiconductors, supercomputers, cars, and machinery are the industries winning trade protection.

Interestingly, import change was not statistically significant, nor was the size of the industry. This suggests that while import change is often cited as the most important reason to give trade protection to an industry, this might not be the actual reason an industry does or does not receive trade protection. Employment was also not statistically significant, suggesting that political "adding machine" models in which the political power of an industry is directly translated into the voting preferences of politicians might not be true in the case of this form of trade protection. While these findings are not consistent with the hypothesized relationships derived from the general literature, they are consistent with the continued disagreements over the multifaceted causes of trade protection.

Change in real GDP and change in unemployment rate are highly correlated ($r = -.93\star\star\star$), therefore both cannot be used in the same model. Model 1 tests the effects of change in real GDP and Model 2 tests the effects of change in unemployment. Both variables are significant in each model, but not in the hypothesized directions. As GDP increases, trade protection is more likely. As unemployment increases, trade protection is less likely. These results highlight the divisions in the literature in which factors might be important explanations of trade protection in some but not all circumstances.

What is most interesting are the findings related to the international political variables. The two significant variables with the largest coefficients are NME and Japan. An industry in Japan or an NME is more likely to face protection in the form of anti-dumping cases than industries in other countries regions. Big Emerging Markets and Other Asian countries were also statistically significant, all in a positive direction.

Model 3: 1985–1999, Cold War Interactive Variable

Model 3 incorporates a cold war interactive variable to test whether there is some difference in the treatment of NMEs in the cold war and post–cold war time periods. The interactive variable is tested only with respect to non-market economies, since the puzzle is whether or not NMEs are treated differently over time by the United States, and if so why.

The cold war interactive variable is not statistically significant, and fails to affect the significance or directionality of any of the variables from the previous models. In essence, there is very little change in this model, suggesting that time period examined does not affect the incidence of trade protection. Specially, the model leads one to suggest that even though there have been changes in the geostrategic structure of the international system and NMEs have made substantial changes to their domestic political and economic systems in the post–cold war period, neither of these changes has had a discernable effect on outcomes. These sorts of changes in outcomes would be predicted based on the traditional political economy variables. The outcome stasis revealed in the statistical analysis remains to be explored in the case study chapters.

Analysis II: Which Factors Determine How Much Protection an Industry Is Granted?

In this series of models, I test which factors affect the size of the trade protection an industry is awarded. The dependent variable is level of protection, operationalized in terms of the dumping margin (continuous variable).[10] This analysis looks only at cases in which an industry is granted protection, either in the form of a dumping margin or a suspension agreement. In the case of suspension agreements the preliminary dumping margins are used to assess the level of protection. The same independent variables are tested.

Model 1: Domestic Economic, Domestic Political, and International Economic Variables

In Model 1, the international political variables are excluded in order to determine how much variation in the dependent variable the variables based on traditional political economy hypotheses can explain. All the variables are statistically significant but not in the predicted directions. Out of six variables, change in real GDP and import change are the only two moving in the expected directions. Declining GDP and import surges do lead to higher levels of trade protection. However change in real GDP is significant at the lowest confidence interval of any of the variables in this model and has the smallest standardized beta. Therefore we can assert that it has the smallest effect on the amount of trade protection received (see table 3.7).

Table 3.7 Which Factors Explain the Size of the Trade Protection Awarded? Analysis II—OLS Regression Model Dependent Variable: Amount of Trade Protection Received

Independent Variables	Model 1	Model 2	Model 3	Model 4
Size of Industry	−0.26**	—	−0.16*	5.85E−03
(Employment)	(0.09)		(0.08)	(0.10)
	−0.18		−0.11	0.004
Value Added by Industry	0.56***	—	0.46***	0.51***
Per Employee	(0.15)		(0.13)	(0.16)
(Lagged)	0.21		0.17	0.19
Industry Profitability	0.78***	—	0.57**	0.27
	(0.20)		(0.19)	(0.24)
	0.23		0.17	0.08
Import Penetration	−1.28***	—	−0.97***	0.09*
(Lagged)	(0.19)		(0.18)	(0.05)
	−0.65		−0.49	0.11
Import Change	1.46***	—	1.07***	0.02
	(0.23)		(0.22)	(0.11)
	0.62		0.45	0.01
Change in Real GDP	−7.87*	—	−8.36**	−10.70**
	(3.70)		(3.39)	(4.05)
	−0.12		−0.13	−0.16
Non-Market Economies	—	1.69***	1.11***	1.30***
		(0.26)	(0.27)	(0.36)
		0.56	0.37	0.5
South America	—	0.28	0.17	0.31
		(0.26)	(0.26)	(0.29)
		0.07	0.01	0.08
Europe	—	0.64**	0.12	0.02
		(0.27)	(0.28)	(0.36)
		0.20	0.04	0.007
Japan	—	1.36***	0.87***	0.87**
		(0.28)	(0.28)	(0.37)
		0.39	0.25	0.26

(Continued)

Table 3.7 Continued

Asian NICs	—	−0.65**	−0.67**	−0.90***
		(0.26)	(0.26)	(0.28)
		−0.19	*−0.2*	*−0.28*
Big Emerging Markets	—	0.56*	0.33	0.16
		(0.26)	(0.26)	(0.32)
		0.22	*0.13*	*0.07*
Other Asian Countries	—	−0.15	−0.18	0.15
		(0.30)	(0.30)	(0.30)
		−0.03	*−0.04*	*0.04*
Constant	44.85**	2.65***	45.25**	54.38**
	(17.00)	(0.23)	(15.70)	(18.97)
Adjusted R2	0.22	0.25	0.37	0.41
Sample Size	281	321	280	203
F Value	14.26***	16.39***	13.42***	11.62***
Durbin-Watson	1.79	1.58	1.80	1.85

Note: 1. Coefficients are unstandardized linear regression coefficients: standard errors in parentheses. Betas in italics. 2. * $p < .05$; ** $p < .01$; *** $p < .001$, $t > 2$ and two-tailed test.

Employment, import penetration, value-added, and profitability all vary in the opposite direction of that hypothesized. Contrary to predictions, smaller industries get higher levels of trade protection than larger industries, and more profitable industries get higher levels of trade protection. Industries with low levels of import penetration get higher levels of trade protection. This suggests that firms already receiving import protection are the recipients of the most new trade protection. The positive relationship between valued-added and level of protection suggests that higher value-added industries get higher levels of protection, contrary to sensitive sector theories. However, industries with already low levels of import penetration get the highest levels of trade protection. This might indirectly support the theory that sensitive sectors receive the most trade protection, even when they already have substantial levels of protection. While some of these findings are contrary to traditional political and economic predictions regarding value-added or profitability as explanatory variables, they do reaffirm the myriad of factors that affect levels of trade protection.

In sum, traditional domestic economic, domestic political, and international economic variables do not present a straightforward explanation of levels of trade protection. Overall this model explains 22 percent of the variation in levels of trade protection. The two significant variables explaining levels of protection are import penetration and import change.

As imports increase, trade protection increases. This suggests that simple economic or political explanations of patterns of anti-dumping protection are insufficient.

Model 2: International Political Variables

In Model 2, I test the explanatory power of the international political variables. The variables are coded as a series of dummy variables, with one category "other" not included in the analysis. Knowing country of origin can explain 25 percent of the variation in level of trade protection. The country designation with the largest beta coefficient was NME, followed by Japan. This suggests that imports from Japan or from non-market economies are more likely to get higher levels of trade protection than imports from other regions, regardless of year or sector. The NME effect is 30 percent greater than the effect of the Japan variable. Moreover, while imports from Europe also have a positive relationship with trade protection, the NME effect is more than twice as great as the Europe effect. Interestingly, there is a negative relationship between being an Asian NIC and levels of trade protection. Imports from Asian NICs are less likely to have higher levels of trade protection, suggesting they are protected from high levels of anti-dumping trade protection even though they are exporting commodities similar to NMEs and Japan.

There is substantial overlap between the export compositions of Japan and the Asian NICs, and between NMEs and big emerging markets. This is interesting because while they are often cumulated on anti-dumping cases together, they exhibit very different patterns of trade protection (see table 3.8). Table 3.8 displays different countries involved in the same anti-dumping cases, against the same commodities, in the same time period, with different patterns of trade protection. These tables demonstrate that NMEs and Japan are almost always the recipients of the highest dumping margins, holding other factors constant. Together with the OLS regression analysis, this suggests that commodity composition alone cannot account for the patterns of trade protection evidenced. Country region of origin is important in determining the magnitude of trade protection an industry is awarded. Explorations of why country of origin matter are broached in later chapters. This preliminary statistical analysis simply demonstrates a lacuna in our understanding of causes of trade protection.

Model 3: All Variables (1985–1999)

In this model all the variables are included across the 15-year time period. This model explains the most variation in the dependent

Table 3.8 Comparison of Dumping Margins in Same U.S. Cases

	Japan and Asian NICs				Non-Market Economies and Big Emerging Markets		
Product/Case	Year	Country	Dumping Margin	Product/Case	Year	Country	Dumping Margin
Cold-Rolled Steel	1999	Japan	39.28%	Mushrooms	1998	China	198.63%
		Taiwan	14.97%			India	11.30%
						Indonesia	11.26%
Steel Beams	1999	Japan	31.98%	Nails	1996	China	118.41%
		Korea	37.25%			Taiwan	2.98%
						Korea	0.00%
Steel Sheet	1998	Japan	40.18%	Steel plate	1996	Russia	185.00%
		Korea	12.12%			Ukraine	237.91%
Steel Wire	1998	Japan	15.20%			South Africa	0.00%
		Korea	0.00%				
		Taiwan	0.00%	Dinnerware	1996	China	7.06%
						Taiwan	3.25%
						Taiwan	0.00%
Stainless Steel	1997	Japan	25.26%				
		Korea	5.19%	Silicomanganese	1993	China	150.00%
		Taiwan	8.29%			Ukraine	163.00%
Alcohol	1995	Japan	77.49%			Brazil	17.60%
		Taiwan	19.21%	Pencils	1993	China	53.65%
		Korea	0.00%			Thailand	0.00%
						Korea	0.00%
Tubular Goods	1994	Japan	44.20%	Ferosilicon	1992	Kazakhstan	104.18%
		Korea	12.17%			Russia	104.18%
Flat Steel Products	1992	Japan	40.19%			Ukraine	104.18%
		Taiwan	0.00%			Argentina	0.00%
		Korea	0.00%			Venezuela	0.00%

variable, roughly 37 percent of the variation in level of trade protection. All of the traditional political economy variables from Model 1 are significant, but their signs remain problematic. Again, only change in real GDP and import change are significant in the expected directions. Import change and import penetration are significant at the 99.99 percent confidence interval. This suggests an important role for both variables in explaining amount of trade protection awarded.

Once again, non-market economies, Japan, and Asian NICs are statistically significant variables. Imports from Japan and from NMEs are highly penalized and imports from Asian NICs are favored. What is most striking about the level of effect of the variables, is that the NME standardized beta is only surpassed in magnitude and expected direction by import change. Therefore one can conclude that the NME dummy variable appears to be having the greatest effect on the level of trade protection received. The higher the trade protection received, the more likely it was that the import originated in a non-market economy.

Model 4: All Variables (1990–1999)
This model tests whether the end of the cold war has some effect on the use of anti-dumping laws. One expects NME status to be less important after the cold war. If NMEs are distrusted because they have different economic and political institutional structures, then in the ten years since the beginning of their economic transitions, one would expect a lessening of distrust fueled trade protection. The results of the model correspond poorly with these predictions.

Of the domestic and international economic factors, value-added, import penetration, and change in real GDP are significant. The profitability of an industry drops out as a statistically significant variable, and import change is not statistically significant. Moreover, the non-market economy variable dominates the explanation. NME is the variable with the largest standardized beta, at the highest confidence level. Instead of being less important, non-market economy status is even more important in predicting levels of protection. This runs contrary to predicted U.S. behavior toward these transitional economies.

This model can account for 41 percent of the variation in the dependent variable. This model suggests that not only are non-market economies still burdened by trade protection in the post–cold war period, but also that country classification remains the best predictor of overall level of protection. Theoretically this model leads one to

Table 3.9 Which Factors Explain Incidence of Trade Protection against Certain Countries? Analysis III: Parameter Values for Logit Model of Anti-dumping Decisions Dependent Variable: Anti-dumping Determinations

Independent Variables	NME	BEM	NICs	Japan	Europe	Oasian	SAmerica
Size of Industry	−0.66★★	0.19	0.02	−0.42	0.33	2.06★	0.01
(Employment)	(0.32)	(0.20)	(0.28)	(0.38)	(0.34)	(1.60)	(0.35)
Value Added by Industry	0.61★	0.83★★★	0.61	0.42	0.20	0.47	0.89★
(Per Employee)	(0.48)	(0.31)	(0.45)	(0.69)	(0.43)	(1.16)	(0.72)
Industry Profitability	0.69	−2.26★★★	−1.14★	0.38	−0.23	−10.73★★	−3.29★★★
	(0.87)	(0.60)	(0.78)	(0.66)	(0.50)	(5.31)	(1.29)
Import Penetration	−0.09	−0.13	−0.08	−0.20	−0.13	−1.46★★	−0.53★
(Lagged)	(0.22)	(0.13)	(0.18)	(0.21)	(0.19)	(0.73)	(0.35)
Import Change	−0.14	0.60	1.09★★	0.34	0.28	−1.69	0.20
	(0.25)	(0.48)	(0.66)	(0.61)	(0.83)	(2.22)	(1.20)
Change in Real GDP	7.37	16.13★★	5.76	43.54★★★	−12.06★	10.54	3.71
	(12.97)	(7.57)	(10.87)	(17.80)	(8.79)	(31.53)	(13.35)
Constant	−24.70	−77.51★★★	−26.81	−196.15★★★	52.00★	−84.36	−20.69
	(59.61)	(35.27)	(51.00)	(81.68)	(40.32)	(137.57)	(61.66)
Pseudo R2	0.07	0.14	0.10	0.12	0.03	0.44	0.16
Sample Size	98	213	97	71	149	37	64
Chi-Squared	7.36	32.36★★★	9.94★	8.99★	4.83	21.26★★★	11.36★★
	p = 0.15				p = 0.28		
Percentage Correctly Classified	68.40%	68.50%	61.90%	73.20%	59.70%	86.50%	57.80%

Note: 1. Natural logs taken in order to make the distribution more normal, since outliers were not removed: margins, value added, employment, import change, import penetration, and profitability.

2. Coefficients are unstandardized logistic regression coefficients; standard errors in parentheses.

3. ★ p < .10; ★★ p < .05; ★★★ p < .01, two tailed t-test.

question whether formal economic or political institutions alone in non-market economies could explain the treatment of their imports. The formal institutions in both NMEs and in the United States have changed during this time period, yet NME status remains an important predictor of high levels of trade protection. This theoretical question raised from these preliminary analyses is explored directly in the case study section of the book.

Analysis III: Can Traditional Political Economy Theories

Explain Patterns of Trade Protection against Certain

Country Groupings but Not Others?

Are traditional political economy theories more useful in explaining patterns of trade protection against some countries rather than others? Are there some countries for which international political considerations trump the domestic political, domestic economic, and international economic factors? In this analysis I separate the anti-dumping decisions by country, and test the ability of the political and economic hypotheses to explain patterns of trade protection against each country group. I segment the data into seven country categories and test the hypotheses using a logit model. The dependent variable is incidence of trade protection, whether there is an affirmative anti-dumping determination or suspension agreement or not (dichotomous). See table 3.9.

The results indicate that the political economy variables work better at explaining trade protection against certain countries regions. The logit models are robust for Big Emerging Markets, Asian NICs, Japan, Other Asian Countries, and South American countries. Between 58 and 73 percent of the cases, trade protection can be correctly predicted by the traditional political economy variables for these country groups. The two regional groups for which the model is not robust are NMEs and Europe. Traditional political economy variables do not correctly predict cases of trade protection or lack of trade protection against imports from NMEs or Europe.

It is also interesting that not all variables are significant across the countries. For example, in trade cases involving BEMs, South America, or Asia, declining industry profitability is a good indicator of trade protection. This is not the case with Japan. The only variable significant in the Japan model is change in real GDP, but not in the expected direction. Equally interesting is import changes are good predictors of trade protection in cases involving the Asian NICs, but not for any of the other country groups. Some political economy variables are more robust in explaining patterns of trade protection against certain countries and not others, suggesting a possible interactive effect between the variables tested here and other political factors.

These findings are particularly notable when one considers the findings from table 3.8 in which there is substantial overlap in anti-dumping cases between the country groups. There are many dumping cases involving the same product, the same domestic interest groups, the same international economic environment, the same domestic economic environment, but different countries. Holding these other factors constant, there are definite patterns in the way different countries and regions are treated on the same cases. The results from the three statistical analyses bear this out for the case of U.S. trade protection.

In sum, Analysis III shows that traditional political economy variables are good predictors of trade protection against most country groupings, except non-market economies. Other factors need to be examined to explain trade protection against NMEs.

Conclusion

This chapter has tested the traditional political economy explanations of level and intensity of trade protection. The traditional hypotheses have done a good job explaining both when and how much trade protection an industry will receive if the imports originate in most countries, except for Japan or NMEs. However, this chapter shows that trade protection against NMEs cannot easily be explained by looking at the nature of their exports, or the political saliency or economic profitability of domestic competing firms. Macroeconomic factors and export volumes fall short in accounting for trade protection against NME exports. All of these factors play a role in explaining trade protection against other countries, but seem to get minimized by an NME effect. The addition of the NME variable to the equations tends to minimize or eliminate the explanatory effects of these variables.

Moreover, the greater effect of the NME variable in the post–cold war period suggests that formal NME political and economic institutions are not the sole cause of the trade protection. NMEs are reforming, U.S. laws are changing, but the patterns of trade protection have not followed suit. In fact, they appear to have gotten worse over the time period analyzed. Since the analyses have demonstrated the utility of these traditional hypotheses in explaining patterns of trade protection against other countries, this makes the treatment of NMEs that much more puzzling. What *does* explain trade protection if the traditional political economy hypotheses have limited explanatory capacity in cases involving (former) Communist countries?

This chapter has not proven that beliefs matter, nor has it proven that NME region of origin explains trade protection. But it has refuted the alternative explanations of trade protection, and demonstrated that interest based accounts and traditional economic explanations cannot explain trade protection against non-market economies. It has also suggested that region of origin has a systematic effect on patterns of trade protection. Proving that beliefs about country or region of origin matter requires different types of evidence, and a more narrative examination of the application of anti-dumping trade remedy laws. I take up an ideational argument in the ensuing chapters, demonstrating that cold war beliefs about the antagonistic and inherently threatening nature of trade with Communist countries have hindered the West's willingness to recognize these countries as "market oriented" and engage in normal trade relations. I examine the mechanism by which these beliefs have limited trade relations, and also explore how this dynamic has impacted the economic development and international integration of these transitional economies.

The Nuts and Bolts of Anti-dumping Laws: Actors and Institutions in the United States and the European Union

Introduction

Because anti-dumping laws are fairly technical laws, and the devil lays in the details of how they are applied, I provide a brief overview of these laws in this chapter. I review their definition and intention, and explain the structure and functions of the trade agencies tasked with administering them in the United States and the European Union. I compare how the International Trade Administration in the U.S. Department of Commerce and the Directorate General of Trade in the European Commission define, interpret, and implement anti-dumping cases, highlighting their unique methods of applying the laws against non-market economies. Finally, I compare the special trade remedy laws designed by the European Commission and the International Trade Administration for dealing with imports from NMEs.

Anti-dumping Laws: Letter and Spirit of this Unfair Trade Remedy

Dumping, at its most basics is the sale of goods at less than fair value. The technical definition of dumping does not vary much by country, hewing rather closely to the GATT/WTO anti-dumping regulations (Article VI, Section 1).[1] Dumping, as defined by European Community regulations, is the "selling of a product in the Community at a price below its normal value" (European Commission 1998b, 3). This is understood to mean that if the "export price [of a product] to the Community is less than a comparable price for the like product, in the ordinary course of trade, as established for the exporting country," then the product is being dumped (Council Reg No. 384/96 1996, Article 2). The United States' anti-dumping law defines dumping as "sales at less than fair value" that cause or threaten to cause material injury to domestic industries (U.S. Department of Commerce International Trade Administration 1991). "Sales at less than fair value most often occur when a foreign firm sells merchandise in the U.S. market at a price lower than the price it charges for a comparable product sold in its domestic market" (U.S. Department of Commerce International Trade Administration 1998, Chapter 6). EU and U.S. legal definitions of dumping are essentially the same. The differences occur in the manner in which each country ascertains "fair" or "normal" value.

Anti-dumping laws were created to protect domestic firms from unfair, predatory competition. Scholars and practitioners who favor the use of anti-dumping laws argue that selling below normal value in order to create monopoly conditions or artificially segment the market drives up prices unnecessarily (Holmes and Kempton 1996, 650; Miranda 1996; Stewart 1991). Anti-dumping laws correct such unfair practices and "level the playing field." "For almost one hundred years international trade policy rules have recognized that 'dumping' is a practice that 'is to be condemned,' and have allowed an importing country to take certain counter measures, at least when the dumped goods cause material injury to competing industries in the importing country" (Jackson 1997, 251). There is a substantial body of literature critiquing the economic basis for anti-dumping laws. Critics argue that anti-dumping laws promote market inefficiencies, and benefit narrow industry interests at the cost of consumer welfare (Bhagwati 1988; Boltuck and Litan 1991; Deardorff 1995; Staiger 1995; Stern 1987; Viner 1923; Wares 1977). They argue that not only do consumers benefit but downstream users of products benefit from cheap inputs as well. Setting aside normative questions about the economic efficiency or necessity of anti-dumping laws, I examine the manner in which they are applied.

United States: The International Trade Administration and the International Trade Commission

In 1921, the United States implemented its first Anti-dumping Act, to be administered by the Department of Treasury. Title VII of the Tariff

Act of 1930 modified the original laws, and is the current basis for U.S. anti-dumping regulations.[2] Since 1930, not only have the agencies responsible for administering the anti-dumping laws changed, but there have been significant modifications to the laws themselves. In 1954, responsibility for administration was split between the Treasury and the International Trade Commission. This was modified again in 1980, when the International Trade Administration was given joint responsibility with the International Trade Commission to render anti-dumping decisions. Parties unsatisfied with the final determinations of the International Trade Administration and International Trade Commission can seek redress from the Federal Courts and International Court of Appeal. The 1979 GATT Anti-dumping Agreements were implemented into U.S. law by the Trade Agreements Act of 1979, and significant changes were made by the 1984 Act, the 1988 Act, the 1990 Act and the 1994 (U.S. Department of commerce; Uruguay Round Agreements Act U.S. International Trade Commission 1995, 1998).[3]

The two agencies currently charged with jointly administering U.S. anti-dumping laws are the International Trade Administration within the Department of Commerce and the International Trade Commission. To be awarded anti-dumping protection, a firm must demonstrate that foreign imports are being dumped, and that the imported goods are the cause of, or threaten to cause, material injury to the domestic competing firm. The International Trade Administration makes the dumping determination and the International Trade Commission makes the injury determination. To be awarded protection, both agencies must concur. See figure 4.1 for a schematic representation of an anti-dumping decision tree, with the actions of each party involved and a timetable for actions.

United States International Trade Commission (USITC)

The International Trade Commission determines whether the domestic industry is suffering material injury as a result of imports of dumped or subsidized products. In rendering decisions, the International Trade Commission considers all relevant economic factors, including but not limited to: domestic industry output, sales, market share, productivity, returns on investment, capacity utilization, employment, wages, growth, and profits (U.S. Department of Commerce International Trade Administration 2001). The law defines material injury as "harm that is not inconsequential, immaterial, or unimportant (Section 771 (7) (A),

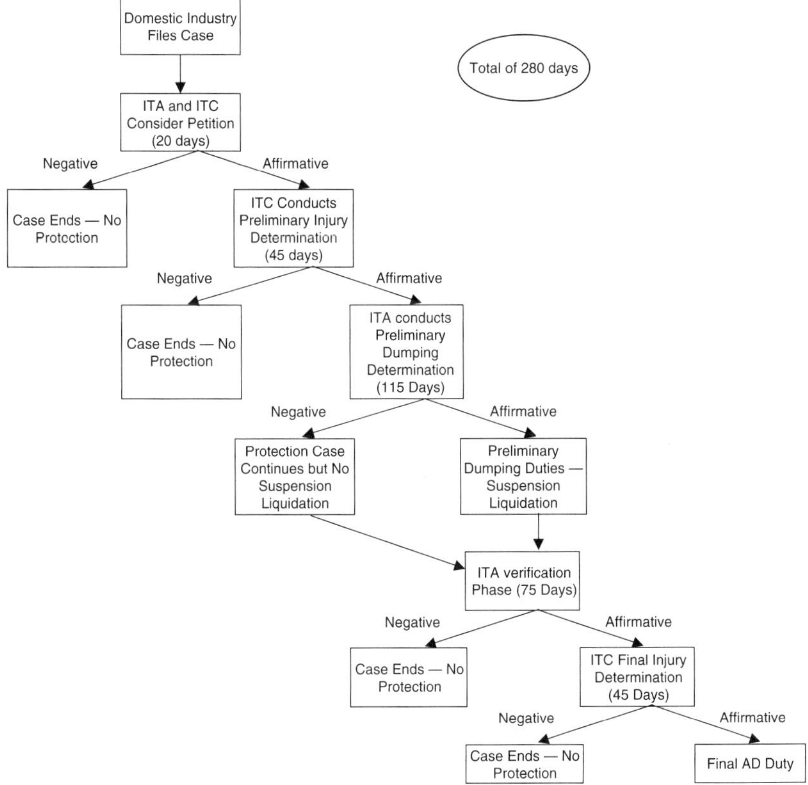

Figure 4.1   U.S. Anti-dumping Decision Tree

Notes: 1. These time periods can be extended by as much as 60 to 120 days depending upon special circumstances 2. Suspension liquidation requies an importer to post a bond guaranteeing that it will pay a duty in the event of an affirmative final determination.

Sources: Author constructed based on U.S. Department of Commerce Anti-Dumping Manual, November 1998 and 19 U.S.C. 1973a.

Tariff Act of 1930, as amended). The definition is intentionally vague and subject to interpretation.

A six court panel of politically appointed commissioners hears cases and determines whether imports have caused injury to domestic firms. The impetus for transferring injury determinations out of Treasury and to the ITC was to improve the fairness of the decision making process, and create an agency more autonomous from congressional, presidential, and special interest political pressure (Baldwin 1985b, 17; Moore 1992, 451).

Congress designed the ITC to be insulated from political pressure. The commissioners serve nine year terms not subject to reappointment, and the Commission's budget is removed from presidential control. These are just two of the ways in which ITC decision making has been institutionally depoliticized (Baldwin 1985b, 104).

International Trade Administration (ITA)

In an anti-dumping case, the ITA determines if the product is being dumped, that is sold at less than fair value. The determination of dumping is a highly formal procedure. The ITA is charged with conducting a formal investigation of dumping allegations, and told how to conduct said investigation. Extensive rules delineate the time frame, parties to be considered, and factors to analyze in the case. When Treasury was removed from the AD process, Congress also removed much of the discretion from ITA decision making. For example, it devoted 247 lines in the Trade Agreements Act of 1979 to instructions regarding the calculation of dumping, and only 40 lines to ITC injury determination (Moore 1992, 451). Moreover, analysts working on the anti-dumping cases are career bureaucrats, not political appointees.

There are four main responsibilities delegated to the ITA. First, ITA analysts accumulate and process the foreign and domestic firm level data used in rendering fair value calculations. The ITA sends detailed questionnaires to interested parties and collects relevant financial, organizational, and political information. Second, analysts determine if a sufficiently representative proportion of an industry supports a petition in order to merit a formal investigation.[4] Third, the ITA determines the scope of an investigation, namely what class or kind of merchandise will be grouped together in the investigation. This is an important component of a case, for, a very general description of commodities can bias the case in favor of petitioners, and a very narrow interpretation of the scope of the investigation can overly hinder petitioners. For example, defining steel products in general terms can make it easier for a domestic firm to show it is being injured because it increases the number of steel products that are potentially facing adverse foreign competition. A domestic firm must only show that one of the steel products under the umbrella of the case is being dumped in order to get protection for all products under the case umbrella. Fourth, analysts visit the facilities of foreign firms to verify the information supplied in the cases and to determine the veracity of financial statements (U.S. Department of Commerce International Trade Administration 1998, Chapter 1).

To start a dumping investigation, a petition is filed with the ITA and the ITC on behalf of a domestic industry alleging that it is being injured by foreign imports sold in the United States at less than fair value. The petition must contain information regarding: (1) the exact nature of the product being dumped, with appropriate Harmonized Tariff Schedule descriptive codes; (2) the countries the petitioners claim are dumping; (3) statistical data and supporting evidence of the volume and value of the imports under investigation; (4) statistical evidence of material injury to the domestic firm during the time of imports; and (5) a calculation of the export price or the constructed export price of the imports to justify the petition's allegations of dumping (U.S. Department of Commerce International Trade Administration 1998, Chapter 1, esp. 31–37).

Based on the information provided by petitioners, the ITC and the ITA can choose to initiate a full anti-dumping investigation. Figure 4.1 shows how the decisions rendered by the ITC and ITA proceed from each other. If the ITC does not find that a domestic firm is being injured, the investigation is terminated before dumping is even established by the ITA. Injury against domestic industries is calculated based on the cumulative effects of imports from a number of exporters. So an anti-dumping case may be a case against a single exporting firm in one country, several exporting firms in one country, or involve multiple exporting firms in multiple countries. This is why there are often several countries named as defendants on any one anti-dumping case. Accusing multiple countries of dumping improves the chances of finding the parties guilty of injury to domestic industries (Hansen and Prusa 1996; Tharakan, Greenaway, and Tharakan 1998).[5]

If a preliminary determination of injury is found, the ITA then renders a preliminary dumping determination. The fair market value (normal value) is compared to the export price; the difference constitutes the dumping margin. There are several ways to determine "normal value." The price for the goods in the exporting country's home market is the preferred measure of normal value. When home market sales do not exist, the export price to a third country is used. The constructed value method, a valuation of production costs, including quantities of raw materials, labor, and energy consumed plus a 10 percent general expenses charge and a 8 percent profits margin is employed as a third best method of determining fair value. In this method, the exporting firm provides costs for its factors of production, and these are added together to arrive at a normal value. The amount by which the normal value is less than the price of the goods imported to the United States is the dumping margin. This margin is used to calculate a duty on subsequent imports

(U.S.C. 19 § 1677e and 19 § 1677b). If dumping can be proven and the dumped good either causes material injury or threatens to cause material injury, duties are assessed.[6]

These methods of determining the fair value of imports from market economies have never applied to non-market economies, in which domestic prices failed to reflect relative scarcities and were divorced from world prices by a system of price equalization. Instead, alternate procedures have been devised, in part reflecting traditional Western presumptions that non-market economies posed a special threat to import competing producers and by extension to the importing country as a whole. The GATT/WTO allows for alternative methods of determining normal value when trading with non-market economies. These alternative methods are discussed later in this chapter. Because the ITA controls the "fair" or "normal" value component of the anti-dumping determinations and is in charge of interpreting and implementing the special rules with respect to NMEs, it is the U.S. trade agency on which this study is focused.

The European Union: The European Commission and the Council of the European Union

The EU anti-dumping laws, as well as GATT/WTO compliant procedures for implementing them, are spelled out in EC Regulation 3283/94, updated and amended by Council Regulation (EC) No. 384/96, (EC) No. 2026/97, and most recently Council Regulation (EC) No. 461/2004. (Council Reg No. 384/96 1996, European Commission 2004a, 2–3). Dumping laws cannot be applied to EU members; they only apply to non-EU member states. Dumping determinations are administered by both the European Commission and the Advisory Committee of the Council of the European Union. The European Commission implements and interprets the anti-dumping laws, and the Council has final veto power over the imposition of trade protection. The European Court of First Instance and the European Court of Justice are the final arbiters of any disputes arising from the legal interpretation and implementation of the laws (European Commission 2004b).[7]

European Commission

The European Commission collectively administers anti-dumping laws for all the member states of the EU. The Directorate General bureau in the Commission with responsibility for anti-dumping is DG Trade (formerly DG I and DGIA).[8] For the EU, dumping is a three part determination: there must be dumping, the dumped goods must be injuring a domestic producer of a like product, and a dumping margin must be "in the Community's interest." The Commission renders all three parts of the dumping decision. Within DG Trade the dumping and injury determinations are made by separate departments (E and C respectively). Although the Commission renders all dumping and injury findings, the decisions are made simultaneously by separate teams of analysts.

In determining if an anti-dumping case is merited, the Commission is instructed to look at "Import terms and conditions, import trends, the various aspects of the economic and commercial situation, and the measures, if any, to be taken" with respect to dumping (Council Reg No. 288/82 1982, 1). With regard to injury, the Commission is instructed to look at: "the volume of imports . . . the prices of imports . . . the consequent impact on the community producers of similar or directly competitive products as indicated by trends in certain economic factors, such as production, utilization of capacity, stocks, sales, ...rate of increase of the exports of the community . . . . And export capacity in the country of origin of export" (Council Reg No. 288/82 1982, Article 9 (1–2)). Finally, the Commission is instructed to consider if the dumping margin is in the interest of the overall Community. The Commission should weigh the costs and benefits to producers and consumers of the product in determining if duties should be levied (Inama and Vermulst 1999, 215). All three components are necessary for dumping duties to be imposed.

To begin an investigation, the Commission typically receives a complaint from a segment of the Community industry with standing, alleging injury from unfairly priced imports (see figure 4.2).[9] In some cases the Commission can self-initiate a case. The complaint must contain preliminary evidence that the product under question is being dumped, that the volume of imports is substantial, that is, represents a market share above 1 percent, and that the dumped goods are injuring the domestic industry (European Commission 2004b).[10] The complaint is then examined by the Advisory Committee of the Council and a representative of the Commission. If the complaint has merit, a proceeding is initiated. The Commission sends out questionnaires to interested parties, solicits comments from Community producers and the foreign exporters. It uses the data it receives to make like product determinations, normal value determinations, injury determinations, and finally calculate dumping margins (European Commission 1996, 1998b; Holmes and Kempton 1996).

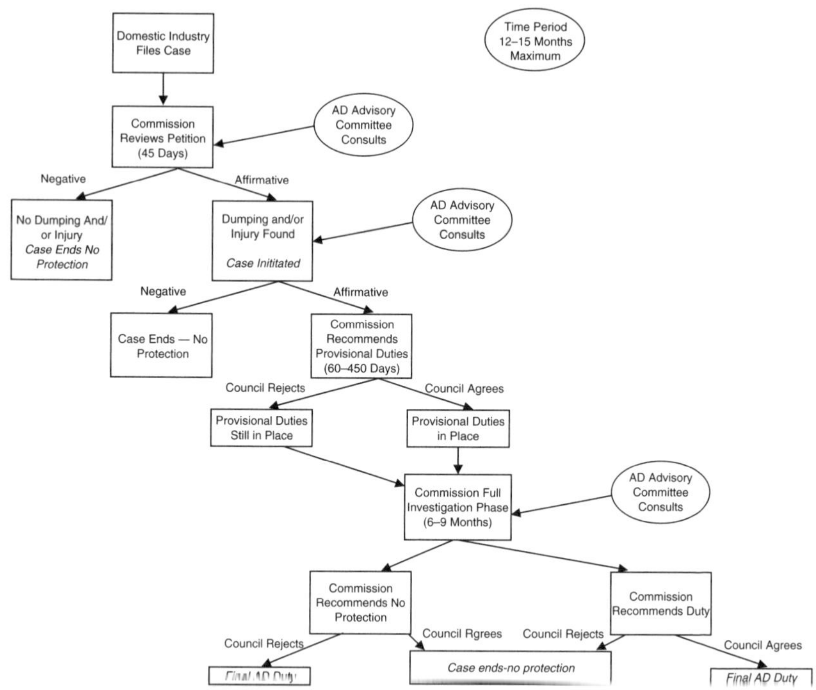

Figure 4.2   EU Anti-dumping Decision Tree

Notes: 1. The Council requires a simple majority or affirm or deny duties.

2. *The AD Advisory Committee* does not have voting power, simply consultative power.

Sources: *Author constructed based on Inama and Vermulst. 199. Customs and Trade Laws of the European Community. The Hague: Kluwer Law Intl.*

As in the U.S. example, what constitutes "normal value" is one of the most difficult questions faced in dumping determinations. Normal value is typically based on the prices paid in the ordinary course of trade in the domestic market. The normal value of the product is then compared to the export price of the product to determine if there is dumping. Similar to the United States, the EU will first turn to home market sales to determine normal value, then as a second best alternative to export sales to third countries, and finally as a third best alternative to a constructed value measure to determine normal value in the absence of sales in the home market (Inama and Vermulst 1999, 249). There are various procedures and rules designed to determine normal value, if there are problems associated with using the domestic prices of an exporting country. This is the problem faced by non-market economies. As such, special rules and procedures have developed to determine what constitutes the "normal value" of products from non-market economies. This is discussed later in this chapter.

Council of the European Union

The Council of the European Union (Council) comprises 25 voting members: one representative per member state. The Council votes twice on anti-dumping cases: once on provisional anti-dumping measures and once on definitive anti-dumping measures. The Council requires a qualified majority to impose or reject the duties proposed by the Commission (Council of the European Union 2004, 30). The provisional measure vote is not binding on the Commission, but the definitive anti-dumping vote is binding. Even if the Council rejects provisional duties, the Commission can continue with a full investigation. Although the Commission is technically in charge of all anti-dumping determinations and aspects of the investigations, the Council does have the final say in ratifying or rejecting Commission recommendations. While it is rare for the Council to vote against final Commission recommendations, there are some exceptions. The Council does not simply rubber-stamp Commission decisions.[11]

There is a competitive power dynamic between the Council and Commission involving the implementation of the anti-dumping laws. The Council's real influence comes through the Anti-dumping Advisory Committee, which consults with the Commission on cases. The Advisory Committee consists of government appointed representatives from member states. These representatives advise firms in their respective countries about the feasibility of filing an anti-dumping case, and are closely tied with national industries (Inama and Vermulst 1999, 212). The Advisory Committee is chaired by the Commission, so there is an informal Commission presence in the intra-Committee bargaining and negotiations. The discussions involving this Advisory Committee are confidential, but personal interviews with Anti-dumping Trade Officials at the European Commission revealed that the Council uses the Advisory Committee to influence the Commission's anti-dumping decisions. In these meetings the Commission gets a sense of Council opinions, and can alter the scope of the case or terminate the case altogether if it does not look like Council approval of a final anti-dumping duty would be forthcoming (Holmes and Kempton 1996, 653–654).

One Commission trade official referred to the Commission-Council-Advisory Committee relationship as a "political game."[12] Sometimes countries will vote nay in preliminary determinations to send a signal to the Commission about their intentions. Voting nay in the preliminary determinations also signals the domestic interest groups in that country that their representatives in the Council have their interests in mind. The Commission may engage in bargaining with the countries on other issues in order to secure yes votes in the final anti-dumping determination. Sometimes the countries will vote nay, in order to bargain or horse-trade their votes with other member states or the Commission on related issues (Buckley 1998).

Council voting decisions are confidential, as are Council discussions of the cases. However, some information regarding voting patterns has emerged that suggests there are two loose blocs of countries that tend to vote en masse for or against protection based on their economic predisposition.[13] Southern countries tend to be more protectionist than Northern countries, and this North/South split tends to hold across countries and commodities. Table 4.1 presents some expository evidence of Council voting patterns. Cases against a variety of countries and a variety of commodities evidence similar North/South voting patterns.

While member states can try and work their national interests into the Council's votes, it is also possible for the Council to try and influence the Commission in terms of overarching EU interests. On more than one occasion, the Council has explicitly told the Commission to keep the Community's political considerations in mind when administering anti-dumping laws (Council Reg No. 2022/95 1995, recital 80). For example, "The Council reaffirmed that the Commission, in making its proposals, must give proper consideration to the Community's stated commitment to encourage trade with Russia in order to facilitate its transition to a market economy (Agence Europe 1995a). This political requirement must be taken into account when adopting anti-dumping measures" (Agence Europe 1995b). Nonetheless, while the Council would certainly like to inject its political will into the determination of anti-dumping cases, the explicit power of the Council lies only in its veto.

In sum, the Council does play an oversight role in approving or denying Commission anti-dumping determinations. This role is not as transparent or direct as the Commission's in the anti-dumping process. While there may be an indirect and non-systemic role for the Council in NME dumping cases, in this project I focus on the European Commission as the primary trade agency. I am most concerned with the process of administering trade laws. Since the Council simply has

Table 4.1 European Council Voting Patterns on Anti-dumping Measures

Country	product	year	For AD Measures	Against AD Measures	Abstained from Voting
Russia and China	Aluminium Foil	1999	Portugal, Spain, France, Italy, Lux, Belgium, Greece, Austria, Ireland	UK, Nether, Sweden, Denmark	
Poland and Ukraine	Fertilizer	2000	Portugal, Spain, France, Italy, Lux, Belgium, Greece, Austria, Ireland	Denmark, Nether, Sweden	
China, S. Korea, Taiwan, Thailand	Hairbrushes	2000	Portugal, Spain, France, Italy, Lux, Belgium	Germany, Sweden, Nether, Denmark, UK, Austria	
China	Coke	2000	Greece, Spain, Belgium, Italy	Germany, Sweden, Nether, Denmark, UK, Austria, Finland	Portugal
China	Glycine	2000	Portugal, Spain, France, Italy, Lux, Belgium	Denmark, Germany, Nether, Austria, Finland	Sweden, UK
United States, Thailand	Electrolytic Capacitators	1999	Portugal, Spain, France, Belgium	UK, Germany, France, Sweden, Finland, Denmark, Ireland, Lux	Italy
Japan, Korea, Malaysia, China, Taiwan	Car CD Players	1999	Italy, Nether, France, Portugal, Belgium, Greece, Austria	Sweden, UK, Spain, Finland, Germany	Denmark, Lux, Ireland
India	Stainless Steel Bars	1998	Belgium, Spain, France, Greece, Italy, Lux, Portugal	Germany, Denmark, Ireland, Finland, Nether, UK, Sweden	Austria
China	Unbleached Cotton Fabrics	1998	France, Italy, Spain, Portugal, Greece, Austria	UK, Germany, Sweden, Denmark, Ireland, Nether, Finland	Belgium, Lux
China, Japan, Korea, Malaysia, Singapore, Taiwan, Thailand	Personal photocopiers	1998	Nether, Austria, Portugal, France, Greece, Finland	Germany, UK, Denmark, Ireland, Sweden	
China, Indonesia	Shoes	1997	Italy, Portugal, Greece, France, Spain, Austria, Finland	Germany, Denmark, Sweden, UK	

(Continued)

Table 4.1   Continued

Country	product	year	For AD Measures	Against AD Measures	Abstained from Voting
Japan	Photocopiers	1995	France, Italy, Spain, Nether, Belgium, Lux, Portugal, Austria	Germany, UK, Sweden	

Note: Information on Council voting patterns is not a matter of public record. The voting patterns are confidential EU documents. Therefore this information is derived from daily press reports that leak voting patterns. This is why the voting record is not complete but simply expository.

Sources: European Information Service and Europe Daily Bulletins, Daily Reports, 1994–2001.

veto power, it is not directly involved in interpreting and administering the trade laws. In addition, available information on Council voting patterns suggests that the Council does not differentiate substantially between trade protection against NMEs and trade protection against other countries (table 4.1). Therefore, this book focuses exclusively on the activities of the European Commission, namely the Directorate General for Trade, in the realm of trade relations with non-market economies.

Anti-dumping Laws and Non-Market Economies

The aforementioned discussions of U.S. and EU normal value calculations and anti-dumping procedures cover dumping that occurs in the "ordinary course of trade." Trade with non-market economies has never been considered "ordinary." Even in 1955 when Article VI of the GATT was implemented, an interpretive note was included with the original draft recognizing the difficulties in determining the normal value of imports from state controlled economies. At that time no suggestions were proffered as to how normal value might be calculated in such dumping cases, but a broad definition of "non-market economy" was included:

> It is recognized that, in the case of imports from a country which has a *complete or substantially complete monopoly of its trade* and where *all domestic prices are fixed by the state*, special difficulties may exist in determining price comparability for the purposes of paragraph 1, and in such cases importing contracting parties may find it necessary to take into account the possibility that a strict comparison with

domestic prices in which a country may not always be appropriate (Bael and Bellis 1990, 66, my emphasis).

For countries in which a complete state monopoly over trade and domestic prices existed, the GATT allowed different anti-dumping rules to be applied. In keeping with this broad description of "non-market," the West devised special GATT compliant trade laws to address the possibility of dumping from Communist countries. In practice, the West created a dichotomy: non-market economies and market economies. Neither the United States nor the EU had clear definitions or criteria to make this distinction. The United States did not come up with a legal definition of "non-market" until 1988. "The term 'non-market economy country' means any foreign country that the administering authority determines does not operate on market principles of cost or pricing structures, so that sales of merchandise in such a country do not reflect the fair value of the merchandise" (See OTCA, Pub. L. 100–418, 1316 (b), 102 Stat. 1107, 1187). In practice, only Communist countries were grouped in the "non-market" category, and singled out for extraordinary trade protection measures and procedures.

United States

The United States developed a "surrogate country method" or a "constructed value method" to determine normal value in cases involving state controlled economies. The surrogate method uses the prices in a third country to determine what constitutes normal value in NME anti-dumping cases. The surrogate country method originated with the Polish Golf Cart case (43 FR 1356 1978). At that time, Treasury was still the implementing agency and it struggled to interpret the Congressional intent of Section 205 (c) of the Anti-dumping Act of 1921, which instructed how to calculate normal value in NME cases (Department of Treasury 1977a). Section 205 allowed use of either the prices in a non-state controlled economy (i.e., a market economy) or, if such prices were unavailable, a constructed measure of "fair" value. There were two primary concerns with the constructed value method. First, a constructed value method would be time consuming and expensive for the United States to administer. Second, a constructed value method might violate congressional intent, which was not to use U.S. prices or other market economy prices to construct a surrogate price (Department of Treasury 1978).

In this case, Treasury tried to determine a fair way to calculate the normal value of Polish golf carts. Traditionally the prices in another market economy that produced the like product would be used to determine the normal value for Polish imports. Because the United States and Poland were the only producers in the world of electric golf carts, following the traditional method of determining normal value would have required the use of U.S. prices as measures of "fair value." As such this would have completely blocked Polish golf carts from the U.S. market. The Polish government became involved in the case, thereby raising its political importance. An internal Treasury Department memorandum commented that "The Poles have chosen to make a major political issue of this case, characterizing it as symbolic of their ability to expand their industrial exports to the United States" (Department of Treasury 1977b).

In the end the Treasury departed from precedent and from congressional intent and adopted a constructed value or surrogate method of determining normal value in NME anti-dumping cases. From its inception this method has been politically charged both within the United States and between the United States and NMEs. This constructed value methodology was supposed to improve the fairness of the anti-dumping laws by not de facto excluding NME exports from the U.S. market.

When administrative authority for anti-dumping laws was transferred to the International Trade Administration in 1980, this method was also continued. In essence, the surrogate country method uses the prices in a third country to determine what constitutes normal value in NME anti-dumping cases. A surrogate is selected, which is at a comparable state of economic development to the NME against which a case has been filed. The ITA then values the physical factors used in producing the allegedly dumped good in the surrogate country's factor prices. The resulting constructed value is converted into dollars at the surrogate's exchange rate to arrive at a dollar foreign market value. In 1988, the Omnibus Trade and Competitiveness Act adopted this "factors of production methodology," as the preferred method for determining the normal value (also called foreign market value) of imports from non-market economies (Willkie 1990, 517).

In practice the surrogate method values the prices for the factor inputs of commodity X in the surrogate country. For example, in a case against bicycles from Poland, a surrogate such as Brazil might be chosen. Then the factors of production that go into the manufacturing of bicycles would be determined, based on information supplied by Poland as well as ITA research. Such a list might include rubber tires, steel frames, plastic tubing, chrome gears, labor costs, the cost of electricity to power the factory in which the bicycles are produced, the cost of gas to power the machines that solder the bike frame together, and the cost of the cardboard boxes in which the bicycles are shipped, etc. These factors of production are then valued using a per unit cost supplied by the surrogate. Profit margins and margins for general expenses are added to the constructed value to arrive at a "normal value."

In market economy cases, each firm alleged to be dumping receives a separate dumping margin. In practice, this means that if five firms export commodity X to the United States, in a dumping case there could be five dumping margins assessed. In an NME there is a single countrywide rate. All industries are assumed to be under the control of the government, and therefore there are no separate rate assessments. "The purpose of applying one country-wide rate in an NME context is to prevent an NME government from later circumventing an anti-dumping order by controlling the flow of subject merchandise through exporters which have the lowest margin" (62 FR 61754 1997). This rule has been modified by the ITA, and in some cases separate rates are assessed if the firm can demonstrate an absence of government control in both law and fact with respect to exports. However, the anti-dumping law as applied to NME stipulates a single countrywide anti-dumping margin, and separate country specific margins are the exception.[14]

In sum, the surrogate country method presumes that prices in NMEs are inaccurate, and substitutes prices in a third country price proxy in order to determine a fair value for traded goods. The crux of NME anti-dumping determinations then revolves around the selection of an appropriate surrogate and the treatment of information supplied by NMEs. These topics are taken up in the next chapter. Both surrogate selection and information assessments are highly subjective, and the lens with which the International Trade Administration views NME cases has substantially affected case outcomes.

The European Union

The EU began applying special anti-dumping trade rules to non-market economies in the 1950s, but it was not until 1979 that the EU codified these procedures as the analogue country method (European Commission 1997a, 3). An "analogue" is the European equivalent of the U.S. "surrogate," namely a third country price proxy for non-market economies. In 1982, the EEC set out *Common Rules for Imports from State-Trading Countries*, in which it outlined the different trading rules for non-market economies (Council Reg No. 1765/82 1982). The document specified that Bulgaria, Hungary, Poland, Romania,

Czechoslovakia, the German Democratic Republic (GDR), the USSR, Vietnam, North Korea, and Mongolia should be treated as non-market economies and special anti-dumping rules applied to them (Council Reg No. 1765/82 1982, Annex). A companion regulation was drafted for China, mirroring the main document and applying the same special NME rules to China (Council Reg No. 1766/82 1982).

The principle guiding the special trade rules for NMEs was the same as that guiding U.S. policy. Non-market economies were assumed to pose an extraordinary trade threat due to the structure of their domestic economic and political institutions and their hostile interests toward the West (Council Reg No. 1765/82 1982, Article 9 (2)). Therefore special rules had to be established to safeguard European industries from unfair trade with NMEs. The original 1982 Council Regulation has been amended numerous times, but has remained consistent with the spirit of the original regulation.[15] In particular, a 1996 modification clarified the use of the analogue country method in the calculation of normal value:

> normal value shall be determined on the basis of the price or constructed value in a market economy third country to other countries, including the Community, or where those are not possible, on any other reasonable basis, including the price actually paid or payable in the Community for the like product, duly adjusted if necessary to include a reasonable profit margin. An appropriate market economy third country shall be selected in a not unreasonable manner, due account being taken of any reliable information made available at the time of selection. Account shall also be taken of time limits; where appropriate, a market economy third country which is subject to the same investigation shall be used. (Council Reg No. 384/96 1996, Article 2(7))

The EU uses the analogue country to determine the normal value of NME imports. Instead of valuing each of the factor inputs in a third country and adding them together to arrive at a surrogate price, as the United States does, the EU uses the price of commodity X in a third country as a substitute for the price of commodity X in an NME. The Commission has four authorized ways of using an analogue to derive prices to be used in an NME case. These include: (1) using the actual prices that a given commodity is sold for in the analogue; (2) using the export price of the commodity from the analogue to another market economy; (3) using a constructed value measure of the price of the commodity in the analogue in the event that there are inadequate domestic sales; and (4) use of the price paid in the EU for the commodity

(Fine 1988, 100–101). However, the EU prefers to use the actual prices of like product in the analogue as a price proxy for the non-market economy commodity prices, thereby favoring the first method (Fine 1988, 102).

For example, in a 1985 dumping case involving ice skates from Hungary, Czechoslovakia, and Romania, the prices incurred by Yugoslav producers of ice skates were used as analogues to calculate dumping margins against Hungary, Czechoslovakia, and Romania (Commission Decision 1985). More recently, Brazil was used as an analogue to determine prices in an anti-dumping case against Ukrainian silicon carbide producers (Council Reg No. 1786/97 1997), and India was used as an analogue for China in a case involving unbleached cotton (COM Reg No. 2208/96 1996). Common analogues for non-market economies in EU anti-dumping cases include Korea, Thailand, Brazil, India, Malaysia, and Indonesia. The analogue used essentially determines the outcome of the anti-dumping case.

In sum, the Commission alone renders decisions regarding the veracity of information in NME anti-dumping cases, and solely selects the analogues used as price proxies. The substantial amount of discretion afforded to the Commission in these determinations has allowed for agency-held beliefs, presumptions, and assumptions about the trade threat posed by NMEs to affect outcomes.

Conclusion

In the world of anti-dumping, one is either a market economy or a non-market economy. There are no special rules for shades of economic gray. It is important to note that other types of developing countries, including countries in which there are state controlled industries, like cotton in Egypt, or metals in Brazil, or chemicals in India, are not subject to these special trade rules. Only non-market economies have their domestic prices summarily disregarded in anti-dumping cases. Once a country is labeled a *market economy*, then the domestic prices *even for state-controlled industries* are accepted as true representations of "normal value," and used by the ITA and the European Commission in administering anti-dumping cases. The opposite presumption exists for NMEs. Once labeled a NME, the presumption of state interference in economic exchange activities permeates the evaluation of all economic information.

In the subsequent chapters I explore the manner in which this special non-market economy anti-dumping law has been institutionalized by the

United States and the European Union, and the way in which beliefs and presumptions of non-market activities have affected the implementation of this trade law. The types of decision making principles used by the European Commission and the International Trade Administration to select price proxies and implement anti-dumping proceedings have substantially influenced outcomes. It is these presumptions, decision making principles, and normative beliefs regarding NMEs that are explored in the remaining case study chapters.

Chapter five examines how the beliefs about the trade threat posed by NMEs have become institutionalized in the practice of the surrogate country method. It compares the practices used by the U.S. and EU trade agencies in their assessments and use of information involving NME trade cases. Chapter six examines two formal rule change to the anti-dumping laws, enacted after the end of the cold war, by both the United States and the European Union. In this chapter the stasis of beliefs is explored in the comparative context of U.S. and EU trade policy toward NMEs. Chapter seven examines a third formal rule change in the post-cold war period. While this rule change has been stymied by belief stasis, it is starting to evidence some outcome change. It provides a nice comparison in terms of both U.S. and EU trade policy, as well as a foil to the case of formal rule change and outcome stasis presented in chapter six.

CHAPTER FIVE

The Institutionalization of Beliefs

Almost everyone, domestic producers and non-market economy exporters alike, agrees that our current system of remedies with respect to imports from non-market economies does not work as well as it should. Current law is so arbitrary and unpredictable that a domestic industry contemplating an import relief petition and a non-market economy exporter seeking to price goods for the U.S. market both face the same problem—neither can accurately predict what constitutes "fair market value" under the law.
—Alan Holmer (Carey, Cunningham, and Abbey 1993).

Introduction

Chapter four outlined the formal mechanism for the implementation of the surrogate country method by the U.S. International Trade Administration and the European Commission. This chapter elaborates how beliefs, norms, and informal practices have influenced the implementation of this special NME anti-dumping method. Specifically it reviews how the institutionalization of cold war beliefs about the threatening nature of trade with NMEs has affected the respective trade agencies' interpretation and implementation of the constructed value methodology. The selection of surrogates, the acceptance or dismissal of information surrounding the case, and the presumptions used to access the veracity of claims all strongly suggest a causal impact for these cold war beliefs on anti-dumping laws even in the post–cold war period.

Trade agents have routinely cited higher levels of corruption, lack of economic freedom, or authoritarianism as reasons why trade with NMEs should be treated more cautiously than trade with other developing countries. In the second part of this chapter, I test these assertions using logit models to determine if indeed statistically significant differences exist or existed between the political and economic institutions in NMEs and other comparable developing countries. These models demonstrate that the presumptions about the different and potentially threatening nature of domestic institutions in NMEs were not supported by empirical conditions.

U.S. Surrogate Methodology in Practice

Surrogate Selection Pitfalls

Surrogate selection is the most crucial component of NME dumping investigations, because it is on the surrogate's prices that the normal value calculation rests. Therefore, the entire determination of dumping is ultimately reduced to the selection of the surrogate. There are official criteria used in the selection of comparable surrogates, and certain procedures and steps in place to direct the ITA in the preferencing and ordering of information and facts. Despite the formal procedures, "Congress provided the Department [ITA] with broad discretion in selecting surrogate countries in NME cases" (65 FR 1139 2000). This discretion left room for beliefs and perceptions about NMEs to affect the implementation of the laws. Within the broad guidelines, it is possible to select a surrogate that will yield more or less disadvantageous results.

To combat the perception that surrogate selection was arbitrary in 2004, the ITA clarified its position on surrogate selection procedures, economic comparability, and merchandise comparability. However, part of the new statute explicitly expanded the discretion afforded to the ITA in such determinations.

The statue does not require that the Department [ITA] use a surrogate country that is at a level of economic development *most* comparable to the NME country and that is the *most* significant producer of comparable merchandise. The statute requires only that the Department use a surrogate market economy country that is at a level of economic development comparable to that of the NME country and that is a significant producer of comparable merchandise. Even these requirements are not binding, as the statute requires that they be met *only to the extent possible*. (U.S. International Trade Administration, 2004b, 2, italics in original)

This memo was the first time in more than ten years of administering the NME statutes that a formal policy outlining a series of steps to follow in the selection of a surrogate was issued. This formalized the discretionary component of surrogate selection. This reconfirmation of NME treatment and the surrogate method suggests intent to continue its use in the near future.

The discretionary power of the ITA has been evidenced in the manner in which it interpreted and administered determinations of economic comparability, the use of multiple surrogates, changes in surrogates mid-way through cases, and ever changing information requirements on NME cases. These determinations were not arbitrary. They reflected the institutionalized belief that NMEs posed an extraordinary trade threat, and therefore the ITA needed to be especially vigilant in the administration of such cases. Each of these components of the decision making process is explored in more detail to elucidate how beliefs matter.

Economic Comparability

The surrogate is supposed to be economically comparable to the NME under investigation in terms of level of development. This is based on the assumption that level of economic development is a good indicator of underlying microeconomic prices. The general guidelines for surrogate selection, based on five objective economic criteria include: overall level of economic development, per capita Gross National Product (GNP), growth rate of per capita GNP, significance as a producer of a like product, and the distribution of labor between the agricultural and nonagricultural sectors (56 FR 60969 1991). In 2004, the ITA further specified that surrogate selection could be a function of (1) economic comparability, (2) comparability of merchandise, (3) significance as a producer, and (4) data considerations, in the order given (U.S. International Trade Administration 2004b). However, in practice the Office of Policy in Import Administration at the Department of Commerce relies on three factors to make surrogate selections: per capita GNP, real growth of GNP, and labor distribution, with a heavy reliance on per capita GNP alone (U.S. International Trade Administration 1996, 1999c, and 1999d).[1]

Table 5.1 illustrates the surrogate selection in several anti-dumping cases when GNP per capita was the sole economic criterion.

Using a surrogate's prices for factor inputs is premised on the existence of a relationship between macroeconomic factors and industry specific costs. There is little empirical evidence to show that comparable per capita incomes are stable predictors of relative factor endowments, hence relative factor prices. This renders the use of the surrogate's factor prices methodologically suspect from the beginning (Holzman 1987b). Intuitively, it is difficult to believe that the cost of labor in Tunisia and Russia, or Oman and the Czech Republic approximate each other simply because these countries have a similar GNP per capita.

Putting aside questions about the appropriateness of the procedure, finding an appropriate surrogate is highly problematic. It is not always possible to obtain information on a surrogate that is a producer of comparable products.[2] This is especially troubling if the product under consideration contains certain factor inputs only found in the country of production. In the case of *Certain Cased Pencils from the People's Republic of China (1994)*, Chinese producers used a special kind of wood for the production of pencils. Wood was the primary input in pencils and comprised over 50 percent of the cost of production. No other producer in the world used this kind of wood. So the prices of "similar" but much more expensive wood inputs were used instead to determine normal value. These "similar" wood products were produced and sold in the United States. In this case, the primary factor input was valued using a more expensive wood and in the prices of the very country alleging dumping (59 FR 55625 1994). In cases against *Magnesium Metal from Ukraine (1995)* and *Beryllium Metal and High Beryllium Alloys from Kazakhstan (1996)*, both countries were using chemicals, raw materials, and/or production processes that were unique (60 FR 16433 1995; 61

Table 5.1   Recent Surrogates Proposed By ITA for Non-Market Economies

	NME			*Surrogates*		
Case #1	Russia	Tunisia	Colombia	S. Africa	Venezuela	Poland
GNP/capita	$1999	$2100	$2250	$3160	$3670	$2270
Case #2	Czech	Brazil	Chile	Malaysia	Oman	Mexico
GNP/capita	$5200	$4700	$5020	$4680	$4950	$3680
Case #3	China	India	Pakistan	Sri Lanka	Philippines	Indonesia
GNP/capita	$750	$430	$480	$810	$1050	$680
Case #4	Romania	Egypt				
GNP/capita	$1720	$1530				

Sources: (68 FR 54418. 2003; U.S. International Trade Administration 1996, 2000d, 2001b, and 2003).

FR 44212 1996). No comparable producers could be found in the world. These unique production activities should have constituted a comparative advantage, and should have stopped the NME application of the anti-dumping case. By substituting price proxies using surrogates that were not even producing related products, any potential comparative advantage would be summarily rejected.

Multiple Surrogates or Changes in Surrogates

In addition to the host of problems associated with the choice of a reasonable surrogate, the ITA determined that multiple surrogates could be used in constructing a value in NME cases. This means that energy prices could be derived from one country, labor prices from a second country, and other factor inputs from a third country. These prices would then be summed to arrive at a "normal value" (59 FR 28053 1994; 59 FR 55625 1994; 64 FR 38626 1999). This method arrives at a value that is anything but "normal." Starting in 2001, the International Trade Administration stated a new preference for using single surrogates over multiple surrogates if possible, although this has not always been possible.[3]

There are many different factors of production included in a constructed value. Typical factors of production include: hours of labor, quantities of raw materials, amount of energy and utilities consumed, representative capital costs, freight charges, profit margins, and packing expenses (U.S. International Trade Administration 1998a). If there are ten factor inputs and four different surrogates used in the same case, it is very difficult to know what the final "normal" value will be.

Table 5.2 illustrates the sheer complexity involved in the calculation of normal value. The table lists a number of the factor inputs involved in the calculation of normal value for a given commodity, and which surrogate was used to price each factor. Because of the large number of factors that go into the production of a single commodity, all of them are not included in the table. Given the number of factors and the number of surrogates, there are an enormous number of permutations possible in the construction of "normal value." This illustrates the arbitrariness of normal value calculations, and how impossible it is for an NME to know *a priori* what price will constitute normal value.

Because no predictable scheme exists for weighting various macro-economic and industry specific factors in the choice of a surrogate, the NME exporter must estimate a range of possible foreign market values

Table 5.2 Surrogates in Selected Recent U.S. Anti-dumping Cases

Case No.	Product	NME	Surrogate	Selected Factor Inputs (Not Exhaustive)
A–485–804	Welded Steel Pipe	Romania	Colombia	marking paint, electricity, zinc, natural gas, unskilled labor
			Thailand	zinc and steel scrap, packing materials, freight, overhead
A–821–807	Ferrovanadium	Russia	South Africa	sodium ash, lime, electricity, labor, freight
			Thailand	thinner, paint, steel sheet,
			Turkey	sulfuric acid
			Brazil	nitrogen
			Poland	natural gas
A–823–806	Pure Magnesium	Ukraine	Indonesia	electricity, diesel fuel, unskilled labor, freight
			Egypt	natural gas
A–834–805	Beryillium	Kazakhstan	Algeria	alumimum hydroxide
			Colombia	red lead
			Ecuador	ammonia water
			Peru	resin, electricity, coal, unskilled labor, plastic bags
			Tunisia	sulfuric acid
				world composite
				beryl ore
			EU	base metal waste scrap, inorganic bases/oxides
			Brazil	freight, factory overhead

Sources: U.S. International Trade Administration 2001. *Index of Factor Values or Other Non-Market Economy countries*. <www.ita.doc.gov/IAFrameset.html>

for each potential export price (Brown 1989). Thus unlike market economy producers who know whether they are technically dumping, NMEs may dump involuntarily simply because they cannot know what price will turn out to be their product's constructed market value. The only sure figure is a cost above the price of like products produced by U.S. firms. However, non-market economies cannot sell their products for the same price as U.S. firms and expect to break into the market. A Senate Trade Hearing acknowledged these problems with the anti-dumping law:

> The current anti-dumping duty law and procedures as they apply to non-market economies do not work well . . . As a result, a non-market economy country typically is unable to predict whether or not a particular U.S. price will be considered a dumped price, and is unable to structure its activities accordingly. In addition, an American industry faced with low-priced competition from a non-market economy producer is unable to determine whether the anti-dumping duty law would provide a remedy. (Senate Report. No 71, 100th Cong., 1st Session, 108 (1987), as quoted in Carey, Cunningham, and Abbey 1993)

Further complicating matters, surrogates can be changed part way into a case, which further confounds the process and ensures that the NME will be kept guessing as to what strike price will be the final "normal" value. For example, in *Tapered Roller Bearings from Romania* (*1997*), the surrogate was changed during the administrative review. First Thai prices were used, and then in the follow-up investigation Turkish prices were used to determine normal value (62 FR 31075 1997). The Romanian firm could not even price to avoid dumping charges because it would have no foreknowledge of the changing "normal value" price target. The only safe price, or price that would definitely qualify as above the dumping threshold, would be so high as to price Romanian goods out of the U.S. market.

Surrogate Selection: Two Examples

The choice of a surrogate can substantially affect the size of the dumping margin, and even the presence of dumping altogether. *Freshwater Crawfish Tail Meat from the People's Republic of China* (*1996*) provides an example of this (62 FR 41355 1997; U.S. International Trade

Administration 1996). Spain was chosen as a "reasonable" surrogate despite the fact that Spain's GNP per capita was $13, 590, while China's was $490. The ITA rejected India, Pakistan, and Sri Lanka as reasonable surrogates, despite more comparable GNP figures and production profiles.[4]

Beyond the disparity in income, Spain was a poor fit as a surrogate for other reasons as well. First, Spain was not a primary harvester of the product, and China was. Spain imported crawfish from Portugal; this added substantially to the cost of production. Second, Spain's industry was so small, and had so many environmental restrictions that the Spanish prices were inflated. In a note to the file, a Department of Commerce Analyst wrote, "The [Spanish] officials told me that crawfish is considered a gourmet item, and because of fishing restrictions, is very expensive in Spain" (U.S. International Trade Administration 1997d). Third, China and the United States accounted for 90 percent of the world production of crawfish and were the only known producers of crawfish tail meat in the world (Sheldon and Mark Attorneys at Law 1997). Therefore, China and the United States were in unique positions because of their size as international distributors. Choosing a very small, niche producer of crawfish was hardly a comparable surrogate. By using a surrogate with a GNP per capita more than 25 times as great as China's, the resulting dumping margin was between 274 and 427 percent. The ITA responded to allegations that the surrogate selection was unfair, by reiterating its discretion over surrogate decisions:

> In this case, we relied upon the import price for Spain, a country which is not economically comparable to the PRC. Respondents do not contest the Department's authority under section 773 (c) (4) of the Act to rely upon surrogate value data from Spain in the absence of data from an economically comparable country.... Section 773 (c) (1) of the Act requires the Department to value the factors of production based on the best available information.... The statute does not specify what constitutes best available information. Therefore, *these decisions are within the Department's discretion.* (62 FR 41355 1997, my emphasis)

Another case that highlights both the discretion enjoyed by the ITA in these decisions, and the substantial effect surrogate selection has on the dumping margin was *Solid Agricultural Grade Ammonium Nitrate from the Russian Federation (2000)* (65 FR 1139 2000). In this case, natural gas was the primary factor input in the production of ammonium nitrate, constituting 30–50 percent of the total cost of production (White and Case Law Firm 2000b). Therefore the selection of a surrogate was very important, as the dumping margin would largely depend on the surrogate's factor price for gas. Poland and Venezuela were initially suggested by the ITA as surrogates, based on per capita GNP figures. Poland was eventually selected as an appropriate surrogate and Venezuela was rejected due to "unspecified, non-specific export subsidies" (U.S. International Trade Administration 1999d).[5]

Poland was an inappropriate surrogate for many reasons. First, the Polish government maintained monopoly control over the natural gas industry, thereby controlling production and pricing. This meant natural gas prices, the primary factor input, were not market determined in Poland. Second, Poland sourced 80 percent of its natural gas from Russia, the very target of the anti-dumping investigation. Therefore, Polish prices for natural gas would be at a premium to Russian prices, since Russia was selling the gas to Poland for a profit. Third, Polish prices were influenced by non-market economy transactions, since the gas was bought from Russia. Any NME influenced prices are supposed to be excluded from consideration in anti-dumping investigations, so using these prices violated legal precedent (see *Titanium Sponge from the Russian Federation* 57 FR 36070 1992). Polish prices were substantially inflated estimates of what Russian natural gas prices would be for the production of ammonium nitrate.

If Venezuelan prices for natural gas were used in this case to construct normal value, the dumping margin against Russia would have been 1.01 percent. A 1 percent margin is *de minimis* and the case would have been dismissed (U.S. International Trade Administration 1999d). Using Polish gas prices, the dumping margin assessed on Russian ammonium exports was 264.59 percent (65 FR 1139 2000).

The selection of surrogates, the use of multiple surrogates, and the preferencing of secondary information have all been problems in the administration of anti-dumping laws to NMEs. The examples demonstrate the substantial discretion the ITA has in administering an NME case and how this discretion can be used to penalize NME imports. The ITA is quite aware of the arbitrary elements in the calculation of a dumping margin using surrogate values. In personal interviews ITA analysts acknowledged the ease of adjusting the numbers up or down in order to come up with a dumping figure that "seemed appropriate" for the case. For example, in an interview with an analyst at the Department of Commerce, the analyst said he had come up with a 700 percent dumping margin on a current Chinese AD case, but would need to "tweak" the numbers to come up with a better margin that would not raise "red flags."[6] There is sufficient discretion built into the law to allow for substantial manipulation of the figures by the ITA.

Information Requirements as Trade Safeguards

The type and quantity of information required of NMEs reflected presumptions both about the inadequacy of NME supplied data, and the need for extra vigilance in considerations of data veracity from NMEs. While these presumptions have become institutionalized in the formal anti-dumping rules, they have also manifested themselves in the manner in which information was interpreted over the period 1980–2004, there has been a tendency in the ITA to reject information supplied by NMEs, even if the information would have technically met the formal requirements. Information sources deemed reliable by the ITA in a case against a developing country have been rejected as unreliable in parallel cases against NMEs. This rejection has not been ad hoc; it has been systematic, reflecting the underlying beliefs about NMEs from which the behavior gave rise. Some examples will demonstrate these assertions.

NMEs have different information requirements than other countries because of their special status. As such, the dumping questionnaire for NMEs is different from that used in other anti-dumping cases, although the time deadlines are the same. The unusual information requirements and the strict time deadlines make the information requirements that much more onerous for NMEs.

After the ITA opens a case, it requests information from interested parties. The questionnaire and request for information sent to the NME are 150-pages long. They require the preparation of a formal report, including information and supporting documentation about all aspects of a firm's business and the businesses of its affiliates. Additional information about the nature of the NME market, third country potential price proxy markets, and the U.S. domestic market is also required. Information about the cost of production of the goods in both the foreign and domestic market is also required. Finally, original and translated versions of all pertinent portions of non-English language documents and financial statements are mandatory. Upon receiving notification from the ITA, a non-market economy exporter has 21 days to respond to these requests.[7]

NME *price* information is completely rejected, but the ITA does solicit *production* information from the NME for possible use. However, even when NMEs submit all known information, it has often been deemed inadequate by the ITA and not used. There is a Department preference for verifiable, publicly available information over information supplied by the non-market economy exporter (59 FR 28053 1994; 60 FR 54472 1995). This preference originated from the belief that NMEs had more of an incentive than other countries to be untruthful in anti-dumping cases. "In typical NME cases, the Department historically has relied on rates supplied by the embassy of the surrogate country, without independently verifying the underlying data" (61 FR 192 1996). Therefore, unverified information from a third country, which might or might not be cooperative, has been preferred over actual information supplied by the non-market economy.

The financial cost of the information requirements poses a barrier to NME trade. NMEs may drop out of an anti-dumping case and simply cease exports because they cannot afford the legal costs. An anti-dumping case can cost a firm anywhere from $400,000 to $1 million and up to defend (Carey, Cunningham, and Abbey 1993).[8] Domestic firms have an incentive to file spurious cases in the hopes of deterring even "fair" trade from NMEs because of the ease of winning protection in NME cases (Olechowski 1990).[9] Even if domestic firms do not win, the mere filing of a case has trade deterring effects (Finger and Murray 1990). In the case of NMEs, it has been demonstrated that the filing of anti-dumping petitions may disproportionately inhibit exporters (Brown and Haas–Wilson 1990). This "harassment effect" persuades the exporter to restrict sales or to raise prices, both because the NME has a low probability of winning a case, and because funding a legal defense against dumping charges is prohibitively expensive.[10]

For example, in the case of *Ferrovanadium and Nitrided Vanadium from the Russian Federation (1998)*, the domestic industry launched an anti-dumping administrative review of Russian exporters because it had read that there were imports of this product into the United States and it wanted to get protection (63 FR 13031 1998). However, the figures were wrong. There were no Russian imports. Therefore the domestic industry was filing a case on the basis of reading that Russia might be exporting to the United States. The domestic industry was not being harmed by the products, because there were no imports. This case highlights how the structure of the law has created perverse incentives for domestic industries to file spurious cases. Moreover, this section has highlighted the way in which information requirements can be structured and used as de facto trade barriers.

Best Information Available

If the ITA rejects the information supplied by the defendant in a case (i.e., the NME) the Best Information Available (BIA) is used (57 FR 61876 1992).[11] Because BIA is typically the information submitted by the petitioners in the anti-dumping case, it practically guarantees that the data will be biased against the defendants and toward the highest possible anti-dumping margins. The ITA has acknowledged the questionable veracity of the information provided by petitioners. "BIA is not necessarily the most accurate information but a choice of information on the record which is usually prejudicial to respondents for non-compliance with the Department's requests for information" (56 FR 19640 1991).[12]

While the use of BIA in the absence of verifiable, publicly available information is the standard used in all antidumping cases, it is particularly prevalent in cases involving NMEs (58 FR 7539 1993). In 85 percent of cases against NMEs filed from 1988 to 1993, BIA was used in final anti-dumping determinations. This means that the information used to determine normal value was largely supplied by the very industries accusing NMEs of dumping (Carey, Cunningham, and Abbey 1993, 7). Not meeting deadlines, not providing information in the form required, providing some but not all information, or providing information that could only be used with difficulty, regardless of the reason, are all justifications for rejection of NME supplied information, and use of BIA (59 FR 22585 1994).

Use of BIA results in substantially larger anti-dumping margins. See table 5.3 for a comparison of dumping margins when the information provided by the NME exporter is used and when BIA is used. "Actual information" does not mean that NME prices are used. NME price data is always rejected and surrogates are used to price the export commodity in question. However, NME production data, input data, transportation data

Table 5.3   Comparison of Anti-dumping Margins: BIA versus NME Information

Case	*BIA*	*Actual Information*
Sebacic Acid from China	243.4%	43.72–85.45%
Steel Plate from Ukraine	237.91%	99.59%
Lug Nuts from China	44.99%	5.44%
Crawfish from China	201.63%	91.5–156.77%

Sources: (59 FR 28053 1994; 61 FR 58514 1996; 62 FR 41355 1997; 62 FR 61754 1997). Information based on comparison of individual rates (using actual data provided by firm) and countrywide rates (using BIA) in Separate Rates Determinations. Note, the actual information is *not* the price actually charged by the NME.

could all be accepted to determine the factor inputs for a commodity, and then those factor inputs could be priced in a surrogate country. The acceptance of this type of data is reflected in table 5.3 column "actual information." The use of BIA signals the outright rejection of the information.

As noted earlier, there are many different reasons why the ITA has rejected NME information and used BIA. For example, in *Certain Cut-to-Length Carbon Steel Plate from Romania* (*1993*), the ITA rejected the information provided by Romanian producers because information provided on one section of the questionnaire did not arrive in a "timely manner." As a result, a 75 percent dumping margin was assessed using BIA (58 FR 37209 1993). In *Heavy Forged Hand Tools from China* (*1991*), BIA was used because the Chinese exporter failed to file returns for all producers, even though the respondent did not have control over the one omitted producer. Moreover the ITA said the information contained disparities and was improperly formatted (56 FR 241 1991), 50 duties were imposed. Finally, in *Ferrosilicon from Russia, Kazakhstan, and Ukraine* (*1992*), dumping was determined based completely on BIA supplied by the petitioners in the case (58 FR 29192 1993). That meant the U.S. firms lobbying for protection supplied all the information used to determine the size of the anti-dumping margin. The ITA rejected the information from Russia, Kazakhstan, and Ukraine arguing it was incomplete, improperly certified, and incorrectly filed (57 FR 61876 1992).

The ITA's practice of disregarding NME information runs contrary to congressional intent for the administration of the laws. Congress stipulated, "If information supplied by an NME country to the Commerce Department permits foreign market value to be determined accurately using the normal methodology, then the Committee expects such methodology to be used by the Commerce Department."[13] However, the ITA does have full discretion over BIA determinations. Therefore, the ITA's BIA use is technically consistent with the letter of the dumping statute.

This section demonstrates the extent to which the ITA has erected information safeguards in cases involving NME transitional economies. Lingering beliefs about the harmful nature of NMEs have affected the way the ITA perceived the facts in NME antidumping cases. ITA discretion over the administration of a case has allowed it the room to act on these beliefs. The creation of extraordinary safeguards and impossible information requirements reflected the underlying beliefs that NMEs were extraordinary and needed to be approached with trepidation. These beliefs have had causal weight in the administration of the trade cases, manifesting themselves in surrogate selection, information decisions, and the tendency to use BIA. The ITA's method over this period was arbitrary. It reflected a systematic dislike of the information supplied by NMEs in anti-dumping cases.

European Union: Analogue Country Selection

As with the U.S. surrogate selection, the analogue chosen by the Commission can make the difference between a positive or negative finding of dumping. The Commission has sole authority to select analogues, and is given ample discretion in rendering such decisions by the vaguely worded European anti-dumping regulations. This discretion has provided room for Commission beliefs and perceptions about NMEs to affect the implementation of the laws.

Analogue Information Problems

The regulations stipulate that the analogue should be selected "not in an unreasonable manner" (European Commission 1997a). Overall, "the conditions of competition in the candidate analogue country and the characteristics of its domestic industry, such as the degree of its rationalization and modernization and its cost consciousness" should be comparable to the NME under investigation (European Commission 1997a, 2). Other factors such as wage comparability, similarity of product, similarity of production method, similarity of access to raw materials or factors of production, and volume of domestic sales are potential analogue criteria. Based on these suggestions for analogue selection, common analogues for non-market economies often include other developing countries such as Korea, Thailand, Brazil, India, Malaysia, and Indonesia (see table 5.4). These countries tend to be the most appropriate proxies in terms of wage levels, sophistication of industry development, size of export/import market, and technological development.

Because of various problems obtaining information about an analogue's costs of production, any analogue that will comply with an investigation is chosen, even if it is a poor proxy for the non-market economy.[14] As a result, the analogue involved in a concurrent or recent anti-dumping investigation will most often be used to price the costs of production for an NME. In such cases the analogue is forced to supply the information to the EU. However, since the analogue is already guilty of dumping, using its costs of production increases the likelihood that the non-market economy will be found guilty of dumping as well.[15]

Table 5.4 Sample of Affirmative Anti-dumping Cases against Non-Market Economies with Developing Countries as Analogues (1990–2003)

Case	NME	Product	Analogue
91/522/EEC, OJL 02/10/91	USSR	Artificial Corundum	Yugoslavia
91/522/EEC, OJL 02/10/91	Hungary	Artificial Corundum	Yugoslavia
EC No. 1189/93, OJL 15/05/93	Hungary	Seamless Iron Pipe	Croatia
EC No. 1189/93, OJL 15/05/93	Poland	Seamless Iron Pipe	Croatia
EC No. 710/95, OJL 01/04/95	China	Color TVs	Singapore
EC No. 2022/95, OJL 23/08/95	Russia	Ammonium Nitrate	Poland
EC No. 2022/95, OJL 23/08/95	Lithuania	Ammonium Nitrate	Poland
EC No. 5/96, OJL 04/01/96	China	Microwave Ovens	Korea
EC No. 1490/96, OJL 30/07/96	Belarus	Polyester Fiber	Taiwan
EC No. 119/97, OJL 24/01/97	China	Ring Binders	Malaysia
EC No. 165/97, OJL 01/31/97	China	Footwear	Indonesia
EC No. 981/97, OJL 31/05/97	Russia	Seamless Iron Pipe	Czech Rep
EC No. 1786/97, OJL 17/09/97	Ukraine	Silicon Carbide	Brazil
EC No. 1931/97, OJL 04/10/97	Uzbekistan	Unalloyed Zinc	Poland
EC No. 1931/97, OJL 04/10/97	Kazakhstan	Unalloyed Zinc	Poland
EC No. 2380/98, OJL 23/01/98	China	Leather Handbags	Indonesia
EC No. 904/98, OJL 30/04/98	China	Fax Machines	Korea
EC No. 1802/99, OJL 18/08/99	Ukraine	Seamless Pipe	Croatia
EC No. 362/99, OJL 19/02/99	Ukraine	Steel Ropes/Cables	Poland
COM Doc. (2000), 504 final	China	Fluorspar	South Africa
EC No. 967/00, OJL 09/05/00	China	Hairbrushes	Korea
EC No. 837/00, OJL 27/04/00	China	Picture Tubes	Malaysia
COM Doc. (2000), 43 final	China	Magnesia	Turkey
EC No. 2605/00, OJL 30/11/00	China	Scales	Indonesia
EC No. 255/01, OJL 02/02/01	China	Lamps	Mexico
EC No. 230/01, OJL 02/02/01	Russia	Steel Ropes	Korea
EC No. 1799/02, OJL274, 11/10/02	Belarus	Polyester Fibers	Poland
EC No. 540/02, OJL083, 27/03/02	Ukraine	Welded Tubes and Pipes	Turkey
EC No. 575/02, OJL087, 04/04/02	China	Sulfanilic Acid	India
EC No. 151/03, OJL025, 30/01/03	Russia	Electrical Sheets	Brazil
EC No. 1627/03, OJL232, 18/09/03	China	Sodium Cyclamate	Indonesia

Source: Commission Regulations and Council Regulations, 1990–2003 *Official Journal*.

There is an enormous problem getting adequate, reliable information from analogue countries.[16] Analogues that are not involved in their own anti-dumping investigations cannot be forced to comply with other EU investigations. The EU needs the cooperation of the relevant firms in supplying information about costs of production, factor inputs, wage levels, etc., since this information is not publicly available. To compound the difficulty, analogue countries have powerful disincentives to comply, as it is costly, time consuming and possibly self-defeating.[17] The information revealed by a cooperating firm could be used against it later should it be accused of dumping in the future. There are also incentives to provide misleading information. The analogue could provide information that might overstate or understate its costs of production. Since the accuracy of the information is vital to determine whether or not non-market economies are dumping, information problems affect the fairness of the anti–dumping determinations.

Poor analogue choices, information problems from the analogues, and presumptions that these second best price proxies are better than the prices provided by NMEs, have all resulted in discriminatory policies against non-market economy imports. The Commission has not made the same presumptions about the quality of information or the adverse intentions of the defendants from other countries. While, the Commission will penalize a company, from any country for intentionally trying to mislead or provide false information, it generally grants companies the benefit of the doubt. For example, in a case involving *Steel Ropes and Cables from Russia, Korea et al. (2001)*, a Korean firm gave misleading information but was not penalized by the Commission. The Commission determined that "given the fact that the party had acted to the best of its ability, and that the information submitted was verifiable, the Commission was able to correct the figures reported in the questionnaire" (COM Reg No. 230/2001 2001, recital 46). NMEs have not received the benefit of the doubt on cases. Mistakes on the part of NMEs have been seen as intentional and therefore reinforced the beliefs about the untrustworthy nature of NMEs. This lack of flexibility has substantially affected the interpretation of "facts" and the determinations that resulted.

In practice, the analogue country method, as it was and continues to be implemented, all but guarantees that the Commission will find the NME guilty of dumping. A trade official said that the Commission knows that using the analogue method would always result in positive dumping findings against NMEs.[18] If the dumping margin was high, that is, over 50 percent, then the official could be reasonably sure there was actual NME dumping. The dumping would probably not be as high as that calculated by the Commission, but the Commission was probably doing right by Community industries by imposing dumping duties. But if the dumping margin was low, then it was possible there was no dumping at all; the figure could be a fiction of the analogue method.[19]

Why did the Commission continue to use a method fraught with such clear information problems and one that yielded such erroneous results? A method that the Commission acknowledged was inaccurate? The answer lies in the institutionalization of cold war beliefs about the harmful nature of trade with NMEs. Using a second best analogue method was still better than using the information supplied by NMEs because non-market economies could not be trusted. There was a chance that analogue country data might reflect economic conditions, but there was no perceived possibility that NME data reflected market conditions. Therefore, this presumption about the non-market nature of economic relationships in NMEs, even against those that have enacted substantial economic transitions, continued to dominate Commission dumping decision making.

Lessons in "Appropriate" Comparative Advantage

Although the intention of the analogue method is to use comparable developing countries as price proxies for NMEs, the Commission has routinely used advanced industrialized countries as price proxies. This contradicts official EU policy stating that such advanced economies were ill suited to serve as analogues for NMEs. For example, Canada, the United States, Norway, even the entire European Union have been used as analogues (table 5.5). Because non-market economies necessarily compete on price to break into new markets, and since the types of goods they tend to export are labor or energy intensive, the use of advanced industrialized democracies as analogues substantially inflated the dumping margin (Laurent 1996).

These cases are particularly interesting because they have been used to "teach" NMEs what constitutes a viable comparative advantage in the international political economy. A review of a few cases will elucidate the EU's way of instructing non-market economies about appropriate market behaviors.

In the case of *Unwrought Magnesium from Russia and Ukraine* (*1995*), the Commission used Norway as a price analogue to determine normal value. The Commission argued that since Norway was a significant producer of this product, had an efficient production process, enjoyed low cost electricity, and had similar access to raw materials (sea water and dolomite), Norway would be an appropriate analogue (COM Reg No. 2997/95 1995). Differences in the quality and purity of Norwegian output and Russian and Ukrainian output were ignored, even though the lower purity of NME output should have lowered its market price. The biggest problem with the use of Norway involved labor costs. Since labor costs comprised a substantial proportion of the cost of magnesium, using Norway as an analogue inflated the "normal value" of the commodity.

Table 5.5 Sample of Affirmative Anti-dumping Cases against Non-Market Economies with OECD Countries as Analogues (1990–2003)

Case	NME	Product	Analogue
EC No. 1937/90, OJL 07/07/90	China	Typewriter Ribbon	EU
EC No. 3642/92, OJL 14/12/92	Poland	Ferrosilicon	Norway
EC No. 3068/92, OJL 24/10/92	Ukraine	Potash	Canada
EC No. 3068/92, OJL 24/10/92	Belarus	Potash	Canada
EC No. 821/94, OJL 13/04/94	Poland	Silicon Carbide	United States
EC No. 821/94, OJL 13/04/94	Russia	Silicon Carbide	United States
EC No. 821/94, OJL 13/04/94	Ukraine	Silicon Carbide	United States
EC No. 137/96, OJL 27/01/96	China	Chamottes	United States
EC No. 600/96, OJL 04/04/96	China	Coumarin	United States
EC No. 1006/96, OJL 05/06/96	China	Powdered Carbon	United States
EC No. 1347/96, OJL 12/07/96	Russia	Unwrought Magnesium	Norway
EC No. 1347/96, OJL 12/07/96	Ukraine	Unwrought Magnesium	Norway
EC No. 1347/96, OJL 12/07/96	Kazakhstan	Unwrought Magnesium	Norway
EC No. 2496/97, OJL 16/12/97	China	Silicon Metal	Norway
EC No. 449/98, OJL 27/02/98	Belarus	Potassium Chloride	Canada
EC No. 449/98, OJL 27/02/98	Russia	Potassium Chloride	Canada
EC No. 449/98, OJL 27/02/98	Ukraine	Potassium Chloride	Canada
98/90/EC, OJL 22/01/98	China	Dihydrostreptomycin	Japan
EC No. 771/98, OJL 09/04/98	China	Tungsten Carbide	United States
EC No. 603/99, OJL 20/03/99	Czech Rep★	Polypropelene Binder	United States
EC No. 603/99, OJL 20/03/99	Hungary★	Polypropelene Binder	United States
EC No. 1238/00, OJL 15/06/00	China	Coke	United States
EC No. 299/01, OJL 12/02/01	China	Potassium permanganate	United States
EC No. 1827/01, OJL248 18/09/01	China	Zinc Oxides	United States
EC No. 215/02, OJL035 06/02/02	China	Ferromolybdenum	United States
EC No. 658/02, OJL102 18/04/02	Russia	Ammonium Nitrate	United States
EC No. 2229/03, OJL339 24/12/03	Russia	Silicon	Canada, Norway
EC No. 1905/03, OJL283 31/10/03	China	Furfuryl Alcohol	United States

Note: (★)—in all these cases the countries had been reclassified as market economies, but analogues were still used in determining normal value

Source: Commission Regulations and Council Regulations, 1990–2003. *Official journal*.

Russian producers argued that Norwegian labor costs were not comparable to labor costs in Russia, and use of this analogue would result in inflated dumping margins (Council Reg No. 1347/96 1996, recital 16). The NMEs argued that their low labor costs should make their exports more competitive than Norway's. The Commission rejected this claim, specifying which costs did not constitute a comparative advantage for NMEs. "A number of claims put forward by the exporters concerned cannot be accepted, as such claims related to certain cost advantages, in particular with respect—to production labor costs—depreciation costs;—environmental costs;—selling expenses;—and raw material costs" (COM Reg No. 2997/95 1995, recital 36). Therefore the Russian and Ukrainian producers' claims that they enjoyed a comparative advantage in terms of raw materials and labor were rejected. In effect, the Commission rejected that low labor costs could constitute a comparative advantage in the production of a commodity from non-market economics.

The Commission then went even further in interpreting what constituted a comparative advantage. It subsequently imposed its interpretation of correct energy and environmental policies on the constructed cost of production for Russia and Ukraine. The Commission explained that not only would it use Norwegian labor costs, but it would make adjustments to the Russian and Ukrainian costs to take into consideration energy and environmental policies that they *should have* followed.

> It has been concluded that the normal value established in the analogue country should be adjusted in order to reflect that the Norwegian production process has a lower yield of by-product [meaning pollution] while being more energy efficient. Such an adjustment was done on the basis of electricity prices prevailing in the analogue and on the basis of an estimate of the prices of the main by-products valued at prices prevailing in the Community adjusted for necessary purification treatment. (Council Reg No. 1347/96 1996, recital 27)

In sum, the Commission ruled that Russia and Ukraine were not allowed to treat cheap labor as a comparative advantage, and were not permitted to waste energy or pollute in the production of products for export. After imposing anti-dumping duties on Russian and Ukrainian magnesium imports, the volume of imports fell by 49 percent and the value of imports fell by 55 percent (COM Reg No. 1002/98 1998, recital 47).

In a similar case against *Unwrought Magnesium from China (1998)* the Commission ruled that the large and conveniently located reserves of raw materials, low investment overhead, low labor costs, and low costs of production that characterized the Chinese industry could either not be quantified or were not considered "relevant" in determining the normal value of Chinese goods (Council Reg No. 2402/98 1998, recital 9). Norway was again used as an analogue for the calculation of normal value, and dumping was found.

In *Powdered Carbon from the People's Republic of China (1995)*, the costs of environmental protection became an anti-dumping issue (COM Reg No. 1984/95 1995). European producers had updated their production methods to decrease pollution, and this was considered the standard to which Chinese exporters should comply. Chinese production costs were revalued, including an "appropriate" cost for environmental protection. In this case, U.S. domestic prices for labor and access to raw materials were used to price Chinese exports to the EU, and costs for environmental protection as well as raw materials usage were added on top (COM Reg No. 1984/95 1995, recital 57). The resulting anti-dumping margin of more than 70 percent resulted in the expected drop in Chinese imports. This case set an interesting precedent of imposing European environmental policies on imports from NMEs. This policy was not followed with respect to other types of developing countries. The surrogate method gave the Commission the opportunity to manipulate the dumping margins in a way that the traditional anti-dumping remedy laws used against other developing countries did not.

In the case of *Potassium Chloride from Russia, Belarus, and Ukraine (1998)*, the defendants argued that they enjoyed a natural comparative advantage in the production of potassium chloride as compared with Canada, the chosen analogue (Council Reg No. 449/98 1998). "The Russian and Belarussian mines [claimed they] enjoyed natural comparative advantages in terms of access to raw materials, production process, proximity of production to customers and special characteristics of the product, i.e., the size of the reserves, the general characteristics of the mines, and their geographical location, and finally the characteristics of the ore" (Council Reg No. 449/98 1998, recital 32).

The EU rejected these claims of a natural comparative advantage and argued that none of these claims could be "clearly demonstrated and evaluated in terms of cost" (recital 34). The largest cost in the production of potassium chloride was transportation, namely getting the ore from the mines to market (recital 29). The prices of Canadian rail and road transport were applied to Russian, Ukrainian, and Belarussian calculations of normal value.

In a 2003 case against *Silicon Originating in Russia* (Council Reg. No. 2229/2003 2003, OJL 339), the Commission determined that Norway should be used as an appropriate analogue in constructing normal value. Electricity was a substantial factor input in the production of silicon. Using Norwegian energy costs substantially inflated the "normal value." Russian producers argued that their low cost of producing silicon was a function of low quality and highly competitive electricity costs. Russian producers emphasized that their "main electricity supplier [was] a majority private-owned company and this low price could [*sic*] be explained by the presence of the world's largest complex of hydro-electric power stations, based on a natural comparative advantage" (Council Reg. No. 2229/2003 2003 2003, OJL 339, section 3.1 (27)). The Commission rejected this claim of a natural comparative advantage in the generation of electricity, arguing that the electricity costs were too low and needed to be brought in line with "the lowest price of representative electricity producers found in the Community" (Council Reg. No. 2229/2003 2003 OJL, section 3.1 (27)). This is an odd lesson in comparative advantage.[20]

Other European actors have questioned the Commission's treatment of NMEs under the current anti-dumping laws. The European Parliament questioned the fairness of using Canada as an analogue in the aforementioned case of potassium chloride, citing the incomparable production costs between Canadian firms and NME firms (European Parliament 1996). The European Court of Justice ruled that the Commission was wrong to say that the comparative advantage of an NME could not be quantified. The ECJ has chided the Commission to work harder at finding comparable analogues and to take potential comparative advantages into account in the determination of normal value (European Court of Justice 1991). The European Foreign Trade Association has also lobbied against Commission anti-dumping determinations, specifically citing the Commission's use of the analogue country method as an unfair practice. It argued that anti-dumping laws were being manipulated "to abusively counteract the lawful comparative cost advantages enjoyed by developing countries" (Agence Europe 1996a).

Other developing countries are *not* treated like non-market economies. India, Pakistan, Egypt, Indonesia, or Thailand do not have the same labor, environmental, or energy standards applied to them. Despite the fact that many developing countries have very low labor rates, or subsidized, state owned, inefficient energy production, or pollute or abuse the environment as a by-product of their production for export, the EU has not used and as a policy does not use its anti-dumping laws to thwart these practices. It is accepted that these types of "comparative advantages" are low value-added, short-term practices to help developing countries earn capital in the international division of labor. As such, non-market economies have been held to a different standard of development than other types of developing countries.

An interview with a European trade official confirmed that an EU policy goal was to create incentives for other countries to use sound energy and environmental policies. The present interpretation and implementation of anti-dumping laws with respect to NMEs was a way to accomplish this larger EU goal.[21] All officials interviewed at the European Commission did not see the need to correct their treatment of NMEs.[22] In interviews with trade officials and heads of units in the Commission, all vehemently denied that labor, energy, or the use of the environment could constitute a comparative advantage for NMEs. In fact, in an interview with the EU official charged with overseeing external relations with China, he could not think of a natural comparative advantage that China might enjoy. Most officials could not think of comparative advantages that other NMEs might enjoy.

How is it that commissioners selectively ignored the contradictions in their policies despite the glaring information abnormalities and inconsistencies, as well as gentle reprimands from other EU institutions? This behavior is consistent with that of a rational information discounting agent. The set of institutionalized cold war beliefs about the potentially harmful effects of trade with NMEs acted as information discounters. The new, contrary information about the economic changes in NMEs was received by the Commission, although it failed to act on this information. These beliefs have become resistant to new information because they were institutionalized in both the formal rules, namely the analogue method, and the informal norms and practices, namely the presumptions about how one ought to treat cases involving NMEs.

Are NMEs Institutionally Different from Other Developing Countries?

The examples discussed in the preceding sections took place in the post–cold war period, mainly from 1995 to 2004. These are anti-dumping cases against NMEs in the midst of economic transitions, but differential trade rules have continued to be applied. While NMEs have enacted many economic and political reforms, perhaps there was still something institutionally different about NMEs that merited their continued differential treatment? Were NMEs more authoritarian or less market oriented than other developing countries? Did NMEs have fewer economic freedoms, which might explain their more onerous anti-dumping treatment? Perhaps NMEs were more corrupt as the trade officials alleged? In essence, could domestic institutional differences explain differences in protectionism?

In this section I test whether there was something significantly different about the domestic institutions of non-market economies from other developing countries during this time period which might account for the difference in their treatment. If this analysis demonstrates statistically significant differences in the domestic institutions of NMEs and other countries, this would work against a belief based hypothesis. If however, there were no substantial differences between NMEs and other developing countries, this suggests that material conditions are insufficient to explain patterns of trade protection. Additionally, it suggests a role for beliefs in an analysis of patterns of trade discrimination.

Data and Variables

I selected 1997 as the year of comparison, in order to compare non-market economies in transition to other developing countries in the post–cold war period only. I compare the domestic institutions of non-market economies and their analogues along four factors to test for significant institutional differences in corruption, democratization, political freedom, and economic freedom. First, NMEs are widely believed to be more corrupt than other countries, which might account for why they are distrusted. Second, NMEs are believed to be less democratic, meaning they have less well-established democratic political institutions than other developing countries. Third, NMEs are believed to be less politically free in terms of civil liberties than developing countries, as a legacy of communism. Fourth, many argue that there is an unusually large state presence in economic activities in NMEs, and that this lack of "market orientation" might explain the discriminatory treatment of NMEs.

In addition, I look at three strategic factors that interact with domestic institutions and might explain why NMEs are seen as "different" from other developing countries, namely: level of economic development, geographic distance from the United States, or EU, and trade importance. First, developing countries have less economic power in the international system than more developed countries. Lower levels of economic development might explain differential treatment. Second, trade importance might factor into calculations of NME trade relations. If a country is of low trade importance, the U.S. or EU might not worry about treating it poorly, for there would be few domestic trade repercussions. Third, geographic proximity could increase the political saliency of the other country's institutions. Trade importance and geographic distance should vary between the U.S. and EU samples.

I used the countries chosen as price proxies by the United States and EU for their NME anti-dumping cases as comparative cases, as the U.S. and EU thought these countries were institutionally comparable (see table 5.6).

Table 5.6   Countries in Logit Analyses (Baseline Year 1997)

U.S. Sample of Surrogates and NMEs

NMEs		Surrogates for NMEs		
Bulgaria	Romania	Brazil	Malaysia	Taiwan
China	Russia	Colombia	Pakistan	Thailand
Czech Republic	Slovakia	Egypt	Peru	Tunisia
Hungary	Ukraine	India	Philippines	Turkey
Poland		Indonesia	Spain	Sri Lanka
		Korea		

EU Sample of Surrogates and NMEs

NMEs		Surrogates for NMEs		
Albania	Lithuania	Brazil	India	Norway
Bulgaria	Romania	Canada	Indonesia	Singapore
China	Russia	Croatia	Korea	South Africa
Estonia	Ukraine	Egypt	Malaysia	Thailand
Georgia	Vietnam	Hong Kong	Mexico	Turkey
Latvia				

Since the United Status and EU treat NMEs slightly differently, I have used different surrogate/analogue countries in the samples, and I ran two separate analyses. For example, since the EU had already reclassified and treated Hungary, the Czech Republic, Poland, and Slovakia as "market economies" by 1997, I have not included them in the sample of NMEs. Excluding them is the more difficult test. If NMEs do not differ from other developing countries, even when the most advanced, market oriented NMEs are removed from the sample, this strongly rejects a theory focused on domestic, political, or economic institutions as explanations for differential treatment. Latvia, Lithuania, and Estonia's market status had not yet been ratified by 1997, therefore they were included. Although Romania and Bulgaria were reclassified as "market economies" in 1993–1994, they had not been treated as such under anti-dumping laws by 1997. Therefore I have included them in the EU sample of NMEs. The samples were chosen to maximize country diversity, and were limited by data availability.

Using a logit analysis, I test whether there are statistically significant differences between NMEs and other developing countries that the United States and European Union have labeled "similar" across these seven criteria: domestic corruption, level of democratization, GDP per capita (as a proxy for level of economic development), economic freedom, political freedom, trade importance, and geographic proximity.

Table 5.7 Summary of Variables

Independent Variables	Expected Sign
Domestic corruption	+
Democratization	−
GDP per capita	−
Economic freedom	+
Political freedom	+
Trade importance	−
Geographic distance	−

The dependent variable is dichotomous country type (1 = non-market/0 = market). Where some of the data are ordinal and bounded, they have been transformed to meet assumptions of normality (See Appendix 1).[23] Table 5.7 summarizes the hypothesized direction of the variables.

Results

Table 5.8 summarizes the analysis of the U.S. data. Because of the high correlation between economic freedom and GDP per capita (r = −.62★★), and democratization and political freedom (r = −71★★), the models test permutations of the variables to avoid problems of multicollinearity. The chi-square test shows all five models are significant and robust. Geographic distance, democratization, GDP per capita, and economic freedom are not statistically significant in any of the models. Domestic corruption is only significant in the model in which trade importance is included (model 5). Political freedom is only significant in the model without trade importance (model 3). This suggests that there might be an interaction between these variables. Surprisingly, domestic corruption varies in the opposite direction of that hypothesized. NMEs are not more corrupt than their developing country surrogates. Also surprising is that political freedom has a negative coefficient. NMEs are not less politically free than other developing countries.

These two findings are important, because contrary to popular perceptions, they show that NMEs are not less free, or more authoritarian, or less market oriented than other developing countries, contrary to popular perceptions. Trade importance is the only consistently significant variable and it is in the direction hypothesized, that is, NMEs are not important trading partners. This could reflect the continuing impediments to exchange relations between the East and the United States.

Table 5.8 Are NMEs Institutionally Different from Other Developing Countries? *Parameter Values for Logit Model (US Data, 1997)*

Dependent Variable: *Type of country (0/1 NME)*	*Model 1*	*Model 2*	*Model 3*	*Model 4*	*Model 5*
Domestic Corruption	−1.02	−0.74	−0.82	−0.78	−1.70★
	(0.91)	0.78)	(0.75)	(0.81)	(0.93)
Democratization	0.04	0.04	—	—	0.04
(Institutions)	(0.03)	(0.03)			(0.03)
Economic Freedom	8.22	5.56	6.59	6.98	—
	(6.16)	(4.87)	(5.00)	(5.85)	
Political Freedom	—	—	−3.18★	−2.50	—
			(1.70)	(1.63)	
GDP per capita	0.90	—	—	—	0.98
	(1.24)				(1.18)
Geographic Distance	−0.04	−0.07	−0.06	−0.05	−0.05
(km)	(0.05)	(0.05)	(0.04)	(0.04)	(0.04)
Trade Importance	—	—	—	−0.91★	−1.19★
(US/EU Exports to Country)				(0.54)	(0.57)
Constant	−16.62★	−3.57	1.64	−5.93	−7.06
	(20.38)	11.77)	(12.26)	(13.66)	(11.97)
Chi-Square	10.67★	10.13★	11.52★★	15.58★★	16.05★★
Pseudo R2 (Cox & Snell)	035	33	0.40	0.46	0.47
% Correctly Classified	76.00%	72.00%	80.00%	88.00%	92.00%
Sample Size	25	25	25	25	25

Note: 1. Coefficients are unstandardized logistic regression coefficients: standard errors in parentheses.

2. ★ p < .05; ★★ p < .01; and ★★★ p < .001, and two-tailed t-test.

However, it does not appear to reflect the underlying political and economic institutions.

The results from the analysis of European Union data are similar to the U.S. results (table 5.9). The models are all robust. Corruption, democratization, GDP per capita, economic freedom, political freedom, and this time trade importance, are not statistically significant in any of the models. The only variable that is significant in the EU analysis is geographic proximity. This variable was not significant in the U.S. analysis. The domestic economic and political conditions of neighbors may be of greater importance to the EU because of the potential spillover effects. NMEs tend to be closer to the EU than other developing countries, and the EU may be more aware and concerned with their domestic institutions as a result of the potential direct effects on the EU. However, geographic proximity alone cannot predict or explain NME treatment.

In interviews, analysts at the Commission said they did not like conducting anti-dumping investigations in non-market economies because of the conditions in those countries. In several interviews, officials independently brought up the corruption in NMEs, and why they should therefore be treated differently from other countries. The Russian mafia or Ukrainian corruption were specifically cited as reasons for these countries not being trusted.[24] Because of the alleged "market disruptions" in these countries, "widespread irregularities" and high levels of corruption, NMEs were perceived to merit much more cautious treatment by the Commission. However, the evidence from this section demonstrates that these beliefs were not borne out by the facts.

NMEs were not institutionally different from other developing countries that were treated like market economies during this time period. Russia, China, and Romania, were not more corrupt, less democratic, or less economically free, on average, than the countries used as price proxies in anti-dumping cases, such as Colombia, India, and Thailand. This suggests that institutional differences between NMEs and other developing countries cannot explain the differential treatment of non-market economies. It demonstrates, in particular, that Commission and ITA perceptions about the corruption in NMEs were not based on accurate measures of corruption levels in NMEs compared to other developing market economies; instead, cold war beliefs held about these countries have continued to influence the investigations. These presumptions have persisted, despite the fact that there were no significant differences in their domestic economic and political institutions.

Table 5.9 Are NMEs Institutionally Different from Other Developing Countries? *Parameter Values for Logit Model (EU Data, 1997)*

Dependent Variable: Type of country (0/1 NME)	Model 1	Model 2	Model 3	Model 4	Model 5
Domestic Corruption	−2.28	−1.49	—	—	−2.26
	(2.09)	(1.87)			(2.16)
Democratization	0.02	—	—	0.002	0.01
(Institutions)	(0.03)			(0.03)	(0.03)
Economic Freedom	0.24	0.28	0.30	—	0.19
	(0.19)	(0.22)	(0.23)		(0.19)
Political Freedom	—	−1.25	0.11	—	—
		(1.80)	(1.78)		
GDP per capita	—	—	—	−1.86	—
				(1.18)	
Geographic Distance	−1.68★	—	−1.29	−2.43★	−1.49★
(km)	(0.81)		(0.85)	(1.41)	(0.86)
Trade Importance	—	−33.77	−27.85	−8.75	−25.67
(US/EU Exports to Country)	(25.28)	(20.82)	(22.09)	(21.65)	
Constant	12.76★	2.86	8.63	33.81★	13.56
	(7.94)	(4.49)	(6.12)	(17.88)	(8.59)
Chi-Square	12.73★★	11.12★★	16.46★★★	17.90★★★	14.27★★
Pseudo R2 (Cox & Snell)	0.41	0.37	0.47	0.51	0.45
% Correctly Classified	83.30%	79.20%	84.60%	80.00%	79.20%
Sample Size	24	24	26	25	24

Note: 1. Coefficients are unstandardized logistic regression coefficients: standard errors in parentheses.
2. ★ p < .05; ★★ p < .01; and ★★★ p < .001, and two-tailed t-test.

Western Presumptions and Beliefs about NMEs

Both the U.S. and the EU trade agencies presumed that non-market forces operated in NMEs in transition. The trade agencies presumed that trade with NMEs was different from trade with other countries. They also presumed that NMEs had an interest and incentive to dump, as well as provide misleading information. These presumptions were grounded in cold war beliefs about NMEs and became institutionalized in trade policy and practice. These beliefs were based on a rational assessment of the capabilities, interests, and incentives of NMEs at one point in time. However, both international conditions and domestic institutions in NMEs have changed since that time. This means that non-market economy internationally determined interests and domestically determined incentives have also changed. The institutionalized beliefs about the threatening nature of trade with NMEs have continued though, and have impeded the ability of both the ITA and the Commission to process fully the new information about the former Communist countries.

Presumptions about the non-market behavior and antagonistic intentions of NMEs have been difficult, if not impossible, for many NMEs to overcome in the short term. A plaintiff in the case of *Climax Paper Converters from China* Case T-155/94 (1996) took the anti-dumping case to the European Court of First Instance, arguing that it was not enough for the Commission or Council to assume non-market activities in cases against NMEs, but the Commission had to prove non-market activities (European Court of First Instance 1996). This would have fundamentally changed the nature of NME cases, and resulted in better treatment of NME defendants. The European Court of Justice rejected this proposal saying the Commission could act on presumptions about the nature of NMEs.

In an interview, an official in Anti-dumping Investigations in DG Trade (then DG I) confirmed that there was a presumption of non-market activities in NMEs, but a presumption of market activities in Asian developing countries. The official pointed out a certain "darkness about their [Asian] market practices," a lack of transparency in Asia, "dark" accounting practices, and specifically the fact that Korean *chaebol* were clearly not market oriented. However, the institutional structures of Asian developing countries were simply not questioned, while those in NMEs were actively questioned.[25] Beliefs about NMEs have caused rigidity in the implementation of cases: an extraordinary questioning of facts and information has resulted in higher levels of trade protection.

Presumptions about the different and harmful nature of economic activities in NMEs caused the ITA and the Commission to more actively question the veracity of information supplied by NMEs. The information supplied by the typical "market oriented" developing country may not have been perfect, but it was not summarily rejected as it was in the case of NMEs. Other countries' information was not subjected to the same level of scrutiny. There was a certain level of trust involved in assessments of other countries' information that was not extended to NMEs.

The rejection of information from NMEs is consistent with belief perseverance theory. Because beliefs are resistant to change, decision makers will often reject information that is contrary to their beliefs. Both the ITA and the Commission have behaved as disproportionate information processors. If ITA and Commission decision makers believed that NMEs were not to be trusted because they had extraordinary incentives and interests to engage in dumping, then information submitted by NMEs contrary to this belief would be cognitively dissonant. One would expect decision makers to prefer information supplied by countries other than NMEs, because of the endemic belief that trade with NMEs was harmful. This is exactly the behavior that was observed on the part of both the United States and the European Union. This proves that the behavior was neither idiosyncratic nor bureaucratically specific, but was rather a systematic function of institutionalized beliefs. The next chapter explores in detail how these institutionalized beliefs have impeded the implementation of formal rule change.

CHAPTER SIX

Rule Change but Outcome Stasis

I too often have the impression that there are some states, China for instance, which are unpopular here, so that things are applied to them that are not applied to others.

—EU Official, in oral comments before the
European Parliament

Introduction

Chapter five demonstrated how belief stasis can impede policy change. But, belief stasis cannot forestall policy change indefinitely. Over the period 1990–2004, the transitions in NMEs were so far reaching as to make it impossible to ignore the scope of the changes. While the ITA and the Commission have been disproportionate information processors (Jones 2001, 158) this still allows them to respond to some of the information about the economic and political reforms in NMEs. Beliefs have not rendered these agencies ossified, simply more resistant to change. As such, the ITA and the Commission have enacted several formal rule changes to NME relevant anti-dumping laws in order to accommodate the reforms in these countries. However (for a period of almost 15 years) the formal rule changes went unimplemented. Outcome stasis in the face of policy change presents an interesting puzzle.

In this chapter I focus on two formal rule changes made to anti-dumping statutes by the ITA and the Commission. Each trade agency self-initiated its formal rule changes; the changes have not been imposed from outside. However, the rule changes have been artfully circumvented in the actual administration of the law by these trade agencies. Over the period 1990–2004, the process of administering the cases has remained largely consistent with the belief that non-market economies were inherently antagonistic and trade with them could be harmful. The self-initiation aspect is important because it demonstrates that the agencies were cognizant of the reform efforts in NMEs. It also rules out a possible explanation that the agencies were simply failing to implement a rule change forced on them by the outside. The curious manner in which cold war beliefs about NMEs continued to impede outcome change even in the face of formal rule change is explored in this chapter.

United States: Formal Rule Change yet Outcome Stasis

The extensive political and economic transitions in NMEs have made some revisions of the anti-dumping law inevitable.[1] Even in 1981, in the case of *Natural Menthol from the People's Republic of China* (46 FR 3258 1981), Commerce began to grapple with both regional and sectoral differences in the pace and scope of reform in transitional economies, and what this would mean for the application of U.S. trade laws. Both the U.S. Department of Commerce and the United States Congress acknowledged that certain sectors or regions in a transitional economy would face market prices more quickly than others. "Attempts by traditional non-market economies to evolve toward market-oriented economies may result in a situation in which a *sector* of a NME may be sufficiently free of non-market economy distortions so that the actual prices and/or costs incurred in the NME could be used in dumping calculations and render meaningful results" (57 FR 24018 1992, esp. 24019, emphasis in original). In an effort to render more accurate judgments in anti-dumping investigations, the ITA began to consider the possibility of a "bubble of capitalism" within a NME.

Bubbles of Capitalism

The rationale behind the bubbles of capitalism argument was to allow those industries in a non-market economy that have converted to market oriented incentives to prove that their inputs and pricing structures were completely market determined. This would thereby allow them to use their own prices for factor inputs in anti-dumping cases. "A market oriented industry determination focuses on overall control of the domestic industry, rather than simply on its export activities, and therefore leads to a decision as to whether home market or third country prices within the industry are sufficiently market driven that such prices may be used to establish fair market value" (62 FR 6189 1997). In order to systematically implement a policy focused on emergent bubbles of capitalism in an otherwise non-market environment, a Market Oriented Industry (MOI) test was developed.

The MOI procedure evolved over several cases (57 FR 15052 1992; 57 FR 29705 1992; 62 FR 4250 1997).[2] At first the ITA tried to combine elements of the surrogate country method with the regular anti-dumping procedure for market economics. When some of the inputs were unambiguously market determined, the ITA used those costs and prices in the anti-dumping determination. Inputs whose prices could not be unambiguously shown to be market determined would be calculated using surrogate values (56 FR 66833 1991). The ITA rendered a decision employing the partial use of domestic factor prices in a case against *Chrome Plated Lug Nuts from the People's Republic of China* (*1991*). The preliminary dumping margin was assessed at 66 percent using only the traditional surrogate method. In the final determination, when some of the inputs were valued using the NME industry's actual prices, the dumping margin was only 4 percent (56 FR 46153 1991). The partial use of domestic factor prices substantially decreased the final dumping margin.

However, as a result of a challenge in the U.S. Court of International Trade and evolving positions adopted in two ITA countervailing duty cases, the ITA remanded its determination in *Lug Nuts* (56 FR 57616 1991). In *Lug Nuts*, the state had a considerable presence in both the steel and chemicals industries (two significant production inputs). It was originally ruled that the industry still sourced the inputs at market determined prices. However, in the remanded case, the ITA stated that its previous standard was based on too narrow a scope of inquiry. "The absence of direct government involvement in specific transactions between buyers and sellers does not mean that the terms of those transactions reflect market-determined prices or values. This is especially the case in a non-market economy environment which is necessarily 'riddled with distortions'" (57 FR 15052 1992, esp. 15053). Even though there was no direct government involvement in the transactions between the lug nut producers and the steel suppliers, the fact that 45 percent of national steel output could be requisitioned by the government at in-plan prices indicated that "the extent of government involvement in the production and pricing decisions for steel generally affects the demand

and supply for individual steel products (56 FR 46153 1991)." The decision stated that if 25–50 percent of production could be government directed, the ITA would consider this "significant" government involvement in the industry (56 FR 46153 1991). This precedent setting case reinforced the presumption that market forces were not at work in a transitional economy: that NMEs were "riddled with distortions." This differed markedly from the presumption of market forces in cases involving developing countries.

In light of the aforementioned cases, the ITA codified new formal criteria—the "Market-Oriented Industry Test"—in order to clarify the definition of what precisely constituted a market oriented industry in a non-market economy:

1. For the merchandise under review there must be almost no government involvement in the setting of prices or quantities to be produced, state mandated production, or allocation of output precludes a MOI;
2. The industry producing the merchandise under review should be characterized by private or collective ownership, although a very small, undetermined, percentage of enterprises could still be state owned; and
3. All significant inputs must be paid for in market determined prices, and for all but an insignificant portion of all the inputs accounting for the total value of the merchandise under review (57 FR 9409 1992, esp. 9411).

To qualify for MOI treatment, an NME industry must meet all three criteria. The first criterion addresses the degree of government involvement in pricing and production decisions. The second criterion explains how different types of ownership could affect the ability of enterprises to "respond to market signals with respect to investment and divestment." The third criterion addresses "inputs and market distortions that may result from central planning activities" (57 FR 24018 1992, esp. 24021). The degree of state control, whether it be indirect or direct, that would negate the industry from being considered market oriented was not specified by the ITA. "There are no set criteria for judging whether, in a particular case, the degree of state control over an economy is such as to make home market prices inappropriate for purposes of foreign market value" (56 FR 46153 1991). This decision is left to the discretion of the ITA.

There are many reasons why an industry would try to quality for MOI consideration. If an industry were labeled a MOI, it would be subject to antidumping procedures similar to those used for market economies. If the actual prices that MOIs paid for their factors of production were used, the comparative advantage of an industry could be demonstrated. Use of a MOI standard would provide industries in economies in transition with more fair and predictable treatment in antidumping investigations, before the country itself was recognized as a full-fledged market economy. Use of the MOI standard would decrease the number of positive final determinations of dumping against NME industries. It may decrease the incidence of dumping complaints against NMEs also, since the determination of dumping would be simpler, less subjective, and less prone to abuse. It could also provide an incentive for industries in non-market economies to push ahead with market reforms in order to garner market oriented treatment. In sum, there are many economic and political incentives for firms in NMEs to try and obtain MOI treatment.

As a result of these incentives, many NMEs have applied for MOI consideration. Since its initiation in 1989, dozens of full MOI cases have been conducted. However, between 1989 and 2004, not a single MOI was found. This is not for lack of trying. Chinese, Romanian, Russian, Ukrainian, and Kazakh firms have all requested MOI treatment on multiple occasions. Various types of industries and commodities within these countries have been considered, ranging from steel products to chemicals to food products to consumers goods. However, in each case, across country and across product type, MOI treatment has been systematically denied. This was no accident. Beliefs about the threatening nature of NMEs have continued to affect the ITA's interpretation of the MOI criteria, de facto negating the formal changes, and resulting in policy stasis.

The Market-Oriented Industry Test

There are four main categories of reasons the ITA has cited for rejection of the MOI test. They focus on information deficiencies and conflicting interpretations of the veracity and scope of information. The reasons cited are important because they constitute a precedent for future cases, and therefore create a running body of case law. They also reveal the rationale and underlying beliefs that affected the manner in which the agency interpreted the law and processed information.

First, the ITA established that only verifiable, documented data would be adequate to prove market determined prices in an NME case. In theory this seems like a reasonable requirement, for market-determined prices must be demonstrated, not simply asserted. However, in practice this has constituted an unattainable goal for transitional economy firms. It is not that an NME cannot produce documents attesting to the supply and demand driven nature of prices. It is that the NME has been unable to produce what the ITA considered "sufficient evidence" to overcome the ITA's beliefs about the non-market nature of business transactions. In essence a shadow of doubt regarding financial data has remained an impossible hurdle. For example, an NME firm can produce documented evidence that it operates under market influences, determines all input purchase decisions, determines volume and type of production, determines prices based on the forces of supply and demand, negotiates all prices at arms-length, has no restrictions on its use of revenues and profits, and has exclusive control over its bank accounts and yet be denied market treatment. A NME firm can show that the government exercises no control over the price of inputs, does not restrict foreign currency use, and does not control firm bank accounts, and still not qualify as an MOI (62 FR 6189 1997). The ITA has routinely disregarded the type of information supplied by NME firms, saying it was not verifiable or was inadequate in some respect. In fact, certain industries in the United States would not even be able to satisfy the ITA's rigid information requirements (62 FR 6189 1997). Disregarding information that is inconsistent with beliefs about NMEs is one of the predictions of a belief based theory.

Second, all of this information must be submitted at the beginning of a case. If the information is submitted past the deadlines, the information is disregarded (62 FR 41355 1997). The information process is time consuming and costly. In practice, the time requirements have constituted a significant barrier to obtaining MOI treatment. Recently Chinese producers of wooden bedroom furniture (69FR 67313 2004) were denied MOI treatment on procedural grounds, based on the ITA's contention that not enough time was given to process the request (U.S. International Trade Administration 2004a).

Third, MOI information is required for the entire industry or virtually the entire industry in a case. It does not matter if the other firms in the industry do not produce goods for export. All firms within an industry have to submit information in order for the single firm or firms involved in an anti-dumping case to be considered for MOI treatment (61 FR 58514 1996). Getting uninterested parties to provide proprietary information on a voluntary basis is impossibly difficult to achieve. Most recently, even though 80 percent of the Chinese television receiver market responded to the solicitation of information, this was insufficient to grant the industry standing for an MOI analysis (69 FR 20594 2004).

In the Administrative Review of *Chrome Plated Lug Nuts from the People's Republic of China (1996)*, the Chinese firm was denied MOI standing because the ITA alleged that information was not obtained from the entire industry (61 FR 58514 1996). However, the Chinese firm had repeatedly provided evidence that it was the only producer of lug nuts in China, so there was no information about other producers. This information was disregarded by the ITA. Moreover, the ITA requested Chinese government corroboration that the firm was the only producer. This was problematic because the firm was not affiliated with the government. "Because the industry is a MOI, there is no government control, and the government cannot certify who is part of that particular industry" (61 FR 58514 1996). So in essence the ITA requested verifiable information from the Chinese government negating the existence of other nonexistent firms in the industry.

Moreover, the firm submitted information about its suppliers, indicating the suppliers were also free of state control. This information was verified by the ITA. Not only was the particular supplier free of government control, but the entire industry was also free of government control. This was deemed insufficient. The ITA argued that the evidence was not thorough enough, because there was not compelling proof that the entire industry in which the supplier was embedded was also market oriented. As such, MOI treatment was rejected.

Fourth, the third prong of the MOI test requires that all significant inputs, and inputs of inputs be purchased at completely market driven prices. Non-market economy firms trying to obtain MOI treatment have contended that the third component of the MOI test requires that the industry under investigation be more market oriented than current market economies. In *Tapered Roller Bearings from China (1997)*, the Chinese firm argued, "to prove an industry in the PRC is market oriented would require proof negating the existence of any state influence over any factor of production throughout all segments of an industry, potentially involving hundreds of business units . . . such a task would be virtually impossible to achieve" (62 FR 6189 1997). Even some industries in market economies use inputs supplied by government owned industries at fixed prices (53 FR 30385 1988; 54 FR 43440 1990; 57 FR 8800 1992). Such a practice would immediately disqualify a firm in a non-market economy from MOI treatment.

For example, in the United States prices for electricity inputs are regulated by the Federal Energy Regulatory Commission. Such government intervention in the energy market would disqualify NME firms from MOI treatment. In an interview, an ITA analyst acknowledged that many U.S. industries would not qualify as MOIs if they were held up to this test.[3] The excessively rigorous application of the third criterion of the MOI test and the assumptions made about the macroeconomic environment of an NME have excluded any industry in an NME from receiving this classification (56 FR 55274 1991). Yet another analyst summarized the trade deterring effects of Part III of the MOI test by saying, "this is the reason why the MOI test is not a test, it is a wall."[4]

The Moldovan steel industry (66 FR 33525 2001), the Kazakh steel industry (66 FR 50397 2001), and the Romanian pipes industry (65 FR 5594 2000) petitioned for MOI treatment and were rejected based upon the third prong of the test. In the Romanian case, the firms supplied documents verifying: no government involvement in the setting of prices or quantities for seamless pipe; inputs sourced from market economies in hard currency; freely negotiated labor contracts; electricity inputs priced at Western comparable levels; and other energy sources paid for in hard currency at market determined prices. Citing "certain weaknesses in the respondents' requests," and the fact that the Romanian firms only supplied information on 80 percent of the industry, the ITA rejected the MOI application (U.S. International Trade Administration 2000e). The analyst working on the case admitted that the United States has always found a way to reject an MOI, and Romania really had no possibility of proving its case.

The Romanian ruling is particularly interesting because the EU had already reclassified the entire country of Romania as a market economy for the purposes of anti-dumping law by that time. That meant the European Union considered that Romania had made sufficient progress on its economic and political reforms to be reclassified as a market economy. Moreover, Romania was a member of the WTO as a market economy. This meant that other countries have also recognized Romania as a market economy. However, the United States still denied MOI treatment to the Romanian pipe industry, which would have been considered market oriented if it were in any other developing country. The Kazakh ruling was also very interesting because parallel with the MOI case was a change in status case as well. The ITA had sufficient evidence to consider reclassifying the entire country of Kazakhstan from an NME to a market economy, but insufficient evidence to grant MOI treatment of a single industry in the country. The method of administering the laws has demonstrated a fundamental contradiction in terms of intent and perception of information.

How Beliefs Affect Policy Outcomes: A Case Example
The case of *Freshwater Crawfish Tail Meat from the People's Republic of China (1997)* illustrates how beliefs have affected the interpretation of

MOI treatment in non-market economy cases (62 FR 41355 1997). This case was relatively simple. There were few factor inputs in the production of crawfish meat: crawfish, labor, bags and boxes for packaging and shipping the meat, and electricity and water in the factory in which the crawfish meat was processed. The Chinese firms provided documented information to prove their MOI claims showing:

1. the government did not control the price of labor;
2. the cost of crawfish was freely negotiated between buyers and sellers;
3. there were multiple suppliers of crawfish who priced competitively to sell;
4. labor costs varied by factory and were freely negotiated; and
5. the government did not control the price of utilities, and even if it did the U.S. government regulates the price of utilities (electricity) so this should not negate MOI status (62 FR 41355 1997).

The only thing that the government did own was the land on which the crawfish were harvested. This is because private fishermen go to public water and fish for crawfish, and then take the catch and sell it to factories. This is similar to crawfish fishermen in the United States, who harvest from public land and do not pay for this privilege. So there is comparability between U.S. and Chinese fishermen's use of public land. In essence, there was no evidence that any part of the crawfish industry was controlled or influenced by the government in China.

The ITA conducted an on-site verification of the information provided by the Chinese firms and found no discrepancies in the accounting ledgers for any of the factor inputs (U.S. International Trade Administration 1997c). This meant that the ITA could find no evidence that the Chinese firms were not being honest in the reporting of their operations. The crawfish industry was the most likely case to find a MOI. It was made up of small, mom and pop firms that had sprung up since the economic transitions in China. Therefore, there was no government involvement and had never been government involvement in this industry (Sheldon and Mark Attorneys at Law 1992).

Nonetheless, the ITA rejected the MOI request arguing that "insufficient evidence was on the record to make such a [MOI] determination" (U.S. International Trade Administration 1997a). The ITA contended that while the crawfish firms involved in the case had supplied information on all the factors of production, they missed some of crawfish firms. Therefore the Chinese firms did not provide information on the *entire industry*. The crawfish industry responded that it was a mom and pop industry. Many individual fishermen did not have sophisticated accounting systems or records in order to satisfy the ITA's information requirements. Moreover, there were too many individual fishermen and processors from which to gather information. Their claims were denied. When I discussed this particular case with an official at the ITA, he acknowledged that in this case if the ITA wanted to declare Chinese firms market oriented industries, there was overwhelming evidence to do so. However, they found reasons to reject the claim because "the ITA was not currently prepared to find a MOI."[5]

This is compelling evidence for the causal role of beliefs. This was a case in which the very decision makers involved acknowledged the overwhelming material evidence that the NME industries were in fact market determined. The decision makers acknowledged that their administration of the case was circumventing the formal rules. Nonetheless, the decision makers were able to rationalize their continued discriminatory treatment of NMEs because they believed that non-market forces were still at work, and that NMEs were not ordinary developing countries. As such NMEs needed to be treated with more attention and caution than other countries. The empirical evidence was trumped by the lingering cold war beliefs.

There have been fewer requests for MOI treatment in the past four years as the negative precedent cases have accumulated. In *Hand Trucks from China (2004)* (69 FR 60980 2004), *Artificial Corundum from China (2003)* (68 FR 55589 2003), *Carbon Steel Plate from Ukraine (2003)* (68 FR 35626 2003), *Steel Beams from Russia (2002)* (67 FR 35490 2002), and *Concrete Reinforcing Bars from Belarus (2001)* (66 FR 33528 2001), MOI consideration was not even requested by the defendants. When asked about this, an analyst at the ITA explained that Chinese firms understood they were not going to get MOI treatment and should not waste their time and energy applying for it. The analyst referred to it as a "cat and mouse" game; the Chinese now understood the rules of the game.[6]

Presumptions and Beliefs as Information Discounters

The U.S. Commerce Department recognizes that governments intervene and regulate certain markets or sectors in many countries treated as market economies. However, in market economy investigations, "there is a reasonable presumption that market economy influences predominate over the influence of any sector or market in which there is government intervention or regulation" (57 FR 24018 1992 esp. 24021). In contrast, it has been assumed that in NMEs, non-market forces permeate the economy (60 FR 22359 1995). "The Department begins with a rebuttable presumption that all companies within a NME country are subject to government control" (U.S. International Trade Administration 1999a). To be treated differently, a firm or industry must "*overcome the presumption of state control*" (60 FR 22359 1995, my emphasis).

> The Department believes that the test for finding a market oriented industry must begin with a strong presumption that such situations do not occur because non-market economies are riddled with distortions. The presumptions against finding a market-oriented industry must prevail unless thorough and convincing evidence is presented on the record which demonstrates that the producers operate in an environment of market based costs and prices (66 FR 33525 2001, *Decision Memorandum*).

All anti-dumping cases involving NMEs have included the phrase, "In an NME anti-dumping proceeding, the Department presumes that all companies within the country are subject to governmental control and should be assigned a single antidumping duty rate," (69 FR 77722 2004) or "We begin with the presumption that all companies within a non-market economy are subject to government control" (69 FR 67313 2004). Every anti-dumping case involving NMEs, every policy memo, and every decision memorandum has included this line regarding presumptions of non-market activities and market distortions. The ITA has acknowledged the importance of these presumptions in the decision making process. "The absence of direct government involvement in specific transactions between buyers and sellers does not mean that the terms of those transactions reflect market-determined prices or values. This is especially the case in a non-market economy environment which is necessarily 'riddled with distortions'" (57 FR 15052 1992 esp. 15053). The presumption that NMEs are "riddled with distortions" has affected the manner in which the ITA has interpreted information regarding NMEs.

With a negative presumption as a starting point, providing sufficient evidence to overcome such a presumption is much more difficult than starting a case with a presumption that market economy forces are at work. The nature of the underlying presumption, be it friend or foe, or trustworthy or untrustworthy, affects the interpretation of subsequent information. Veracity of information is a subjective determination. It is partially a function of perceptions about the reliability of the party supplying the information. The assumptions about NMEs have differed markedly from other developing countries. Other developing countries do not have to prove market forces, they are assumed. If transitional economies are always assumed to operate under less than market determined conditions, then no amount or type of information would prove the existence of a market oriented industry in an NME.

Analysts in the Office of Anti-dumping Investigations in the ITA have acknowledged in personal interviews that there have been numerous cases in which the NME industries in question met the formal criteria for MOI treatment. The analysts confirmed that the ITA initiated changes that it was not prepared to administer, and they therefore had to find reasons to deny NME firms market-oriented industry treatment.[7] The fact that the analysts have acknowledged that firms in NMEs have met the objective criteria of the MOI test, but that the ITA denied MOI treatment because they did not trust NMEs, strongly demonstrates the lingering effects of Cold War beliefs on recent trade policy.

An inability to process new disconfirming information is consistent with an understanding of organizations as disproportionate information processors (Jones 2001; Simon 1985). Even evidence provided by objective third parties would be discounted by the prevailing beliefs and presumptions. In 1996 the World Bank issued a report stating that "the establishment of a market economy in China was an objective and undeniable fact. The Chinese Government no longer intervenes in an enterprises' production and management or allocated their products" (China Daily 1999). However, this World Bank affirmation did not affect the manner in which the ITA administered cases. If decision makers were using their preformed beliefs to make determinations, one would expect them to continuously reject disconfirming evidence. One would also expect the decision maker to legitimize his actions by questioning the veracity, scope, presentation, and timing of the information provided. This is precisely the kind of systematic information rejection evidenced by the ITA.

European Union: Sticky Beliefs and Sticky Outcomes

In the post–cold war period, the European Commission also amended its NME anti-dumping laws to improve their fairness and transparency. In this section I discuss two such formal rule changes: Individual

Treatment and the Market Economy Treatment determinations. In theory, these changes were designed to give NME industries more beneficial treatment under the law. However, the formal rule changes have also been circumvented by the manner in which the rules have been applied. As with the case of the MOI test in the United States, the European Commission has carefully avoided giving NME industries the benefits of the rule changes.

There are important comparisons to be highlighted in the way the EU and United States have chosen to address trade issues with respect to NMEs. Differences and similarities are emphasized for what they reveal about belief stasis and belief change. In the case of both Individual Treatment and Market Economy Treatment, the EU evaded true implementation of the spirit of the law for many years, only to gradually start to implement the statutes. This gradual shift in policy toward NMEs provides fledgling evidence of belief change.

Individual Treatment

In a typical NME anti-dumping case the Commission assesses a single countrywide dumping margin to all firms named in the case (Council Reg No. 384/96 1996, Article 9(5)). This means that if five Chinese firms are named in an anti-dumping case against bicycles, all five would receive the same dumping margin, regardless of differences in their pricing or market share. The single countrywide anti-dumping rate was thought necessary because of the peculiar nature of domestic economic institutions in non-market economies. It was assumed that a level of state intervention permeated all firms making a product. Firms were not really individual corporate entities, but all part of a supply structure controlled by the state. Therefore the state could potentially circumvent anti-dumping duties by channeling exports through the firm or firms with the lowest dumping margins or no dumping margins (Commission Decision 93/377/EEC 1993, recital 8). As such a countrywide dumping margin against all producers of a given commodity was assessed, regardless of the differences between firms within an industry.

In the early 1990s, the Commission instituted a change in this countrywide dumping rate policy, potentially allowing for the individual treatment of NME firms in an anti-dumping case. The idea behind individual treatment was to allow firms in transitional NMEs to demonstrate their market orientation and reap some benefits from their reforms. If a firm could prove sufficient freedom from state intervention in its export activities, the Commission would establish a separate export price and consequentially a separate dumping margin. Individual dumping rates are the norm in regular anti-dumping cases against market economies. Therefore recognition that a firm in a NME could receive individual treatment was an acknowledgment by the Commission of the market oriented reforms underway in NMEs. It was particularly targeted toward China and Russia, who because of their size and the uneven pockets of reform in different parts of their countries, would be most likely candidates to find some market oriented industries.

The Commission set out conditions specifying how a firm could qualify for individual treatment. Firms needed to "demonstrate a degree of legal and factual independence comparable to that which would prevail in a market economy country and which would justify a departure from the determination of a single countrywide rate" (COM Reg No. 230/2001 2001, recital 101). The Commission outlined criteria to guide its decisions, including: (1) firm level freedom to repatriate capital and profits; (2) firm level freedom to determine export prices and quantities; (3) firm level freedom to carry out business activities; (4) no state interference in the management of the company or of the major shareholders of the parent company; and (5) the firm using market determined factors of production (COM Reg No. 550/93 1993, recitals 34–36; European Commission 1997b, Annex). The actual level of freedom that was "sufficiently free of state control" to permit individual treatment of NME firms has proven to be very slippery in practice (Council Reg No. 467/98 1998).

The discretion afforded to the Commission allowed it to systematically reject individual treatment requests from its inception in 1993 until 2000. Over this seven-year period, the Commission routinely found "state inference" sufficient to reject individual treatment. It was not until the Commission initiated a modification of individual treatment in 2000 that the Commission actually started to find affirmative cases (European Commission 2001d 21).

In the 2000 Annual Report, the Commission clarified the difference between individual treatment and market status treatment. Individual treatment does not use a firm's actual costs to calculate normal value, but instead relies on the use of analogues. The firms' domestic costs are substituted with the prices of third county proxies. Individual treatment looks only at the export price of each firm as part of the anti-dumping procedure. Therefore the use of individual treatment does not jeopardize the use of analogues. Market Economy Treatment, on the other hand, does jeopardize the use of analogues. Therefore, I argue, it is easier for the EU to start to implement changes to its individual treatment test because it does not undermine the institutionalized analogue method. However, any modifications in rule and in practice would indicate an evolutionary change in the Commission's interpretation and implementation of NMEs. This indication of a change in beliefs is an important component of any theory of belief change.

(Mis)Application of the New Rule

The Commission has stressed the need for vigilance and caution in making determinations of individual treatment for NMEs. While "individual treatment may be given to certain exporters in non-market economy countries, in particular where they have demonstrated their independence from the state in the conduct of their export policy and in the fixing of their export prices, it was considered that the *utmost prudence* was required in this matter" (Council Reg No. 1006/95 1995, recital 34). This "utmost prudence" resulted in the rejection of all requests by NME firms for individual treatment through 2000, although during this time some foreign firms and joint ventures located in Hong Kong and China received this preferential treatment. Until 2000, NME exporters were unable to present sufficient evidence to the Commission to win individual treatment. This was primarily because they were unable to overcome presumptions of non-market activities or links to the state.

In *Non-Refillable Pocket Lighters from the People's Republic of China (1993)*, three Chinese exporting firms requested individual treatment (Commission Decision 93/377/EEC 1993). The Commission denied all the individual treatment requests citing state interference in the companies. Both *direct* state interference, such as state ownership of shares in the company, and *indirect* state interference, such as the state controlling shares in companies that had invested in the Chinese firm under investigation, were grounds for denying individual treatment. This was one of the earliest individual treatment cases, and it was interesting because it set a precedent whereby both direct and indirect state influences were interpreted as excessive state involvement. In this case, the EU clarified its position:

> Individual treatment is appropriate only in *exceptional cases* where the producer concerned has shown that its business decisions are taken independently of the state authorities . . . Indeed individual dumping margins or anti-dumping duties are inappropriate when the state, through any form of control on the exporters concerned, can take advantage of differentiation of the anti-dumping duty and thus

undermine the effectiveness of the measures taken. (Commission Decision 93/377/EEC 1993, recital 8, my emphasis)

Chinese firms began to routinely request individual treatment.[8] It was just as routinely rejected. Some examples illustrate the rationale being employed by the Commission. In *Ferro-Silico-Manganese from the People's Republic of China (1997)*, all twelve Chinese exporting firms involved in the case requested individual treatment and provided the Commission with full cooperation in the investigations. Individual treatment was rejected because the Commission found problems with some of the information provided (COM Reg No. 1778/97 1997, recital 17), and the companies were not entirely free to determine the quantities sold on the export and domestic markets" (recital 19).

In *Ring Binders from the People's Republic of China (1996)*, the Commission denied individual treatment because it did not think the firms were sufficiently independent in their method of conducting business and in their procurement techniques (COM Reg No. 1465/96 1996, recital 39). In *Glyphosate from the People's Republic of China (2000)*, the Chinese firms did not send information to the Commission in the correct format (European Commission 2000a). In *Coke from the People's Republic of China (2000)*, unspecified state interference was to blame (Commission Decision 1238/2000/ECSC 2000). In *Color Television Receivers from the People's Republic of China (1994)*, the Chinese firms had agreed to sell some of their output through a state directed exporting company (Council Reg No. 710/95 1995). All of these issues were sufficient reasons to deny an NME firm individual treatment.

State ownership of shares in a firm is often cited as a reason to deny individual treatment to firms in NMEs; however state ownership of firms in India and Egypt have not caused these firms to experience similar discriminatory treatment in anti-dumping cases (COM Reg No. 773/98 1998). In fact, state owned firms in India were used even as surrogates for "state influenced" firms in China (Council Reg No. 1334/1999 1999). When I asked about this somewhat irregular occurrence, Commission officials chastised me for thinking too narrowly about the legitimate role of the state in economic activities in market economies.[9] State ownership of firms in "market economies" was fine, but state influence, not even ownership, in NMEs has precluded individual treatment under the anti-dumping laws. State involvement in pricing, input sourcing, energy regulation, and export arrangements was allowed if you were labeled a "market economy" but not allowed if you were labeled an NME.

In rejecting individual treatment in the aforementioned *Color Televisions* (1994) case, the Commission argued "this [company level economic] freedom can only be seen as conferring at most a quasi-autonomous status within an economic and political system that still retains a large degree of centralized control and which clearly does not correspond to that which pertains in a market economy country" (Council Reg No. 710/95 1995, recital 25). This suggests that macro-economic irregularities would impede the finding of individual treatment of firms in NMEs, even NMEs in transition. However, the Commission has not had a problem giving individual treatment to foreign owned firms operating in China. The macroeconomic environment was the same, but the Commission acted upon different presumptions about the firms working within it.

In the aforementioned case, the Commission denied individual treatment to all the Chinese exporters but awarded individual treatment to the two Sino-Japanese joint venture exporters. The Commission explained that this was justified because "the Chinese exporters, even if they appear as independent companies which invoice their customers directly, have in fact a very limited, if any, degree of independence in their relationship with importers in other countries as they lack the possibility of establishing export prices and any other conditions or terms of sales by themselves" (Council Reg No. 2093/91 1991, recital 20). The Commission said it was able to "establish to its satisfaction that these [Sino-Japanese] companies, even if they did not operate fully on a market economy basis, enjoyed a high degree of independence in their opera-tions" (Council Reg No. 2093/91 1991, recital 20).

Again in *Microwave Ovens from the People's Republic of China (1995)* (COM Reg No. 1645/95 1995), *Leather and Plastic Handbags Originating in the People's Republic of China* (1997) (Council Reg No. 1567/97 1997), *Ring Binders from the People's Republic of China* (1997) (Council Reg No. 119/97 1997), *Fax Machines from the People's Republic of China* (1998) (Council Reg No. 904/98 1998), and *Footwear with Leather or Plastic Uppers from the People's Republic of China et.al.* (1998) (Council Reg No. 467/98 1998), the Chinese firms were denied individual treat-ment and Hong Kong based or "foreign owned firms" were awarded individual treatment. In these cases the macroeconomic environment was the same for all the firms operating in China, but perceptions about the influence of that environment on the firms were very different in the case of NME firms versus foreign ventures.

Individual treatment makes a difference in the size of the final dump-ing margin. Table 6.1 provides some examples of comparative dumping

Table 6.1 Country Wide Rates versus Individual Treatment

Product	Country Wide Dumping Margin	Individual Treatment Dumping Margin
Footwear/China	47.6%	1.3% (no dumping)
Lamps/China	74.4%	29.8%
Plastic Handbags/China	151%	64.3%
Compact Disk Boxes/China	20.1%	9%
Ring Binders/China	129.22%	96.6%
Steel Ropes/Russia	50.7%	35.8%
Urea/Russia	41%	28.5%
Leather Handbags/China	83.5%	0–7.7%

Source: Commission and Council Regulations, 1985–1998. *Official Journal.*

margins when countrywide rates are applied and when individual treatment is granted. Individual treatment duties are lower than analogue method duties. Therefore the inability of Chinese firms to garner individual treatment had significant trade deterrent and development effects.

Even more odd than the previous cases were cases in which reclassified non-market economies have been unable to garner individual treatment for their firms. Legally, once a country is reclassified as a "market economy" it cannot be subjected to NME trade rules, such as individual treatment considerations. However, there have been cases in which firms in reclassified countries have also been denied individual treatment. Romanian firms in *Seamless Pipes and Tubes (1997)* (COM Reg No. 981/1997 1997), and Czech and Romanian firms in *Steel Pipes (1997)* (Council Reg No. 2320/97 1997) are examples of supposedly market economies that were denied individual treatment. This not only violated the letter of the European anti-dumping statutes but also violated GATT/WTO anti-dumping provisions.

Individual treatment is an example of a formal rule change that was self-initiated by the European Commission, yet subsequently one which they actively worked to circumvent. Employing a causal role for belief stasis helps to understand this apparently contradictory behavior. In interviews, the Commission officials acknowledged that this formal rule change was conceived for joint ventures, not NME firms. Of course, NMEs were not apprised of this. In 1999, during the interviews, the officials said that the Commission still believed that Chinese firms could not possibly qualify for individual treatment so they found reasons to reject them.[10] "The situation in China makes it even more difficult, if not impossible, to establish whether a Chinese company or a foreign company manufacturing goods in China is truly independent of the state" (Agence Europe 1996b). Beliefs about the antagonistic interests and threatening nature of NME trade continued to permeate the Commission, and affected decision making regarding NME cases. The selective rejection of disconfirming information, the hesitancy to acknowledge the scope of reforms in NMEs, and the contradictory treatment of foreign and domestic firms in NMEs are all examples of the Commission behaving as a disproportionate information processor (Jones 2001, 9).

Rule Layering and Belief Change

In 2000, there was a significant change, when the Commission awarded individual treatment to Russian firms in *Urea and Ammonium Nitrate* (2000) (COM Reg. No. 617/2000 2000, OJL 75; European Commission 2001d, 62). After that precedent setting ruling, several more positive individual treatment cases were found, including *Steel Ropes and Cables from Russia et al.* (2001) (COM Reg No. 230/2001 2001), *Fluorescent Lamps from China* (2001) (COM Reg. No. 255/2000 2000, OJL 38), and *Urea from Ukraine* (2002) (Council Reg. No. 92/2002 2002, OJL 17). These cases signaled an important shift in the manner of interpreting and implementing a previously circumvented formal rule change. Understanding how the shift in policy took place hinges on an appreciation of the gradual change in the underlying beliefs about NMEs.

In the two Russian cases, one of the Russian firms involved in the investigation was able to demonstrate sufficient independence from the state to be awarded individual treatment. In the provisional duty deter-mination, the Russian firm was originally denied individual treatment (COM Reg. No. 617/2000 2000, recital 23–25). It was only after further analysis and continued lobbying and rebuttals on the part of the Russian producers that a positive individual treatment determination was rendered. Each of the firms had also requested and been denied Market Economy Treatment (to be discussed in the next section). Individual treatment was awarded as a kind of second best compensa-tion. I argue this change in policy implementation was a function of changing options faced by the Commission, as well as a small shift in the Commission's beliefs about trade with NMEs.

The formal "Market Economy Treatment" rule change in 1998 officially conferred on Russia "transitional economy" status, thereby permitting Russian firms to request consideration as market oriented on a case by case basis. However, as we see in the next section, the

Commission was not prepared to actually implement this formal rule change either. As such, the Russian ammonium nitrate case confronted the Commission with a problem. The Russian producers had requested both Market Economy Treatment and Individual Treatment. Market Economy Treatment would have obviated the possibility of using an analogue. Individual treatment, however, does allow the use of analogues, by only accepting export prices, not actual domestic production prices. As such, in the end the Commission gave the lesser of the two benefits to the Russian producers, namely individual treatment.

To formally recognize Russia's "transitional economy" status in 1998, change the Market Economy Treatment rules, and change the Individual Treatment rules, while still refusing to implement any of these rule changes in practice was politically compromising, but not impossible. Subsequent to the Market Economy Treatment change, the Commission rejected individual treatment requests by Russian, Chinese, and other NME producers (Council Reg. No. 215/2002 2002; Council Reg. No. 151/2003 2003; Council Reg. No. 1627/2003 2003). The political situation had not changed enough to *force* a change in the Commission's implementation of the Individual Treatment rule. However, in the end the Commission did choose to actually implement the individual treatment determination in the case of an NME. What explains this change in outcome?

I argue that the "layering" of rule changes on top of cold war beliefs about the antagonistic and threatening nature of trade with NMEs created cognitive dissonance in the Commission (Goldstein 1993).[11] A series of formal rule changes had been layered on each other. These formal rule changes were based on recognition of the market oriented reforms in NMEs. Yet the foundational cold war beliefs still remained institutionalized in the Commission's policies. The layering of promarket formal rule changes on top of cold war beliefs became substantial enough to create a critical tipping point, by which the Commission recognized the inconsistency between formal rules and policy implementation. It would have been an extreme example of cognitive dissonance on the part of the Commission to recognize the extent of the transitions in Russia by conferring "transitional economy status" on the country, and yet continue to reject all NME requests for individual treatment. As such, I argue that the fair implementation of the individual treatment rule is an indicator of the beginning of belief change on the part of the Commission about the market-oriented changes going on in transitional economies.

There are other indicators of fledgling but not wholesale belief change. The Commission's use of the hybrid term "transitional economy" to describe Russia and Ukraine, as well as China in 2004, is an indicator of belief change (European Commission 2003, 12 and 29; Council Reg. No. 398/2004 2004 OJL 66, section 19). A transitional economy is qualitatively different from a non-market economy. The Commission highlighted this qualitative difference in the wording of its status change legislation. This affected the frame of reference used to interpret facts in anti-dumping cases. The presumption of non-market activities permeated NME cases. The burden fell on NMEs to refute the presumption. Conversely, the presumption of market activities holds for market economies, therefore in those cases it is up to the Commission to provide evidence to refute this presumption (Clark 2002a). Transitional economies are somewhere in between, and presumptions about them lie in the middle as well. The shifting of underlying presumptions and therefore beliefs was apparent with this change in labeling. It was not yet a rejection of previously held Cold War beliefs about NMEs, but it was an indication of the start of belief change. Consistent with a theory about the Commission as a disproportionate information processor, one would expect to see critical moments of cognitive dissonance between old beliefs and disconfirming evidence resulting in some change in not only outcomes but also in the underlying belief structures.

The EU has found other cases of individual treatment in subsequent anti-dumping investigations, and has also rejected requests for individual treatment. Therefore one cannot conclude that the situation compelled the Commission to find individual treatment. Material, situational, or even bureaucratic explanations for the EU's behavior would not hold true in this case. Also, one cannot conclude that cold war beliefs about NMEs have completely changed. What one *can* say is that a combination of material interests and cognitive dissonance associated with inconsistent beliefs and empirical evidence caused a change in the EU's behavior. Individual treatment was a very minor concession to NMEs. Analogues are still employed and the prices in NMEs are still ignored. In essence the institutionalized understanding of analogues remained in place. However, it was a symbolic first step, signaling a shift in belief certainty.

Market Economy Treatment (MET)

Market Economy Treatment was the Commission's second major formal rule change to anti-dumping laws. This is a much more potentially substantive rule change that forgoes the use of analogues and accepts the actual prices in NMEs/transitional economies. There has been less policy change on this formal rule change than on individual treatment. However, it is a good example of the slow change of belief certainty even in the face of mountains of disconfirming evidence.

Market Economy Treatment cases have involved orthodox core countries, those predicted to be the most resistant to Commission belief change. Deviant satellites and core countries were not considered for Market Economy Treatment. These countries were simply treated as either non-market economies or market economies. By comparison, the reform efforts in orthodox core countries and orthodox satellites have been much more difficult for the EU, to acknowledge. As such, a special "transitional economy" status was invented to address the reform efforts in these countries, since the EU was unwilling to call them true "market economies." Therefore, one would predict that beliefs about orthodox countries would be most resistant to change, and moreover that a formal rule change targeted exclusively at orthodox core and satellites would confront the most policy stasis.

In 1998, China and Russia were removed from the list of "state-trading countries" (Council Reg No. 905/98 1998, Article 1). Ukraine, Kazakhstan, and Vietnam were officially removed in 2000 (Council Reg. No. 2238/2000, Article 1).[12] Once removed from the NME list, these countries were considered "transitional economies," neither market nor non-market economies (European Commission 1998b, 7). The not actually "market" nature of this classification was repeatedly emphasized to me in interviews with Commission officials.[13] This transitional status simply opened up the possibility that market-oriented industries in these countries could be treated as such under the anti-dumping statutes.[14] Essentially a variant on the United States's MOI test, this change was designed to take into consideration the extensive market reforms in these countries in a way more generous than the individual treatment test.

On a case by case basis, if an industry in a transitional economy could prove with documented evidence that all of its inputs were market determined, then its domestic prices would be used in the anti-dumping investigation. It was believed that this would allow industries to demonstrate a comparative advantage in the production of certain commodities. It would most likely result in substantially lower anti-dumping margins. With these changes, the Commission promised to "take a more *systematic approach to issues of individual treatment and natural comparative advantage*" of Russian and Chinese enterprises (European Commission 1998b, 7, emphasis added).

However, as with the previous formal rule changes, there was much delaying by the Commission in the actual implementation. There have been very few affirmative cases of MET, despite efforts by firms in transitional economies. By one count, 111 Chinese companies had requested MET from 2000 to 2004 (Meller). The Commission has consistently found a reason to deny Chinese and Russian firms market-oriented treatment. It was only in 2003 that the first fledging case of a positive MET for NME firms was actually awarded in practice. A review of cases illustrates the Commission's implementation of MET, and elucidate the manner in which cold war beliefs have affected the Commission's interpretation of the laws.

Overview of the Rules

The Market Economy Treatment (MET) decision was designed to treat qualifying firms within transitional economies as market oriented (Council Reg No. 905/98 1998, Article 1(b)). Under this rule, industries in a transitional economy could potentially use their own prices to determine normal value instead of analogue price proxies. Since the use of analogues to determine the normal value of an NME results in affirmative dumping determinations, it was assumed that using an NME firm's actual prices would be fairer and provide the exporting firm with a real opportunity to demonstrate a comparative advantage.

The criteria required to qualify for Market Economy Treatment include but are not limited to the following:

1. Decisions of firms regarding prices, costs and inputs, including, for instance, raw materials, cost of technology and labor, output, sales and investment, are made in response to market signals reflecting supply and demand, and without significant state interference in this regard, and costs of major inputs substantially reflect market values;
2. Firms have one clear set of basic accounting records that are independently audited in line with international accounting standards and are applied for all purposes;
3. The production costs and financial situation of firms are not subject to significant distortions carried over from the former non market economy system, in particular in relation to depreciation of assets, other write-offs, barter trade, and payment via compensation of debts;
4. The firms concerned are subject to bankruptcy and property laws that guarantee legal certainty and stability for the operation of firms, and

5. Exchange rate conversions are carried out at the market rate. (Council Reg No. 905/98 1998, Article 1(c); European Commission 1997b, Annex I).

The Commission requires information about the costs of all main factor inputs, such as audited accounts, pricing and quantity information, and production process information. The defendant would have to provide this information over the past two years of business, and translate all relevant documents into English. The petitioning firm would also have to provide official documentation on loans, debts, fixed assets, and other business related expenses. Letters from the company's bank and bank statements showing a sample of banking records would also be required to confirm the information provided by the firm (European Commission 1998b, 8). This information must be submitted to the Commission within three weeks of the initiation of the anti-dumping process.

Most of the official reasons given for rejecting MET have revolved around information insufficiencies, "state interference" and not meeting deadlines, although there are many other possible reasons. The Commission has acknowledged that very few companies have obtained MET, however they have continually asserted that "the criteria were relevant, realistic, and attainable" (European Commission 2001d, 20). The following section examines cases of outright MET rejection, partial MET determinations, and rescinded MET determinations in order to trace the rationale used by the Commission in the interpretation and administration of this formal rule. The cases in which MET have been awarded are particularly important because they signal a change in beliefs about these transitional economies. Moreover, they demonstrate the same "layering" of formal policy changes on top of cold war beliefs that precipitated policy change in the case of individual treatment.

Outright Rejection of MET

Information problems are routinely cited to justify the outright rejection of an MET petition by an industry. Information problems could mean the information was not complete, did not comply with Commission specifications, was not correctly formatted, was not turned in within the allotted deadlines, or was not considered reliable. For example, Chinese firms were initially granted MET in *Sodium Cyclamate from the People's Republic of China (2003)*, but it was then rescinded due to unspecified information deficiencies (COM Reg. No. 1627/2003 2003, recitals 27–28). In *Ammonium Nitrate from Russia (2002)* and *Steel Ropes and Cables from the Russian Federation (2001)* information deficiencies were simply cited as reasons to reject MET (Council Reg. No. 658/2002 2002; COM Reg. No. 230/2001 2001, recitals 92–94).[15]

Information provided to the Commission by any firm petitioning for MET must encompass the entire industry of which it is a part. Even if only one firm exports to the EU, that firm must somehow convince the entire industry to provide information to the EU regarding its financial activities in order for the Commission to consider MET claims. In *Glycine from the People's Republic of China (2000)*, the five Chinese companies requesting Market Economy Treatment were rejected for several reasons, including not providing information on the entire chemicals industry in China (COM Reg. No. 1043/2000 2000, recital 11).[16] In *Sulphanilic Acid from the People's Republic of China (2002)*, the MET request was denied because it did not include the "whole group involved in the production and sale of the product" (COM Reg. No. 575/2002 2002, recital 32). As with the MOI test administered by the United States, it is particularly difficult to obtain industry-wide information, deemed reliable by the Commission, and within the deadlines specified by law.

State interference in wages, export activities, domestic sales, or factors of production are reasons to reject Market Economy Treatment for NMEs. In *Coke or Coal Pieces from the People's Republic of China (2000)*, the Chinese firms were denied MET because of unspecified "state interference in wages and exports" as well as information problems (Commission Decision 2730/2000/ECSC 2000, recital 27). In *Electronic Weighing Scales from the People's Republic of China (2000)*, insufficient information, not meeting deadlines, and unspecified state interference in domestic sales, *not foreign sales* were cited as reasons to deny MET to the Chinese firms (Council Reg. No. 2605/2000 2000). In *Colour Television Receivers from the People's Republic of China (2002)*, the single petitioner was rejected MET consideration because he simply did not meet all of the criteria (Council Reg. No. 1531/2002 2002, recital 19). Both indirect and direct forms of state interference, either formal or informal, constitute excessive state interference in firm level economic activities.

Selling output to the state is grounds for rejection of MET because this could allow indirect state interference in industry pricing, since it is presumed that sales to the state would not be at market determined prices. The Chinese firms in *Cast Iron Tube or Pipe Fittings from the People's Republic of China (2000)* were refused MET because they sold some of their product to the state, and because of state interference in the form of tax rebates (European Commission 2000d, recitals, 116–188). Likewise, significant state influence in the form of selling some of the commodity to the state and state ownership of land were given as reasons to deny Market Economy Treatment to six Chinese firms in *Hot-Rolled Steel from the People's Republic of China (2000)* (Commission Decision 1758/2000/ECSC 2000, recital 13).[17]

One analyst said that the EU's treatment of China in many of these cases was really "the pot calling the kettle black." Member states of the EU have many state controlled firms, such as utilities and transportation companies. Industries can sell their output to the government at preferential prices, and not be considered "non-market." There is also state ownership of some public lands, such as fisheries, that does not make the EU fishing industry non-market. Therefore, the analyst commented that the EU was going to have to accept in theory that if one of the inputs was state controlled in a MET case, this would not necessarily negate a positive market industry finding.[18]

. The question is really what *degree* of state interference is sufficient to disqualify Market Economy Treatment. Since there are no set economic indicators for deciding what constitutes excessive state interference, this has remained a subjective decision rendered by the Commission alone. Qualitative evaluations of the completeness and reliability of information have been influenced by beliefs that transitional economies continued to operate under less than market oriented principles, and that therefore their economic activities should be carefully screened.

Since the Commission does not really know what degree of state interference in the context of NMEs would disqualify them from market consideration, or even if there is such a figure to be used, the Commission has sent contradictory messages about the legitimate role of the state in economic development. In *Glycine from China* (2000), the Commission argued that there were some selling restrictions imposed by the state, therefore this state involvement invalidated MET (COM Reg. No. 1043/2000 2000, recital 13). However, in *Fluorspar from the People's Republic of China (2000)*, the EU requested state involvement in limiting export sales and was going to impose anti-dumping duties if the state refused to get involved in regulating the market (Council Reg. No. 2011/2000 2000). Therefore, state involvement per se was not the reason for rejection of MET. The real problem was the belief that somehow state involvement by former non-market economies was different from other types of state involvement. The presumption has remained that state directed economic activities in these transitional economies were somehow extraordinary, potential threatening, and certainly cause for caution.

Positive MET Determinations but Incomplete Implementation
There have been a number of positive MET rulings. However, a positive MET finding does not mean that an NME firm actually received the

benefits of market-oriented treatment. Being awarded MET and actually having MET implemented are two different things. There have been rulings in which MET was found for the foreign firms but not the domestic firms in the transitional economy. There have been positive MET determinations that were rescinded in the final determination. There have also been positive MET determinations that were only partially implemented. What is rare is the actual implementation of the MET statute. A few cases will illustrate the range of possibilities in MET determinations.

As with the individual treatment rule, there have been several cases in which foreign venture type firms in China have been awarded Market Economy Treatment. In *Steel Fasteners from the People's Republic of China (2000)*, the Chinese firms were denied Market Economy Treatment, but the Swedish affiliated companies were awarded MET (Council Reg. No. 2570/2000 2000). Similarly, in *Fluorescent Lamps from the People's Republic of China (2001)*, one wholly owned foreign firm and one joint venture were awarded MET. The Chinese firms that also petitioned for Market Economy Treatment were rejected because they were unable to show they were not encumbered by the Chinese macroeconomic system (COM Reg. No. 255/2001 2001). However, the joint venture and foreign firm operating under the same macroeconomic constraints were able to sufficiently demonstrate their market independence from the overarching macroeconomic environment.

There are two very interesting aspects to the fluorescent lamps case: how the ruling affected the final dumping margins, and what the ruling implied about the causal impact of the macroeconomic environment. First, using different methods of determining normal value resulted in very different final dumping margins for the firms involved. The export prices of all the firms operating in China were basically the same; they sold their products to the EU for similar prices. However, the wholly owned foreign firm got to use its prices in the dumping calculation, and was subsequently not found guilty of dumping (de minimis). The joint venture had a constructed value measure taken in which some but not all of its prices were used. It received a 39.2 percent dumping margin. The Chinese firms had normal value calculated using a price analogue and received dumping margins of 74.4 percent (COM Reg. No. 255/2001 2001). This is a clear indication of the way in which the analogue method inflates the final dumping margins.

Second, this case was revealing for what it demonstrated about the way the Commission interpreted the impact of the macroeconomic environment on the business decisions of firms. The Commission ruled that a foreign owned firm operating in a "non-market or transitional economy" was market oriented. The Commission was able to suspend its belief about the distorting effects of the NME macroeconomic environment on the business decisions of foreign firms. It has not been able to do the same for Chinese firms. Beliefs about the pervasive nature of state influence in NMEs continued to affect the way the Commission perceived and acted on information from NME firms. This suggests that the overall NME macroeconomic environment was not the decisive factor in the Commission's decisions. The Commission was not simply rejecting MET to firms because they were located in a non-market economy; it was rejecting Chinese firms in a non-market economy. This provides compelling evidence that lingering beliefs about the nature of NMEs have impeded the implementation of formal rule changes.

There have also been cases in which MET has been awarded and then rescinded. In *Ferromolybdenum from the People's Republic of China* (*2002*), MET was initially approved for one of the ten petitioning firms. However, after further investigation, the Commission overturned its decision and imposed the regular analogue method (Council Reg. No. 215/2002 2002). In *Certain Zinc Oxides from the People's Republic of China* (*2001*), three Chinese firms were awarded MET, but then in the end their prices could not be used because they appeared "below market prices" (COM Reg. No. 1827/2001 2001, recitals 46–47). Constructing a normal value and ignoring the actual prices is not a true implementation of the MET, which is supposed to be the use of the actual prices paid by the firms.

There have been other cases in which MET has been awarded but not fully implemented. So on the surface it looks like the firms have benefited from MET, but this belies actual treatment. An affirmative MET determination does not necessarily mean that rules have been implemented. In the landmark case of *Aluminum Foil from Russia* (*2001*), the first MET was awarded to a Russian firm. However, in the final implementation, the Commission determined that Russian prices could not actually be used in the dumping determination and a value was constructed to approximate the Russian prices (Council Reg. No. 950/2001 2001, recital). In practice this meant that the normal value was established based on a constructed value of costs of production adding a "reasonable amount for selling, general and administrative costs" (recital 41). These costs were valued in the analogue for the case—the United States. The use of the United States as a partial analogue for this case was not consistent with the intent of the MET statute. In essence, a Russian firm was awarded MET, but then failed to receive it in practice.

In Ukraine's first affirmative MET case, *Urea from Ukraine et al.* (*2002*), it received Market Economy Treatment but this was only partially implemented (Council Reg. No. 92/2002 2002). Two of the three petitioning Ukrainian firms passed the MET criteria, in what was an important affirmation of Ukraine's new transitional economy status. Upon further examination, one of the firms could not actually receive MET because of noncompliance by an associated supplier (recital 59). The second firm's prices needed to be partially amended using the transportation rates applicable in the analogue country—the United States. Therefore neither firm actually received full MET despite being formally awarded (recital 34).

The closest Russian firms came to full MET was the case of *Silicon from Russia (2003)*, in which all three petitioning Russian firms were granted near complete MET (COM Reg. No. 1235/2003 2003). In the end, the prices for electricity were modified to approximate the prices in the Community; however, other than that, the Russian firms' prices were utilized in determining normal value. The EU made a point of rejecting that Russia could have a comparative advantage in electricity costs in this case, so the Commission was still using its special anti-dumping rule leverage to shape the market activities in Russia. However, this was very close to unencumbered market treatment.

Starting in 2003, Chinese firms began to apply for MET in record numbers. The Commission's behavior toward China started to change as well, with some Chinese firms receiving MET in name and in practice. For example, in the 2005 case of *Polyester Filament Apparel Fabrics from the PRC (2005)*, 49 Chinese firms requested MET (COM Reg. No. 426/2005 2005). The increased number resulted in more firms being granted MET. *In Okoumé Plywood from the PRC (2004)*, four of the eight petitioners were granted MET, but the four recipients all had their prices adjusted by the Commission (COM Reg. No. 988/2004 2004, recitals 48–51). In *Barium Carbonate from the PRC (2005)*, two of five requests were provisionally granted (COM Reg. No. 145/2005 2005), and in *Magnesia Bricks (2005)*, two of eight were granted MET but a constructed value for their prices was used in the end (COM Reg. No. 552/2005 2005, recitals 24–25). Therefore although there are more cases in which MET has been awarded, implementation is still incomplete. Receiving MET has not guaranteed that the rules would be fully implemented.

Rule Layering and Policy Tipping Points

Russia offers a compelling example of how the layering of formal rule changes can create critical policy tipping points. In 1998, Russia received special transitional economy status. In 2000, Russia received the unrealized possibility of Market Economy Treatment. In 2002, Russia was officially reclassified as a market economy (Council Reg. No. 1972/2002 2002; European Commission 2003, 12).[19]

The full country reclassification should have obviated the need for a MET determination, since the entire country was reclassified as a "market economy." But as will be detailed in chapter seven, the Commission structured even the country reclassification to circumvent its implementation. Therefore, subsequent cases have continued to treat Russia differently, applying MET treatment to it and even denying MET treatment to firms in Russia, which is blatantly discriminatory since the firms should have been assumed to be market oriented under the new reclassification scheme (Council Reg. No. 1891/2005 2005). In another case Russia was allegedly treated as a market economy, but all its prices were not used because they were not considered "normal" (COM Reg. No. 862/2005 2005, recital 49). Therefore, EU behavior provides a nice example of policy layering and tipping points.

The Commission was unwilling to implement any of these formal rule changes when they were enacted. The Commission invented a "transitional economy" status change as a way to forestall a complete status reclassification for China and Russia. The Commission was, however, not willing or not able to make the cognitive adjustments necessary in order to implement this change. The Commission's yearly report said as much, when it explained that despite anti-dumping reform promises, "neither economy has evolved sufficiently to justify more concessions during anti-dumping probes" (Europe Information Service 2000b). When asked about the timing and intent of the "hybrid" classification for China and Russia in 1998, Commission officials admitted that this formal rule change was a "political gift" to these countries, which they were unprepared to administer under the present conditions.[20] Moreover, Sir Leon Brittan, the former EU Commissioner in charge of trade policy, pushed for this rule change from inside of the agency because he wanted personal recognition for them before leaving office.[21]

Commission officials also admitted that the 2000 MET formal rule change was more in name than in substance, and at that time they had no intention of administering the more beneficial rules to Chinese and Russian firms.[22] One analyst laughingly referred to the rule change, saying it could not be applied to Russia since the industries were basically all "Stalingrad companies."[23] The formal rule change was structured to allow the Commission to interpret the laws as it saw fit. Making the formal rule changes administrable on a case by case basis ensured that the Commission would have ample leeway to act according to its beliefs and perceptions of NMEs. However, the Commission enacted yet one more level of rule change—a complete reclassification. As such the Commission had layered three types of formal rule changes atop a foundation of beliefs anathema to those very changes. This created conditions ripe for a tipping point of policy change.

With the 2003 silicon case, the Commission faced a dilemma. The Commission could not evade implementation of its policy changes indefinitely. However, it was still firmly wedded to its belief that trade with NMEs was extraordinary and should be treated with caution. The Commission started the silicon case leaning in the direction of no policy change. It selected an analogue for Russia in the preliminary determination, "just in case" it needed to be used (COM Reg. No. 1235/2003 2003, recital 12). This "just in case" demonstrates the lingering presumption that Russian prices could not actually be used, since analogues are never assigned to market economies in preliminary dumping determinations just in case their prices cannot be used. In the end the Commission chose the lesser of two options; it granted MET rather than full market status treatment. It did not even grant full MET, but rather modified the electricity costs, as noted above. The same holds for the Chinese MET cases, in which an avalanche of new cases has resulted in a trickle of MET determinations.

I argue that this layering of policy change on top of former beliefs created a policy tipping point. Even disproportionate information processors are forced to accept the mountain of disconfirming evidence at some crucial point, and start to alter outcomes as well as underlying beliefs. Russia and China have been pressuring the EU for a change in policy implementation for many years, but this only worked when it tipped the policy outcome because of the layering of unimplemented formal rule changes. This policy change does not mean that underlying cold war beliefs about NMEs changed. Discussion in chapter seven of country reclassifications demonstrates that lingering cold war beliefs have continued to affect policy implementation. However, as with the case of individual treatment, this fledgling change in outcome is a signal of a shift in the foundational beliefs.

Belief Perpetuation

There are various overt as well as more subtle methods by which beliefs about NMEs have been transmitted within the trade agencies and in the international system in general. Trade agencies are bureaucracies with formal rules and hierarchies, as well as informal norms, procedures, and understandings. New members of these trade organizations are directly and indirectly taught both the formal rules and responsibilities of their positions, and the collectively understood mandates, objectives, and interpretations of their positions.[24]

In the case of the United States, new trade agents are given an Anti-Dumping Handbook, instructing them about the legal method of administering U.S. trade law. To complement the handbook, senior trade officials work with new trade agents in the writing of policy relevant memos and decisions.[25] This oversight of cases by senior officials has ensured that policy interpretation and implementation remained consistent between senior and junior members of the organization. On cases involving NMEs, senior officials have "helped" with policy memos and decisions. One relatively junior trade analyst commented that he "goes along with the analysis of higher ups."[26] This is a typical feature of most bureaucracies in which new members are schooled in the formal and informal rules of the organization of which they are a part. This is especially true for NME cases, which are particularly complicated. Junior bureaucrats refer to senior advisors as well as receive larger policy direction from the Office of Policy in the International Trade Administration on these cases. Finally, there is also a required reliance by trade officials on the boiler plate language that has been used in previous cases. These boiler plate policy memos and decisions are used when possible, thereby ensuring continuity between investigations.

The European Commission is an interesting organization, because trade analysts from all the member states work together in DG Trade on the administration of EU-wide trade policy. This means that analysts with similar degrees, but potentially very different national backgrounds, educational experiences, and ideas about trade policy are brought together to administer EU anti-dumping laws. As such, while one cannot argue that national differences are nullified, there is a common socialization process binding the trade analysts together. It is an organizational process reproduced in the trade agency itself by educational programs in the administration of EU anti-dumping laws, as well as through more informal interactions between the trade agents. Policy statements by European officials have also reinforced negative perceptions of NMEs. In speeches and public forums, one is reminded about the extraordinary nature of NMEs and their unusual capacity and incentive to dump (Laurent 1996). There are various direct methods of instructing members of an organization about the appropriate ways of exercising their responsibilities.

There are indirect methods of socializing trade agents as well. The evolving case law demonstrated the appropriate way to interpret "facts" in trade cases, particularly with respect to NMEs. If previous cases focused on the threats posed by NMEs, this set the frame of reference with which the facts in future NME cases should be viewed. For example, in EU case law, dumping determinations have focused not only on actual imports from NMEs, but also on the latent capacity in these NMEs (COM Reg. No. 394/1996 1996; COM Reg. No. 2997/95 1995; Council Reg. No. 495/98 1998). In several cases, the EU has reimposed duties on NME exporters because they had the capacity to export to the EU, even though they were not actually doing so at the time. These precedent setting interpretations, combined with the practice of using boiler plate language in the administration of new cases, has resulted in the reproduction of a similar way of interpreting facts from one case to another and from one analyst to another.

Outside of the trade agencies themselves, domestic interests and other related bureaucratic institutions have also contributed to maintaining the belief that NMEs posed a disproportionate trade threat. Special interest groups perpetuated these beliefs by painting a picture of NME exporters as agents with both the capacity and institutional incentive to dump (Agence Europe 1997f; European Commission 2000c; Union des Confederations de l'industrie et Employeurs d'Europe 1996). The Council has echoed the Commission's sentiments about the different and potentially threatening nature of trade with transitional economies and NMEs. Specifically with reference to China, the Council argued that there were "secret laws, laws which are not published and to which foreigners do not have access, dealing in particular with external economic and trade relations" (Agence Europe 1996b). And therefore on the basis of the possibility of secret agreements, extraordinary care should be taken when dealing with China. In sum, belief perpetuation has both an internal as well as an external dimension, through which beliefs about the unusual and threatening nature of trade with NMEs have been kept alive despite contrary information.

Conclusion

The evidence from this chapter demonstrates that the treatment of NMEs by the ITA and the Commission has not simply been a case of trade agencies maximizing trade protection for their constituents. There was a systematic pattern of distrust of NMEs, resulting in trade protection. The cases discussed all took place in the post cold war periods and most over the past decade. These examples are addressing trade with economies in transition, not centrally planned economies in the middle of the cold war. Despite changed international circumstances and domestic institutional conditions, trade discrimination continued into 2004.

Information supplied by NMEs was questioned and ignored. Extraordinary safeguards in the form of unattainable information requirements were erected. NMEs were treated in a very different manner than other developing countries, even when they were labeled "transitional economies." Beliefs about the threatening nature of trade with NMEs acted as information discounters. The trade agencies often failed to synthesize or act on all of the information actually provided by the NME. Disconfirming information was discounted by both trade agencies. The trade agencies were able to look at the same objective macroeconomic conditions and render different determinations based on the involvement of NMEs or "market industries." Empirical conditions and interest based accounts of the trade agencies' actions therefore are insufficient to explain their treatment of NMEs.

This conclusion about the causal role of beliefs is not based on an analysis of trade outcomes, per se. Outcomes have not really changed—there is still trade protection. What is curious about the NME cases was the process of administering anti-dumping laws remained the same despite the direct formal rule changes that should have changed the process. In order to appreciate the causal role for beliefs, one must focus on the process, not the outcome. As such, the process of administering the cases combined with the interview data and the trade agencies' policy pronouncements provide compelling evidence of the causal effect of beliefs on trade policy.

The next chapter explores the conditions under which beliefs about NMEs will change. Belief certainty continues to play an important role in discounting new information about transitional economies; however, the European Union has started to change some of its policy behavior toward NMEs. The findings from this chapter alluded to fledgling cases of belief change. In the next chapter I examine how the continued layering of unimplemented formal rule changes on the preexisting belief structures created the opportunity for a reevaluation, although not wholesale rejection, of the cold war belief system.

CHAPTER SEVEN

Belief Stickiness and Belief Change

The anti-dumping rules [against NMEs] teach the capitalists to behave like socialists, not the other way around.

—Finger 1993

Introduction

A series of rule modifications or improvements to the non-market economy anti-dumping law is a second best choice for NMEs. These economies want their transitions to be recognized with full scale country reclassifications as "market economies." A reclassification would be the ultimate formal rule change to the anti-dumping laws. It catapults a country from the sphere of special anti-dumping trade laws to regular anti-dumping laws. A reclassification is desirable for both political and economic reasons. Politically it is an affirmation of the reforms in NMEs and the first step toward reintegration into the international political economy. Economically it improves the fairness of the application of anti-dumping laws by no longer subjecting NMEs to the constructed value method of determining normal value. Using the actual prices in a reclassified NME instead of price proxies would allow the exporting firms to demonstrate they had a comparative advantage in the production of certain commodities, and should decrease both the size and incidence of protection against NME exports. With country reclassifications there would no longer be recourse to third county price proxies, therefore the economic and political stakes are quite high for both Western trade agencies and non-market economies.

In this chapter I examine the last example of formal rule change—country reclassification. Country reclassifications are interesting examples of both belief stickiness and belief change. Predictions regarding the information discounting effects of belief certainty on rule change have proven true in the implementation of this legal procedure. There has continued to be incomplete implementation of formal rule change on the issue of status reclassifications by both the United States and the European Union. However, there has also been fledging belief change on the part of the United States and European Union. Examining the role that institutional safeguards, iterated exchanges, and information flows have on belief change will illustrate the multifaceted manner in which beliefs persist and change over time. Finally, country reclassifications highlight the differences between the European Union and the United States, demonstrating how relative differences in degree of belief certainty predictably affect the propensity for belief change and commensurate policy change on the same issue.

Predicting Reclassifications: Materialist
Explanations

As of 2005, the United States had reclassified a number of countries across the various typologies (see table 7.1): Poland in 1993 (58 FR 44166 1993), Slovakia in 2000 (65 FR 1110 2000; U.S. International Trade Administration 1999a), the Czech Republic in 1999 (65 FR 5599 2000; U.S. International Trade Administration 1999b), Hungary in 2000 (U.S. International Trade Administration 2000b), and Kazakhstan in 2002 (67 FR 15535 2002). The former German Democratic Republic (GDR) was absorbed by Germany, and there was no formal reclassification (61 FR 27049 1996). Lithuania and Estonia were removed from the list of NMEs as of 2003 (U.S. International Trade Administration 2003a). Latvia started to be treated as a market economy in anti-dumping cases in 2001 (66 FR 33530 2001). Russia obtained a quasi-reclassification in 2002 (U.S. International Trade Administration 2003c) and Romania in 2003 (68 FR 54418 2003). Bulgaria received a technical reclassification in 2004 (U.S. International Trade Administration 2003b). China (63 FR 72255 1998), Ukraine (62 FR 61754 1997), and Moldova (67 FR 55790 2002) have had their formal reclassification requests denied in 1997, 1998, and 2002 respectively. In 2006, Ukraine received approval for a reclassification (States News Service 2006).

For the European Union, Association Agreements have facilitated the reclassification of most of the countries in Central and Eastern Europe.

Table 7.1 Summary of US Status Reclassification Requests

Country	Year	Policy Implementation
GDR	1991	Absorbed by FDR
Poland	1993	Real market treatment (2000)
Czech Republic	1999	No real market treatment yet
Slovak Republic	2000	No real market treatment yet
Hungary	2000	Real market treatment (2002)
Latvia	2001	No real market treatment yet
Ukraine	2001	Rejected Reclassification Request
Moldova	2002	Rejected Reclassification Request
Kazakhstan	2002	Continued NME treatment
Russia	2002	Symbolic reclassification—NME treatment
Lithuania	2003	No dumping cases to test treatment
Estonia	2003	No dumping cases to test treatment
Romania	2003	Continued NME treatment
Bulgaria	2004	No dumping cases to test treatment
China	All requests	Rejected Reclassification Request
Ukraine	2006	Symbolic reclassification

The GDR was the exception, having been unofficially reclassified when it unified with West Germany in 1990 (Council Reg. No. 2684/90 1990). Poland, Hungary, Slovakia, and the Czech Republic were removed from the list of state trading countries in February 1992, following the conclusion of Association Agreements (Council Reg. No. 517/92 1992).[1] As of 1994, Bulgaria and Romania were no longer included on the list of non-market economies (Council Reg. No. 519/94 1994; Council Reg. No. 3382/94 1994; Council Reg. No. 3383/94 1994). Latvia, Lithuania, and Estonia signed European agreements on trade related matters in 1995, and as of 1998 were no longer on the list of NMEs (Council Reg. No. 905/98 1998; European Community 1998a, 1998b, and 1998c). Russia received a hybrid reclassification in 2002, and Ukraine and China's requests for reclassification were rejected in 2003 and 2004 respectively (see table 7.2). However, Ukraine's reclassification request was finally approved in 2005, to take effect 2006 (Bellaby 2005).

Explaining the timing and the sequencing of reclassification on the part of the ITA and the Commission might be a simple function of the degree of economic freedom or extent of economic reforms in the NMEs. Perhaps interest based or institution oriented theories explain reclassifications. For example, NMEs that are more economically liberal than other similarly situated developing "market" countries should be

Table 7.2   Waves of EU Country Reclassifications

First Wave (1992)	Second Wave (1994)	Third Wave (1998)
Poland	Bulgaria	Estonia
Hungary	Romania	Latvia
Czech Republic		Lithuania
Slovakia		

reclassified. Or, NMEs that liberalized first should be reclassified first, and so on. If the United States or European Union reclassified NMEs according to the degree of economic liberalization of these countries, then there would be no real need to explore a causal role for beliefs, even if one existed. Parsimony would dictate that interest based accounts be privileged. However, if the timing or sequencing of reclassifications has not hewed closely to what would be predicted by the objective economic and political conditions in NMEs, then there is room for an explanation incorporating cold war beliefs and ideas about non-market economies.

Table 7.3 compares levels of economic freedom across non-market economies and other developing countries over three different time periods.[2] To determine if economic conditions predict reclassifications, one could compare the relative rankings of the countries with the information about sequencing and timing of reclassifications presented in tables 7.1 and 7.2. A look at 1995, and a straight economic assessment would suggest that most so-called non-market economies should have already been reclassified as market economies. Not only were countries in Eastern Europe more economically free than most Western trading partners, but even orthodox core countries like China, Russia, Ukraine, and Belarus were also more economically free than other "market-oriented" developing countries like India or Nicaragua. Since India was classified and treated as a "market economy" in 1995, and according to the measurements of economic freedom India was less market oriented than Russia or China, by extension China and Russia should have been reclassified as market economies, if one was focused on an interest based account or materialist account of trade policies.

The rankings in 2000 and 2004 bear out this assessment as well. For example, the 2004 economic freedom scores list China as more economically free than Bangladesh, Romania (a reclassified country), Kazakhstan (another reclassified country), Venezuela, and Nigeria. Ukraine is on par with Argentina and more economically free than

Table 7.3   Index of Economic Freedom

1995		2000		2004	
Country	*Score*	*Country*	*Score*	*Country*	*Score*
Korea	2.15	Hong Kong	1.3	Hungary	2.6
Czech Rep.	2.2	Czech Rep.	2.2	Armenia	2.63
France	2.3	Estonia	2.2	France	2.63
Estonia	2.35	Germany	2.2	Poland	2.81
Malaysia	2.4	Denmark	2.25	Mexico	2.9
Italy	2.5	Italy	2.3	Bulgaria	2.98
Spain	2.5	Korea	2.4	Moldova	3.09
Sweden	2.65	Spain	2.4	Brazil	3.1
Portugal	2.7	Peru	2.45	Albania	3.1
Argentina	2.75	France	2.5	Croatia	3.11
Slovakia	2.8	Hungary	2.55	Georgia	3.19
Turkey	2.8	Latvia	2.65	Kenya	3.26
Mexico	2.85	Malaysia	2.7	Egypt	3.28
Colombia	2.9	Greece	2.75	Kyrgyz Repub	3.36
Hungary	3	Poland	2.8	Azerbaijan	3.39
Pakistan	3.15	Philippines	2.85	Pakistan	3.4
Ecuador	3.2	Lithuania	2.9	Russia	3.46
Philippines	3.2	Mexico	3	Argentina	3.48
Brazil	3.3	Slovak	3	Ukraine	3.49
Poland	3.3	Armenia	3.1	India	3.53
Russia	3.4	Ecuador	3.1	China	3.64
Indonesia	3.4	Romania	3.3	Romania	3.66
Bulgaria	3.5	Bulgaria	3.4	Kazakhstan	3.7
Bangladesh	3.6	China	3.4	Bangladesh	3.7
Albania	3.6	Pakistan	3.4	Yemen	3.7
China	3.6	Brazil	3.5	Nigeria	3.95
Romania	3.6	Croatia	3.5	Belarus	4.09
Belarus	3.7	Indonesia	3.5	Venezuela	4.18
Ukraine	3.7	Kyrgyz	3.6	Uzbekistan	4.29
India	3.8	Ukraine	3.6	Turkmenistan	4.31
Nicaragua	4	Kazakh	3.7	Zimbabwe	4.54
		Russia	3.7		

Note: 1. No 1995 data available for Lativa, Lithuania, and other Soviet Republics

2. Total 161 countries in sample

Source: The Heritage Foundation, *The Index of Economic Freedom*. <www.heritage.org/research/features/index/downloads/Pastscores.xls.>

India. Albania is on par with Brazil and more economically free than Egypt, Kenya, and Pakistan. In sum, over the past decade neither the order of U.S. country reclassifications, nor the timing of reclassifications, nor the decision to refuse reclassifications has been consistent with simple economic based predictions.

In the case of the European Union, by 1995 Poland, Hungary, the Czech Republic, Slovakia, Bulgaria, and Romania had been reclassified as market economies. Estonia ranked higher in terms of economic freedom than Italy, Spain, Sweden, and Portugal in 1995, but it was not reclassified. In 2000, Russia, China, Ukraine, Armenia, and Kyrgyzstan were all more economically free than supposedly "market oriented" European trading partners, but they were still classified and treated as NMEs. In 2004, Romania, one of the second wave reclassifications was less economically free than Russia, China, and Ukraine, counties not yet reclassified. Material economic conditions yield little explanatory leverage over the EU's scope, timing, or sequencing of reclassifications.

Despite the fact that anti-dumping laws are alleged to be economic determinations, political liberalization is often cited as an important component of the reform process in non-market economies (European Union 1995; European Council 1999, 9). As such political freedom indicators might affect reclassifications decisions. Table 7.4 ranks selected countries in terms of economic and political freedoms. Combining political and economic freedom scores does not, however, yield a stronger explanation about the timing and sequencing of reclassifications. Poland, the Czech Republic, and Hungary should have been the first countries reclassified. In fact, they were the first countries reclassified by the European Union. However, Slovakia was also in the first tier of countries, and its political-economic freedom index shows it was behind Lithuania, Estonia, and Latvia. The Baltics should have been reclassified before Slovakia, and they should have been the second major tier of countries reclassified. This did not happen. The Balkans were reclassified by the Commission before the Baltics, in spite of Bulgaria and Romania's relatively low political-economic freedom scores. Combinations of political and economic freedom scores cannot predict the EU's reclassification patterns. Moreover, they prove completely inadequate in explaining the ITA's behavior.

One could argue, especially in the case of the European Union, geographic proximity combined with political and economic factors affected behavior toward NMEs. For example, countries that were less politically or economically free and were geographically closer could have negative spillover effects on the EU. Perhaps the EU was willing to treat India favorably despite its low level of economic freedom because India was relatively far away and thus posed fewer potential negative externalities.

The empirical evidence does not fully support this assertion. Croatia and Bosnia are not NMEs, and have never been treated as NMEs. Bosnia

Table 7.4   Index of Political and Economic Freedoms Combined

Country	Score	Country	Score
Poland	3.11	Croatia	8.02
Czech Republic	3.5	Russia	8.42
Hungary	3.67	Ukraine	8.64
Slovenia	3.86	Albania	8.88
Lithuania	4.08	Armenia	9.00
Estonia	4.56	Kyrgyzstan	9.46
Latvia	4.89	Kazakhstan	9.96
Slovakia	5.75	Azerbaijan	10.50
Romania	6.77	Yugoslavia	10.83
Bulgaria	6.98	Belarus	12.69
Macedonia	7.11	Uzbekistan	12.69
Georgia	7.75		

Note: Scores 2–14, 2 is most free and 14 is least free.

Source: Freedom House, 2000. *Nations in Transit, Country Reports*. <www. free-domhouse.org/ research/nitransit.>

has an economic freedom score of 4.4 on the Freedom House's *2000 Country Reports*. This is lower than Russia (3.7), China (3.4), and Ukraine (3.6) (see table 7.4). Similarly in 2000, Croatia was less market oriented than China, but China was classified as an NME and Croatia was not. In spite of the low levels of economic freedom of Croatia and Bosnia and their geographic proximity to the EU, which allowed for potential spillover effects, these countries did not experience discriminatory treatment by the Commission with regard to anti-dumping laws. Geographic proximity might play a role in the Commission's decision making, as was tentatively supported in the statistical analysis in chapter five. However, geographic proximity is not decisive in explaining either when a country would be reclassified, or who would receive reclassification. It is also not a factor at all in the United States' behavior toward non-market economies.

In sum, this analysis of levels of economic and political freedom has demonstrated that the timing and sequencing of country reclassifications on the part of both the European Union and the United States is not a function of materialist considerations alone. Institutional differences cannot explain the timing or sequencing of reclassifications. A window of opportunity has thus been opened to present an explanation of *if* and *how* beliefs and ideas about NMEs have impacted reclassification decisions. In the following section I first review the criteria for reclassification specified by both the ITA and the Commission, and then examine the actual implementation of those criteria in order to understand how beliefs matter.

Country Reclassification Criteria: When Is an Economy Market Oriented?

United States

In the 1988 Omnibus Trade and Competitiveness Act (OTCA), Congress for the first time statutorily defined the term "non-market economy country." Prior to the formalization of the definition, "non-market economy" had simply been enumerated as a list of countries. But given the transitions in NMEs and the possible need to consider reclassifications sometime in the future, the definition was finally spelled out. "The term 'non-market economy country' means any foreign country that the administering authority determines does not operate on market principles of cost or pricing structures, so that sales of merchandise in such a country do not reflect the fair value of the merchandise" (see OTCA, Pub. L. 100–418, 1316 (b), 102 Stat. 1107, 1187). Section 771 (18) (B) of the OTCA instructed Commerce to consider several factors when trying to determine if a country should be treated as a non-market econ omy or reclassified as a market economy, under the law. Subsequent to this Commerce added other factors for consideration. These included:

1. the extent to which the currency of the country is convertible;
2. the extent to which wage rates are determined by free bargaining between labor and management;
3. the extent to which joint ventures or other investments by firms of other foreign countries are permitted;
4. the extent of government ownership or control over the means of production;
5. the extent of government control over the price and output decisions of enterprises; and
6. the degree of centralized government control over the allocation of resources or inputs (51 FR 25085 1986, esp. criterion 6; 54 FR 12941 1989).

These criteria are subjectively understood, as each represents not a specific economic or financial state but more a continuum between state directed economic activity and market determined exchange activities. In addition, there is no method to weight the relative importance of the factors. Therefore, no single factor or group of factors would definitively constitute a non-market economy. In fact, if applied without any political frame of reference, many countries currently classified as "market oriented," such as India, Brazil, or Thailand, would fail this test.[3]

For example, the first criterion—currency convertibility—does not prove or disprove the market orientation of an economy. While wage rate controls may distort market signals, the second criterion has been acknowledged as largely insignificant and more a political than an economic consideration.[4] The third criterion is not a sound indicator of market status either, as there are many market economies with restricted foreign penetration, and almost all economies have limited foreign investment in specific sectors. The Department of Commerce has stated that the issue of both currency convertibility and degree of foreign investment are international economic indicators and as such have "little effect on internal market forces" (56 FR 46153 1991). Therefore the degree to which these factors would undermine domestic market mechanisms is suspect. These indicators of "market orientation" are also economically suspicious because only Communist countries have ever been labeled NMEs, and not even every Communist country.[5] Wage controls, or currency inconvertibility, or price controls have not caused other developing countries to be treated as "non-market" for the purpose of anti-dumping laws. In essence, the economic criteria weakly mask the political intent of the law.

In rendering market economy determinations for reclassification cases, the International Trade Administration has both sole responsibility and unusual authority (19 U.S.C. §1677 (18) (c) (ii)). "Section 1316 (b) of the 1988 Act implemented a final procedural change of note by exempting the Commerce Department's determination of market and non-market status from judicial review" (Harris 1993, 418). Anti-dumping decisions are normally subject to judicial review, improving both the final oversight of decisions and accountability. However, the status change was placed above judicial review, giving the ITA an unusual concentration of power over this issue. As one scholar noted, Commerce had been given virtually unfettered discretion to make such political decisions (Neeley 1989, 549). The decision making autonomy of the ITA, combined with the discretionary latitude in the structure of the rules created perfect conditions for cold war beliefs to continue to affect policy outcomes.

European Union

In contrast with the U.S. approach, the European Union has no official market criteria to determine when a country should be reclassified. Based on past behavior, preliminary negotiations for European Agreements have corresponded with country reclassifications. Although Interim Agreements on trade do not include reclassifications, they have facilitated negotiations for Association agreements in some cases, and have been helpful in starting reclassification discussions in other cases.[6] European agreements on trade or preliminary Association Agreements do not exclude future members from anti-dumping investigations. The EU retained the right to apply anti-dumping laws to even reclassified NMEs up until the moment that they become full members of the European Union (European Coal and Steel Committee 1991, recital 5).

By not providing specific economic criteria for reclassification, the Commission guaranteed a substantial amount of discretion for itself in the interpretation and implementation of its trade laws. Therefore, both political and economic criteria could potentially affect reclassification decisions. Beliefs and perceptions could also play a causal role. However, since this highly discretionary approach was tied to Association Agreements, this posed a problem for dealing with countries for whom there was no hope of becoming an EU member, such as Russia, Ukraine, or China. These issues are taken up in the next section in which EU behavior toward each typology of country, from deviant satellites to orthodox core, is addressed.

Country Reclassifications: Using Beliefs to
Square the Circle

Reclassifications are a good test of a theory of belief change. Specific predictions are generated, controlling for information changes, iterations, and institutional safeguards, regarding the order of country reclassifications. According to the logic of belief change set out in this project, beliefs held with less certainty will be more likely to change before beliefs held with greater certainty. Certainty levels affect the relative resistance of beliefs to change.

Degree of belief certainty is a function of internationally determined interests and domestically determined political and economic incentives. (See figure 7.1). It is easier to change the beliefs that resulted from internationally determined interests than domestically determined incentives. Internationally determined interests are clearly defined and changes to

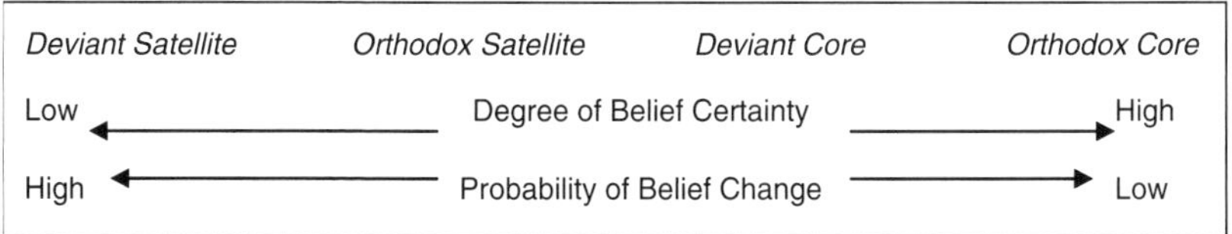

Figure 7.1 Belief Certainty as Predictor of Belief Change

them can be easily recognized—core/periphery. In contrast, domestic institutional incentives include complex assessments of combinations of political and economic institutions. As such, domestic institutional incentives and changes to them are much more difficult to specify. By logical extension, it is easier to change beliefs about satellite states before core states, and easier to change beliefs about economically and politically deviant states before economically and politically orthodox states. Satellites had less interest in harming the West than core countries. Economically and politically deviant countries had fewer domestic incentives to harm the West through trade.

The reclassification predictions based on a model of belief certainty are different from the predictions generated by material, economic, and political conditions. A belief change hypothesis based on degree of belief certainty specifically predicts that Poland, Hungary, the Czech Republic, and Slovakia should be reclassified first. Romania, Bulgaria, Albania, and Vietnam should be reclassified second. Latvia, Lithuania, and Estonia should be reclassified third. China, Russia, Ukraine, and other orthodox core countries should be reclassified last. The next sections examine U.S. and EU reclassification behaviors to test the extent to which belief certainty helps us to better understand trade practices toward NMEs.

United States

A number of deviant satellites, orthodox satellites, and deviant core countries have been reclassified or considered for reclassification by the United States (See table 7.1). The actual decision making process evidenced by the ITA in these cases is instructive for what it reveals about the underlying role for beliefs. It is not necessarily the case outcome, but the process by which the case is decided that illustrates how beliefs can impede full policy implementation. Both the positive reclassification decisions, such as the Polish, Czech, and Slovak cases, and the failed attempts by Ukraine, China, and Moldova evidence the same logic of belief stasis and belief change. I also examine the quasi-reclassification of Russia and explain how a theory of belief change helps to make sense of the symbolic classification. A look at each of these categories of countries—deviant satellites, deviant core, orthodox satellites, and orthodox core—evidences a similar logic of belief stasis and belief change held together by an examination of relative levels of belief certainty.

German Democratic Republic: Deviant Satellites

Although it was never officially reclassified, the German Democratic Republic was the first country to be renamed a market economy. As soon as West Germany and East Germany united, all the firms in East Germany were automatically "market oriented" (58 FR 37315 1993; 61 FR 27049 1996). When asked about the treatment of the GDR, analysts at the International Trade Administration saw no problem with this immediate change in perception of GDR firms. In fact, they did not even consider it a reclassification.[7] The strong ties that the GDR had with West Germany, and Western beliefs that the GDR was anomalous among the NMEs facilitated a rapid change in perceptions about GDR trade. Suddenly the GDR was market oriented, regardless of its economic institutions.

This treatment of the GDR is not consistent with a strict interest based appraisal of the economic institutions in the GDR, but consistent with a belief based hypothesis. It was easy for the United States to change its beliefs about the GDR because they were held with the least certainty of any NME. Belief change was also facilitated by the unification of the Germanys. German reunification acted as a form of institutional contracting, layering West Germany institutions on East Germany institutions. As such, low initial belief certainty plus very strong institutional safeguards and a history of positive interactions yielded a rapid change in both ITA perceptions and actions toward the GDR.

Poland: Deviant Satellite

In the 1993 anti-dumping case *Cut-to-Length Carbon Steel Plate from Poland*, the ITA reclassified Poland (58 FR 44166 1993). This was somewhat surprising given that Poland did not meet many of the formal criteria outlined for status change: the currency was not fully convertible; there was extensive state ownership of many enterprises responsible for industrial production; there were price controls on utilities; and the Polish firm involved in the anti-dumping suit was entirely state owned

(Herzfeld and Rubin 1992). In spite of these seemingly insurmountable impediments to a status change, Poland was declared a market economy retroactive to January 1, 1992.

The Polish case supports the contention that countries with which cold war beliefs were held with lesser certainty would be reclassified first. Poland was one of the countries for which the West held antagonistic beliefs with the least certainty. Poland's refusal to collectivize agriculture, its Solidarity Movement in the 1980s, and Shock Therapy in the 1990s were all signals to the West about the economically and politically deviant nature of Poland.[8] Poland was not a "true Communist believer." Even though Poland was less economically free than Estonia at the time of reclassification, and, even though seven years later it was still less economically free than Estonia and Latvia, the West began to change beliefs about it more readily than the other countries.

Western perceptions about Polish reforms were different because the United States level of certainty with respect to the antagonistic nature of Poland was relatively low among NMEs. Poland had been actively trying to shake off the Communist yoke for a decade prior to the fall of the Berlin Wall. As such, the United States' perceptions of Poland had been changing for some time. Certainty acts as an information discounter. Higher certainty discounts more information and low certainty discounts less information. Therefore, as predicted, the United States did not substantially discount new information about Poland, and was able to see Poland for the market economy that it was trying to be. An analyst involved in this reclassification admitted that Poland did not meet the formal economic criteria, but the United States was willing to extend a political gift to Poland to assist it in its reform efforts.[9] This "gift" was only possible because of relatively weak ITA beliefs about the antagonistic nature of the Polish system.

Institutional safeguards may be necessary, but they are not sufficient to understand Poland's reclassification. Poland was not yet a member of NATO. While Poland had concluded Interim European Agreements in March 1992, so did Hungary and the Czech Republic, and neither of these countries was reclassified by the United States until 2000 and 1999 respectively (European Commission 2001b). Poland was a member of the GATT, but it had been a member since 1967. The Czech Republic was a founding member as well and not reclassified until 1999. International institutional safeguards may be necessary, but one needs to think about the way they interact with existing beliefs and perceptions to unravel why NMEs were treated as they were by the West.

Despite the official reclassification, Poland continued to be treated as an NME in practice until 2000. Poland was involved in an anti-dumping case in 1993, and was subjected to NME treatment by the ITA (58 FR 44166 1993). The Polish firm took the Department of Commerce to court alleging that its retroactive status change should mean that the surrogate country method was no longer applicable.[10] The Court sided with the ITA, ruling special trade practices could still be used against former NMEs despite the status change. It was not until the 2000 Polish sunset review of *Carbon Steel Plate* that Poland was given full market economy treatment (65 FR 18054 2000). The actual change in policy implementation came eight years after its reclassification as a market economy.

This precedent, in which the firms involved in the status change cases were themselves denied market economy treatment, was repeated in the Czech, Slovak, Hungarian, Romanian, and Kazakh reclassification cases. This demonstrates the trouble that decision makers had eschewing old beliefs about NMEs. Even after reclassifying NMEs as market economies, the trade agents still treated the firms involved in the status change case as non-market. This contradictory behavior is consistent with theories about belief stasis and belief change. Beliefs are sticky and change in disjointed manners. Therefore tentative belief change in the form of country reclassifications can be coterminous with resistance to treating NME firms as market oriented. Each of these actions is logically consistent when viewed as part of the process of belief change. Using this lens, I provide examples from each of the other reclassification cases.

Czech Republic: Deviant Satellite

As part of the case of *Certain Small Diameter Carbon and Steel Alloy Seamless Pipe from the Czech Republic*, the Czech government requested revocation of its non-market economy status in the context of the anti-dumping laws (65 FR 5599 2000). While the ITA was reviewing the status change request, it continued with the investigation. It treated the Czech firm accused of dumping as an NME in spite of the eventual retroactive reclassification of the entire country. The Czech government was particularly outraged for several reasons.

First, according to the U.S. definition of an NME, the Czech Republic should have been reclassified years before. By 1999, the Czech currency was convertible, prices had been liberalized and were market determined, tariffs had been reduced, the country was open to foreign direct investment, wages were free of government involvement, and privatization of virtually the entire agricultural, service, and manufacturing sector was in place (U.S. International Trade Administration 1999c, 22–23). The Czech Republic was more economically liberal than

Poland, which had already been reclassified. The Czech Republic had less government intervention in its economy than Germany, Denmark, France, and Italy, but was still classified as an NME.[11]

Second, the Czech Republic had already signed Association Agreements with the European Union, and been reclassified by the EU as a market economy. The United States would not recognize this reclassification. This is a nice illustration of the difference in belief certainty between the United States and the European Union. As predicted, the United States's relatively higher levels of belief certainty about NMEs combined with less frequency of interactions and fewer institutional safeguard arrangements made the United States slower to change its policies than the EU.

Third, and most important, the Czech Republic was a full member of GATT and the WTO (Haus 1991, 164). Once a country becomes a member of the WTO it should not be subjected to special anti-dumping laws, because it is recognized internationally as a market economy.[12] According to the GATT bylaws, imports from a country may be treated as non-market where there is a *"complete or substantially complete monopoly of trade and where all domestic prices are fixed by the Stat."* (Note 2 AD Paragraph 1 of Article VI-Antidumping and Countervailing Duties in Annex I to the GATT 1994). In accordance with the GATT definition, the Czech Republic should not have been classified as an NME. U.S. trade related court cases confirmed that whenever possible U.S. law should be interpreted in a manner consistent with international obligations.[13] As such, the United States was in violation of its WTO obligations to start an anti-dumping case against the Czech Republic using NME standards. WTO obligations required that the United States change the status of the Czech Republic prior to initiating the anti-dumping case.

Even more egregious, the ITA treated the Czech firm as a non-market economy for this case, in spite of the eventual reclassification of the entire country (U.S. International Trade Administration 2000g). This is strong example of the inadequacy of international institutional safeguards to change the treatment of NMEs. While these institutions may facilitate information flows and promote increased interactions between the contracting parties, institutional safeguards alone are unable to dislodge beliefs and perceptions about the other.

Slovak Republic: Deviant Satellite

The case of *Certain Cold-Rolled Flat-Rolled Carbon-Quality Steel Products from Slovakia (2000)* was similar to the aforementioned Czech reclassification case (65 FR 1110 2000). The Slovak Government requested a formal change in status. The ITA confirmed that Slovakia's extensive economic and political reforms merited a change in status, citing Slovakia's founding membership in the GATT, its subsequent membership in the WTO in 1995, and its associations with the EU and OECD as proof (U.S. International Trade Administration 1999a, 20). After much debate and near failures, Slovakia was eventually reclassified. However, in the anti-dumping case in which status change was broached, the Slovak firms were treated as non-market industries (U.S. International Trade Administration 2000h).

Slovakia's reclassification was curious because in terms of economic and political liberalization, it should have been reclassified after Lithuania, Latvia, and Estonia. Each of the Baltic countries had enacted more economic reforms than Slovakia, and achieved a measure of market orientation still not reached by Slovakia in 2000.[14] However, given the combination of interests and incentives used in assessing the strength of Western beliefs, one would have predicted that Slovakia would be reclassified before the Baltics. U.S. cold war beliefs about Slovakia were held with less certainty than beliefs about the Baltics; therefore it was easier for the United States to reclassify Slovakia than the Baltics. A belief based theory predicts that deviant satellite countries would be reclassified before deviant core countries, and this is what we have seen happen in the U.S. case.

Latvia, Lithuania, and Estonia: Deviant Core

The Baltics were interesting cases because the extent of economic and political reform in those countries merited reclassified long before they actually were. In this book's typology the Baltics constitute the deviant core. Latvia was the first of the three deviant core countries to be reclassified, prompted by an anti-dumping case in 2001 (66 FR 33530 2001). Lithuania petitioned for market economy treatment in 2002, and with Estonia was granted market economy treatment in 2003, retroactive to 2002 (67 FR 57393 2002). Of interest and significance is the ease with which the deviant core received reclassification, once the ITA did in fact decide to recognize the extent of their transitions. There were no formal policy announcements and no cautionary language regarding their reclassifications. These countries did not even appear on the 2001 list of non-market economy wage rates, despite not yet being reclassified (U.S. International Trade Administration 2003a). In a 2003 case involving *Steel Reinforcing Bars from Latvia*, no mention at all was made of a change in status and Latvia was treated as a regular market economy for the purposes of the anti-dumping investigation (68 FR 71067 2003).

Apart from the relative lateness of their reclassification, it is clear that beliefs about these countries were already changing prior to their formal reclassifications. Moreover, subsequent to reclassification, none of these countries was treated as anything but a full market economy. The reclassification of the deviant core came after belief change and therefore there was a substantive change in the implementation of the formal rule change. This was in contrast to the Balkans or the orthodox satellites. While there has been formal rule change going on with respect to orthodox satellites and orthodox core countries, beliefs about the different and potentially threatening nature of economic activity in those countries have continued to impede the implementation of real policy change.

Romania and Kazakhstan: Orthodox
Satellite and Core

As of 2004, Romania and Kazakhstan were the only orthodox countries to have been reclassified by the United States. Although Romania was a satellite and Kazakhstan was a core, according to the categorization offered here, both were part of the orthodox group of true Communist believers. Both were treated with the same sense of policy inconsistency on the part of the ITA, in which some of their reforms have been recognized officially, but not acted upon in practice. Since there is such a small number of orthodox countries for which reclassification by the United States has been considered, they are grouped together here.

In the 2003 case of *Standard Line and Pressure Pipe from Romania*, Romania petitioned for MOI treatment and a status reclassification (68 FR 54418 2003). This was not the first time Romania had requested either formal rule change. The ITA reclassified the country retroactive to January 1, 2003 (68 FR 12672 2003), but denied it MOI treatment. Interviews with ITA officials at the time confirmed that it still perceived Romania to be a non-market economy.[15] As such, Romanian firms were rejected as market oriented enough for MOI treatment, but the country as a whole was reclassified as a market economy. Despite the reclassification, Romania continued to receive NME treatment and Egypt was used as a surrogate on subsequent anti-dumping cases. Since Egypt was ranked less economically free than Romania, the continued lack of implementation of formal rule changes was especially pronounced.[16]

Similarly, Kazakhstan in *Hot Rolled Steel from Kazakhstan* was denied MOI treatment because "[the main firm] failed to provide thorough and convincing evidence that a significant portion of its supplier industries, either local or external, are free from government control and state production levels" (66 FR 50397 2001, 3). In a seeming contradiction,

Kazakhstan was granted country reclassification. Despite being reclassified as a market economy, the NME surrogate country methodology was used to price Kazakh inputs. In both the Kazakh and Romanian reclassification cases, the country reclassifications did not result in a change in policy implementation. Moreover, reclassifications accompanied votes of no confidence in the market orientation of firms within the overarching macroeconomy. The treatment of Romania and Kazakhstan highlights that rule change was insufficient to guarantee a change in policy implementation.

Using a theory of belief certainty, one might hypothesize that Romania should be more likely to experience real market economy treatment before Kazakhstan. Members of the orthodox satellite group (Romania) should experience true belief change on the part of the United States before members of the orthodox core group (Kazakhstan). The actual outcome remains to be seen. However, predictions about belief certainty can only get one so far. Actual economic changes in the countries matter. If Romania failed to continue its economic reform programs, one could not presume that beliefs about the non-market nature of Romania would change. Belief certainty must be considered in concert with economic conditions in order to make sense of which countries were reclassified and when those countries were in fact treated as regular market economies. I am not arguing that beliefs alone determine outcomes. However, I am arguing that economic conditions alone are insufficient to explain outcomes. One must marry economic conditions and beliefs or perceptions of those economic conditions in order to better understand outcomes.

Russia: Orthodox Core

Russia received an unexpected partial reclassification in 2002. The reclassification was not a full status change though, and two years later Russia still had not been treated as a market economy. By the special wording of the reclassification in Russia's case, it appeared unlikely to actually receive the market economy benefits of reclassification. In the policy memos surrounding the reclassification, the Department of Commerce sought to clarify its thinking surrounding the status of Russia.

> The Department recognized when it granted Russia market economy status that Russia continues to be in transition and it explicitly stated that the Department will closely examine Russian values in future market economy Russian cases and reject values that are not reflective of market considerations. . . . There will

necessarily be a period of time during which antidumping duty rates, based on the non-market economy calculation methodology, will remain in effect. For existing antidumping duty orders, the non-market economy-based rates will remain in effect until they are changed as a result of a review, pursuant to section 751 of the Act, of a sufficient period of time after April 1, 2002 (U.S. International Trade Administration 2003c, 8).

As of 2004, Russia has not been treated as a market economy in subsequent cases. In *Urea Ammonium Nitrate from Russia (2003)*, the regular NME treatment was used. Egypt was selected as a representative surrogate, and the Russia-wide anti-dumping duty rate was calculated at 239.14 percent (68 FR 9977 2003). In *Silicon Metal from Russia (2003)*, the NME method was used to administer the case to Russia (68 FR 6885 2003). In essence, the symbolic reclassification did not result in a change in the implementation of the trade laws. Given the qualified nature of the reclassification, this status change was partial at best.

The symbolic but unimplemented reclassification of Russia is a good example of belief perseverance in the face of policy change. The extensive market oriented transitions in Russia to date, the high profile nature of Russia in international affairs, the involvement of Russia in many international institutions, and the treatment of Russia by other countries as a market economy have made the continued labeling of Russia as a non-market economy politically problematic. However, despite the changed economic circumstances in Russia and the international system, beliefs about the extraordinary nature of trade relations with Russia have persisted.

The symbolic reclassification of Russia does indicate a slow recognition on the part of the International Trade Administration that policy change must come. What is interesting about the Russian reclassification is that belief certainty helps us to understand why Latvia, Lithuania, and Estonia were actually being treated like market economies before Russia. Although Russia was "reclassified" before Lithuania and Estonia, the reclassification was in name only. In practice the implementation of policy has followed the predictions associated with a theory incorporating belief certainty. Such a theory predicts that the Baltics (deviant core) would receive market economy treatment before both Romania (orthodox satellite) and Russia (orthodox core). This is precisely what we have seen. Although reclassifications have come temporally close together, the actual implementation of policy changes has continued to reflect beliefs about the perceived nature of threats posed by the countries.

China, Ukraine and Moldova: Orthodox Core

As of 2004, China (63 FR 72255 1998), Ukraine (62 FR 61754 1997), and Moldova (67 FR 55790 2002) all had their formal reclassification requests denied. According to the GATT/WTO definition of a non-market economy, none of these countries should be treated as a non-market economy. The United States has been quite clear that it did not intend to reclassify China in the near future.[17] It recently augmented its separate rates practices and surrogate selection criteria explicitly with China in mind, in an effort to streamline anti-dumping procedures and reduce the uncertainty (69 FR 77722 2004). This is partially a function of the large number of cases that have been filed against China and partially a function of the resolve the U.S. has had to continue to treat China as a NME.

The GATT changed Ukraine's status from an NME to a "country in transition" in 1994, acknowledging the extent of the economic and political reforms in the country (General Agreement on Tariffs and Trade 1994). In a "Joint Statement on Expansion of Trade and Investments" signed between Ukraine and the U.S. government in 1994, even the United States officially recognized Ukraine as a country in transition (U.S. International Trade Administration 1997b). However, this did not translate into a status change for the purpose of trade laws.

In 2005, Ukraine initiated another official status change request, coinciding with an impassioned plea by the new president Yushchenko before the U.S. Congress right after the "Orange Revolution."[18] The new Ukrainian president linked Ukrainian economic development and political stability to Ukraine's continued integration into the international trading system (AFX News Limited 2005). According to a theory of belief change, one would expect a status change to be forthcoming. Given the political and economic crisis Ukraine faced during the "Orange Revolution," this exogenous shock to the belief system of the U.S. trade agency might force a reassessment of conditions in Ukraine. Consistent with these predictions, Ukraine was "symbolically" reclassified in February 2006 (RIA Novosti 2006; States News Services 2006). What this means for actual policy implementation based on past U.S. behavior is uncertain.

Moldova petitioned for a status change in 2002, after it was already accepted into the WTO as a member in 2001 (67 FR 55790 2002). Moldova argued that WTO rules required the Department of Commerce to apply MFN treatment to all members, and therefore the United States could not treat Moldova as a NME. The United States rejected this claim and supported the petitioner's contention that WTO membership did not preclude treatment as a NME (U.S. International Trade Administration 2002a, 4).

All three of these countries are members of the orthodox core. As such, one would expect beliefs about the threatening nature of trade with these countries to be particularly durable. In terms of economic development, these countries have reached levels that the international system recognizes as market oriented, and that the United States has recognized as market oriented in other countries. However, the economic conditions in these countries were not sufficient to effect a change in policy. Institutional safeguards were also necessary but not sufficient to change policy. Only when one adds a consideration of belief certainty does the continued treatment of these countries as NMEs in the post–cold war period appear rational and consistent.

European Union

Similar to the United States, beliefs about the extraordinary and potentially threatening nature of trade with NMEs have continued to impact the way in which the EU has implemented its country reclassification policies. The EU is both a foil and a complement to the U.S. case. Even though the EU was quicker to reclassify countries than the United States, at the time of reclassification it was not completely ready to implement this formal rule change either. There have been several cases in which the Commission has reverted to NME practices in administering anti-dumping laws against countries reclassified as "market economies" (Council Reg. No. 603/1999 1999; Council Reg. No. 2320/97 1997). Nonetheless, the EU has been more willing to change the status of NMEs, and has implemented the formal changes sooner than the United States. Examining both who the EU has reclassified and how it has treated reclassified countries will illuminate the impact of beliefs on policy implementation. Comparing the U.S. and EU cases will help illustrate how information changes, iterated interactions, and institutional safeguards can encourage belief change.

Deviant Satellites, Orthodox Satellites, and Deviant Core Countries

The European Union reclassified the deviant satellites *en masse* in 1992, the orthodox satellites in 1994, and the deviant core countries in 1998. The reclassification decisions have accompanied Accession negotiations. Once the countries started to negotiate the terms of their EU membership, they were officially recognized as "market economies." The EU chose to reclassify countries in waves or in blocs (see table 7.2). The blocs have corresponded closely to the typology of country type adopted in this project.

These reclassifications did not follow the pace and scope of economic and political reforms in the region. Estonia, Latvia, and Lithuania (deviant core) were all more market oriented than Slovakia (deviant satellite), but Slovakia was reclassified first. Estonia (deviant core) was more market oriented than Poland (deviant satellite), but it was not reclassified in the first tier of countries. Poland was less market oriented than all the Baltics, but was the first country considered for reclassification. The theory of belief change and the way in which beliefs are processed help us to understand why the EU would conceptualize of countries according to blocs of similarly situated countries rather than as individual cases, and why these might contradict objective economic measures of market orientation.

Despite the reclassifications, the Commission chose to construct normal value in anti-dumping cases involving former NMEs, thereby obviating the market benefits of using a country's own prices. For example, in *Zinc from Poland (1997)*, the Commission constructed a normal value for the commodity for part of the determination and used actual price information from the exporter for part of the determination (COM Reg. No. 593/97 1997). The Commission questioned the reliability of the information provided, due to overarching concerns about the Polish macroeconomic environment. The Polish Foreign Minister protested the way in which the anti-dumping laws were applied, and the manner in which the Commission collected and rejected information (Agence Europe 1997b). However, the Commission's practices, while unusual in market economy cases, were legally permitted.

The Commission has also used single countrywide rates instead of individual dumping margins in anti-dumping cases against reclassified NMEs. As was explained in the section on Individual Treatment, NMEs are subjected to single countrywide dumping margins while market economy firms receive individual dumping margins. The single countrywide margin prevents the central government in an NME from channeling exports through the firm with the lowest dumping margin. In the case of *Steel Pipes from Hungary, Poland, Russia, the Czech Republic, Romania, and the Slovak Republic (1997)*, Polish, Czech, and Romanian exporters were assigned single countrywide rates (Council Reg. No. 2320/97 1997). The EU questioned the market independence of the exporting firms in each of the countries, and penalized them with former

NME measures. This is the norm in NME cases but not market economy cases.

The Commission was aware of the contradictions in its trade policies. In 1999, a Deputy Head of Unit at the Commission acknowledged that Estonia was more market oriented than some current EU members, but he was still unwilling to treat it as if it were a market economy.[19] All of these seemingly contradictory practices are logical if one considers the degree to which belief certainty has affected EU decision making in this issue area.

Residual tension remained between the European Commission and the reclassified NMEs over anti-dumping laws up until their full membership in 2004. The former NME countries questioned the large number of cases and the objectivity of the application of the law. The Commission remained wary of the potential export capacity of these countries. To "ally certain fears" between anti-dumping officials and representatives of Central and Eastern European industries, Sir Leon Brittan hosted a seminar entitled "Problems of Anti-dumping with Regard to Central and Eastern European Countries (CEEC)" (Agence Europe 1997e). The seminar was framed as a medium for addressing fears and perceptions about the parties involved in trade relations, even though almost all of the Central and Eastern European countries in question had already been reclassified as market economies three years earlier.

In the seminar Sir Brittan emphasized that anti-dumping measures against CEEC were "legitimate and perfectly normal instruments of trade policy" and that there was "no question of conducting some sort of industrial policy" nor were any countries in the group singled out (Brittan 1997b). However, he also legitimized the interpretation of anti-dumping laws against CEEC by highlighting various problems in these countries, such as state aid and competition problems, that made it necessary for the EU to maintain its current extraordinary use of anti-dumping laws (Agence Europe 1997c).[20] As of the May 2004 EU enlargement, most countries in Central and Eastern Europe became full members of the EU, and therefore could not be subjected to any type of anti-dumping investigation. The ultimate form of institutional contracting—membership—has obviated the vehicle for acting on cold war beliefs with respect to these countries.

In spite of some setbacks, the Commission has generally been administering anti-dumping laws against reclassified orthodox satellites and orthodox core countries in a fair manner. This does not mean that there has been less final protectionism against reclassified countries. Reclassified countries have still been subjected to a high number of anti-dumping cases. But the *process* of administering the anti-dumping laws to these countries changed. For example, in the cases of *Hot-Rolled Steel from Romania (2000)* (Commission Decision 1758/2000/ECSC 2000), *Ropes and Cables from the Czech Republic (2001)* (COM Reg. No. 230/ 2001 2001), *Urea from Poland (2000)* (European Commission 2001c), *Steel Ropes and Cables from Poland and Hungary (1999)* (COM Reg. No. 362/1999 1999), and *Hardboard from Bulgaria, Estonia, Latvia and Lithuania (1999)* (Council Reg. No. 194/1999 1999), all of the defendants were found guilty of dumping. But in all these cases, the process of administering the case was normal, in the sense that the rules were applied to former NMEs the way they would be applied to any other developing market economy. A change in process is a strong indicator of a change in beliefs about former Communist countries.

The treatment of deviant satellites, deviant core countries, and orthodox satellites is consistent with a theory of belief change. The Association Agreements have functioned as institutional safeguards, creating virtuous cycles of information exchange and positive interactions. In concert the three have worked to change beliefs about the threatening nature of trade with former Communist countries. Of these fourteen country specific hypotheses, only Albania and Vietnam have not followed according to predictions. Albania and Vietnam (orthodox satellites) were not reclassified before the Baltics (orthodox core), and as of 2004 had not been considered for reclassification. However, these "outliers" are actually reminders of the role that information flows have in facilitating belief change. The original model of belief change suggested that changes in beliefs were a function of information changes discounted by belief certainty. While Vietnam has renewed trade talks with Europe and even broached the topic of market economy status recently, the level and intensity of discussions has remained decidedly limited (VNA News Agency 2005). Similarly Albania has only managed fledgling trade dialogues and limited trade agreements with the EU thus far, unlike its Balkan neighbors (The European Commission's Delegation to Albania 2005). As such, the continued relative isolation of these countries, resulting in both information limitations and limited interactions, has acted as an important qualifier on the cases of Vietnam and Albania.

Russia and Ukraine: Orthodox Core

For orthodox core countries, EU membership is not a possibility. Therefore the terms of reclassification are different from that of deviant and orthodox satellites. This section focuses on the failed reclassification attempts of China, Russia, and Ukraine. Each has launched massive public relations efforts to get reclassified by the European Union. China's efforts failed in 2004, and Ukraine has been continually rebuffed by the European Union, finally obtaining a promise of reclassification in early 2006 (Bellaby 2005). Russia was officially reclassified in 2002, with many caveats from the European Union and no actual policy change to date.

Russia was reclassified as a market economy in 2002 (Council Reg. No. 1972/2002 OJL 305, 07/11/02). Symbolically, this was a formal acknowledgment of the progress Russia had made in "respecting market principles." In terms of policy, that meant that Russia would be treated as a market economy in the context of all trade instruments. "In practical terms, this meant that the calculation of dumping margins [would] no longer be based on information from an analogue country, but that, in all cases, the Russian companies' own costs and prices [would] be taken in consideration" (European Commission 2003, 12).

However, in the exact same legislation used to reclassify the first orthodox core country as a market economy, the Commission also included a number of changes to its anti-dumping and antisubsidy laws that would countermand the reclassification. In the very same Council Regulation, the Commission amended its anti-dumping law to allow it to use price proxies against *market economies* (Council Reg. No. 1972/2002 2002, Article 4; Clark 2002b). If "it [the Commission] decides a company does not reasonably reflect its production and sales costs in its records, it allows the Commission to increase the cost of production of an exporting company by a reasonable amount under a particular market situation" (Clark 2002a). This change effectively gave the Commission the discretion to use analogues for prices in market economies, if it felt that prices did not adequately reflect true market mechanisms. As such, the Commission gave itself the right to legitimately use analogue or price proxy methods against any reclassified country. Grouping this change with the Russian reclassification in the same amendment left no room to question the intent of the rule change.

At the time of the pseudo-reclassification, sentiment regarding the status change was mixed. The optimistic assessment was that although the political reclassification could be obviated by its technical application, perhaps the presumptions surrounding Russia would be different. "The advantage of the new status is that the onus of proof will no longer be on the side of the exporter. It will be the Commission, which has to demonstrate that certain exporters do not meet market standards" (Clark 2002a). The "onus of proof" reflected an understanding of how presumptions and beliefs have affected both issue framing and the processing of information. If instead of *presuming* non-market activities the Commission actually had to *prove* non-market activities, perhaps the application of the laws would be more fair to Russia. However, the pessimists have pointed out that the contradictory policies meant "Russia will be formally regarded as a market economy country, but the attitude of the European countries toward Russia will not change" (Ilina, Reut, Skogoreva, 2002).

Unfortunately, the pessimistic predictions about the treatment of Russia have been correct thus far. Despite the reclassification, Russia did not even receive market treatment for *Certain Grain Oriented Electrical Sheets Originating in Russia (2003)* (Council Ref. No. 151/2003 2003) or *Silicon Originating in Russia (2002)* (Council Reg. No. 2229/2003 2003), or *Potassium Chloride Originating in Belarus, Russia, or Ukraine (2005)* (Council Reg. No. 1891/2005 2005). In the case of *Granular Polytetrafluoroethylene Originating in Russia and the People's Republic of China (2005)*, Russia was allegedly treated as a market economy, but all its prices were not used because they were not considered "normal" (COM Reg. 862/2005 2005, recital 49). Therefore, this is not a case of market economy treatment in practice.

The pattern appear to be repeating itself, whereby formal rule changes remain unimplemented in practice for some time. Beliefs and presumptions about the different nature of trade with Russia and other orthodox core countries have continued to permeate Commission trade decisions. The simultaneous enactment of a formal rule change and an amendment to circumvent that rule change highlights the extent of the cognitive dissonance the Commission has experienced with respect to former NMEs.

Through 2005 Ukraine had been unsuccessful in its reclassification attempts. Reclassification and market status have been the subjects of continual negotiations between the countries. Market status has been a particularly rankling issue to Ukraine because of Russia's reclassification (European Information Service 2004). The EU argued that Ukrainian pricing and bankruptcy law issues impeded its reclassification, and that reform would be required in those areas prior to being granted market status (British Broadcasting Corporation 2004; European Commission 2004c). The UK supported a status change for Ukraine, (Ukrayinska Pravda 2005) and at the end of 2005 Ukraine was promised status change for early 2006 (Bellaby 2005).

Interviews affirmed a role for belief stickiness in affecting EU decision making. One European Commission official explained his theory of crisis induced change, namely that it would take a crisis to bring about a change in attitude toward Ukraine and Russia. Essentially, the EU was only willing to think about change when faced with such a breakdown of the present system.[21] This official was unknowingly explaining the causal impact of beliefs on EU decision making. Crisis in the form of a threatened economic breakdown or regime reversal in Ukraine or Russia might be necessary in order to prompt EU belief change about these countries. Since these countries are orthodox core countries, according to the belief based theory, these countries should be most resistant to belief change and as such might require a complete shake up of the system in order to effect conditions for true belief change. The "Orange Revolution" in Ukraine might have encouraged a rethinking of the status in Ukraine, since the UK started to press for a status change for Ukraine one month later (Ukrayinska Pravda 2005). The timing of Ukraine's reclassification supports the "crisis induced theory" of change proffered by DG Trade.

China: Orthodox Core

The EU formally considered a Chinese reclassification request in 2004, and rejected it following a lengthy investigation. The EU cited "too much state interference, the weak rule of law, and poor corporate governance" as justifications for its refusal to grant China market economy status (Asia Pulse 2004). Specifically the European Commission cited four broad areas in which reform would be required in order to merit a status change. "The EU would not grant the status until all SOE's were privatized, corporate governance was improved, laws protecting property rights and allowing bankruptcy were strengthened, and transparency was injected into the financial system" (Cheng 2004a). The United States was involved in a simultaneous country reclassification evaluation initiated by China, and also rejected China's request.

China made a case for reclassification based on a host of objective economic facts and figures. "About 70 percent of China's economy is market-based, above the recognized minimum level of 60 percent for a market economy. About two-thirds of China's gross domestic product growth is created by the non-state sector. In state owned companies, more than 89 percent make decisions free of government influence and have introduced a modern corporate system" (Financial Times Information 2004a). In addition to economic indicators, China cited international memberships and institutional safeguards as reasons for its reclassification. Other WTO members had already reclassified China as a market economy, such as Singapore, Malaysia, Thailand, Benin, and Kyrgyzstan (Asia Pulse 2004). According to MFN, once one member has recognized a country as market oriented, all countries should extend the same recognition. These justifications did not result in a status change.

In 2005, more discussion of a status change ensued prompted by Iceland's formal recognition of China as a market economy and Britain's call to have China reclassified (Comtex News Network 2005). At the time Britain held the rotating EU presidency, and used its power to point out the contradictory treatment of China. Britain highlighted how Russia had been granted market status in 2002, although it was still not a WTO member (Europe Information Service 2005). China was a WTO member and had enacted far reaching economic reforms, which had been recognized by the international community and formalized in a policy report from the OECD. The OECD report confirmed the market determined nature of the Chinese economy, and even estimated private sector contributions to China's GDP at 57–65 percent (McGregor and Minder 2005). In pre-Thatcherite Britain in the 1980s, one-third of British output was contributed by state owned enterprises, similar to China today (Xinhua News Agency 2005). Nonetheless, the EU Commissioner rejected the reclassification request and argued that he did not believe and he did not think Britain actually believed that China was really a market economy (Agence France Presse 2005; Beattie 2005).

Consistent with a theory about the staying power of beliefs, neither a mountain of disconfirming economic evidence nor the presence of institutional safeguards would be sufficient to prompt a formal reclassification of China. The Commission, acting like a disproportionate information processor, selectively disregarded the empirical evidence that ran counter to its foundational belief system.

International Institutions and Institutional Safeguards

Institutionalists contend that institutions encourage exchange relations by providing mechanisms for enforcing rules, and by providing more information to and increasing the certainty of exchange relations. However, institutional safeguards have not had the predicted impact on formal rule change or implementation with respect to the treatment of NMEs in the realm of international trade.

Membership in the World Trade Organization, the quintessential example of trade contracting and safeguards, illustrates the point. In 2004, many countries considered NMEs by the United States and

European Union were members of the WTO, including Albania (2000), China (2001), Georgia (2000), Kyrgyzstan (1998), and Moldova (2001). Others were WTO members while being treated as NMEs, such as Romania (1995), Bulgaria (1996), and Latvia and Estonia (1999), to name a few.[22] International affiliations have not by themselves conferred a change in treatment of the countries, nor facilitated changed beliefs about these countries. Institutions, while necessary, are not sufficient conditions to effect belief change.

The inadequacy of contracting to facilitate a change in treatment is all the more apparent in the U.S. case, because the Department of Commerce has actively worked to override any influence these international institutions might have exerted. The Department of Commerce was aware that its continued treatment of GATT/WTO members as non-market economies was in violation of the terms of the agreement in a number of ways. In an internal memorandum regarding the case of *Uranium from the Russian Federation (2000)*, the Department defiantly argued "United States law not the WTO controls the Department's conduct of this review" (U.S. International Trade Administration 2000f). Interviews with policy analysts at the ITA revealed they were cognizant of the contradiction between international obligations and trade policy practice. One analyst affirmed that he knew the United States was violating its WTO obligations, and he would continue to administer the laws as such until the United States was taken to court.[23]

Knowing that WTO membership might force the ITA and the Commission to treat China as a market economy, part of the agreement negotiated between China and the United States and the European Union explicitly required China to forsake a change in its status for 15 years (White and Case Law Firm 2000a).[24] The United States and European Union both wanted to retain their ability to treat China as a non-market economy well into the future. In the 2004 case of *Wooden Bedroom Furniture from China* the contradiction between WTO membership and NME treatment was raised by the Chinese plaintiffs. However, the Department of Commerce dismissed the connection (U.S. International Trade Administration 2004a, 9). Even the World Bank's classification of China as a "market economy" has not been a sufficient institutional safeguard to encourage the EU or the United States to treat China as a market economy.

The United States and the EU have evidenced similar calculations regarding the relative importance of institutional safeguards. Neither NATO membership, EU membership, EU Association Agreements, nor WTO membership has definitely changed the ITA's or the

Commission's behavior with respect to NMEs. While this is not meant to dismiss the important information facilitating and contract affirming nature of institutional safeguards, they have a supporting role rather than a causal role in affecting policy change. Belief change might be more likely as a result of mechanisms in place to guarantee the security of exchange relations between parties, but belief change cannot result from institutional contracting alone. Institutions are not a substitute for trust in the behavior of the other; they are complements.

Conclusion

The typology of country types, based on internationally determined interests and domestically determined institutional incentives, has yielded substantial predictive and explanatory leverage over European Union and U.S. country reclassifications. The Commission and ITA have hewed closely to the predictions generated by a theory focused on belief certainty as a discounter of new information. Those predictions have demonstrated why Commission and ITA behavior toward NMEs was not internally inconsistent or counterintuitive. Rather, the trade agents have behaved as disproportionate information processors, allowing the degree of certainty of their beliefs about the interests and incentives of NMEs to affect policy implementation.

Reclassifications are a good example of the process of belief change because they demonstrate that beliefs change in halting, punctuated steps. Chapter six focused on issue layering to help understand this punctuated process. For example, in the case of the United States, NMEs received market oriented industry test treatment only after they had been granted full country reclassifications. While on first glance this appears contradictory, once one considers the policy stymieing effects of beliefs, this behavior makes sense. While the United States was unwilling to actually implement a policy consistent with reclassifications, the reclassification decision caused them to finally accept full MOI implementation. However, there is no additional formal rule change to enact on top of reclassifications in order to prompt the full implementation of this status change. Reclassifications mark the final rule change possible to NME anti-dumping laws. Therefore long time periods between the enactment of country reclassifications and the implementation of the trade rules according to those reclassifications would be expected. Only with time, interactions, and continued information flows could one expect true belief change and commensurate policy implementation.

Thinking about the dynamics of belief change in terms of the certainty with which initial beliefs are held yields explanatory power. First, it accounts for the differential treatment between NMEs and other similarly situated developing countries. Second, it explains why certain NME countries were reclassified before others. Belief certainty helps explain why the dynamic of reclassification followed a logic slightly contradictory to what materialist hypotheses would predict. Third, it also accounts for differences in the United States and EU's behavior toward NMEs. The United States held beliefs toward all NMEs with relatively more certainty than the EU. The United States also had fewer institutional safeguards, fewer interactions, and less information exchange than the EU. All of these factors fed into the relative durability of the United States' beliefs. As such, while belief certainty is not an explanatory panacea, combined with other factors it does improve our ability to understand differences between rule formation and policy practices.

A cautionary remark is in order. Beliefs do not change in a vacuum. Beliefs are a function of perceptions, and those perceptions are affected by iteration, information flows, and institutional safeguards. While this chapter has demonstrated that information flows alone will not change beliefs and that various forms of institutional safeguards have alone proven ineffective in changing beliefs about NMEs, both have played an important supporting role. They are necessary but not sufficient factors affecting the implementation of policy. As such, to bridge the distance between rule change and rule implementation, increased information, and increased iteration facilitated by contracts and institutions remain the most effective means of dislodging beliefs.

CHAPTER EIGHT

Integrating Non-Market Economies into the International Trading System

Introduction

"After competing in the cold war, the arms race, and the space race, the United States and Russia are still locked in an epic competition. This time it's over who can raise plump, affordable chickens" (Birch 2004). Disputes over chicken parts do not appear to be the stuff of which high politics is made, however this trade dispute was elevated to the level of congressional debates and arguments in the Russian Parliament (Birch 2004). It was even cited as a major stumbling block to Russia's WTO membership bid (Alden 2003). It became an outlet for frustration over Russia's continued treatment as a non-market economy, and served to galvanize debate about the appropriate use of anti-dumping trade remedy laws.

As of 2004, Russia was the largest market for American chicken exports, accounting for more than $600 million in 2001 and an estimated $700 million in 2003 (Birch 2004; Delovoi Peterburg 2003). The large volume of imports from America hurt the domestic Russian chicken market. American frozen dark meat chicken parts sold for less than domestically raised whole, unfrozen Russian chicken. The low priced imports caused some Russian farmers to go out of business and dissuaded others from entering the market. In addition to the economic impact, the Russian Minister of Agriculture as well as other Russian interest groups argued that the frozen chicken was less healthy, full of unnatural chemicals, and was an example of how the United States had turned. "Russia [us] into a garbage dump" (Financial Times Information 2004b).

The health and safety issues combined with anti-competitiveness allegations led Russia to take punitive trade action against the United States. Russia accused the United States of dumping dark meat chicken and initiated an anti-dumping case against U.S. poultry imports in 2001.[1] U.S. sales to Russia had markedly increased, going from $11 million in 1992 to $700 million in 2003 (Birch 2004). Domestic chicken consumption increased in the United States over the past five years, causing domestic producers to raise more chickens, thereby increasing the amount of domestically unwanted dark meat for sale on the international market (Interfax News Agency 2001c). Therefore there was evidence of rapid market penetration and surplus capacity. According to anti-dumping trade remedy laws, such conditions merit an anti-dumping investigation.

Moreover, in the U.S. market, white meat sold at a price premium to dark meat, as a function of differential demand. U.S. producers sold the excess dark meat at lower prices around the world.[2] However, the cost of production for the dark meat was the same as that of white meat chicken. Therefore according to anti-dumping definitions used by the United States, dark meat and white meat were like commodities and should be similarly priced. Since the United States, sold white meat in its home market for substantially more than its export price of dark meat, according to its own trade laws it was guilty of differential pricing (Interfax News Agency 2001d). The increase in export capacity combined with unfair differential pricing of like commodities technically constituted dumping. Using the U.S.'s logic for anti-dumping determinations, Russia imposed import quotas on U.S. chicken in 2003.

Although this example sounds rather ridiculous, it is emblematic of NME anti-dumping cases. How could quality differences, domestic supply/demand factors, and preference differences not be considered in dumping determinations? The question holds true for both the United States and Russia. In the case of the United States, it is easy to see why changes in domestic demand for a product, might affect international export volumes. A change in American export capacity of chicken is not perceived to be a function of ulterior interests or suspicious incentives; it is a function of market mechanisms. In this scenario, Russian anti-dumping allegations against the United States appear unfounded and unfair.

Conversely, the incentives and interests of Russia, and other NMEs for that matter, are perceived more malevolently. After the collapse of the Soviet Union, Russia and NMEs had to find alternative export markets for things like steel and chemicals. They needed to reorient trade toward the West, in pursuit of hard currency and with the purpose of plugging themselves into the international trading system. However, their "excess" export capacity was viewed as a potential trade threat instrumentally manipulated by Russia and other NMEs, instead of as an attempt to maximize a relative comparative advantage. Using a different frame of reference about perceived interests and incentives, one comes up with different conclusions about Russian's intentions. In this scenario, continued U.S. vigilance toward trade with Russia and other NMEs would seem not only prudent and necessary, but fair. This is because beliefs about the interests and incentives of NMEs have continued to cloud perceptions about NME economic activities.

This single case of a "reverse" anti-dumping suit against the United States by Russia serves as an example of how beliefs about the interests and incentives of the trading partner affect perceptions of "fair" trade. It also provides a harbinger of potential trade problems between NMEs and other countries. Other policy implications from this book are broached in detail later in this chapter, including how these sorts of trade disputes might impact the ability of non-market economies to continue to integrate into the international trading system.

Before addressing the policy implications for NMEs, I first review the key findings from this examination of Western trade discrimination against non-market economies in the post–cold war period. This will include a cautionary remark about the inherent limitations of any theory focused on a causal role for beliefs. Next, I present some larger theoretical contributions to be drawn from this book, specifically as it relates to institutionalism. Finally, I conclude with several possible policy implications for non-market economies as they continue with their economic and political transitions.

Key Findings

The book started by asking two questions. First, why did the United States and European Union continue to differentiate trade with NMEs from trade with other developing countries in the post–cold war period (1989–2004), resulting not only in differential but discriminatory treatment? Second, why did U.S. and EU trade agencies fail to implement changes to the formal trade rules as applied to NMEs? What explains policy stasis in the face of institutional change?

These questions are puzzling and perplexing for a number of reasons. First, institutionalists predict that when formal rules change, outcomes should change. If formal rules change, but trade policy remains the same, this is puzzling. Second, if both EU and U.S. trade agencies were behaving similarly toward non-market economies, then the behavior cannot be explained away as a function of bureaucratic idiosyncrasy. Third, the U.S. and EU's behavior was not simply a case of maximization of trade protection, since there was ongoing policy innovation and alleged improvements to reduce unnecessary barriers. Moreover, the unusual patterns of trade protection only applied to non-market economies. Finally, if the United States and European Union were committed to assisting in the transitions being effected by former Communist countries, then explicitly contradictory behavior on the part of the U.S. and EU trade agencies appears perplexing.

Before constructing a belief based argument, I needed to address two empirical questions. I needed to prove trade discrimination, and I needed to demonstrate that traditional interest based and institution based accounts of trade protection were unable to explain patterns of Western trade protection against NMEs. Demonstrating that differential treatment constituted a systematic policy of trade discrimination against NMEs was an important policy finding. While NMEs repeatedly condemned the discriminatory trade practices of the United States and the European Union, their accusations lacked teeth because they often appeared ad hoc and unsubstantiated. Second, using a quantitative analysis of trade cases, I demonstrated that while traditional explanations of trade protection were fairly good at explaining protectionism against imports from most countries, they were unable to explain patterns of trade protection against NME imports. NMEs evidenced distinct patterns of trade protection, not easily explained by domestic political theories, international economic theories, or domestic economic theories. I was thus able to highlight an empirical and theoretical lacunae in the literature. This gap between what interest based accounts would predict and the actual trade policy that we saw created room for a theory about trade protection in which beliefs and perceptions could be shown to affect policy outcomes.

I then presented a theory of Western trade discrimination against NMEs based on belief stasis and belief change. I demonstrated both theoretical and empirical findings. First, I established that beliefs about a trading partner could affect the implementation of trade policy, and could impede the actualization of formal rule change. Second, I demonstrated that belief change was not irrational or idiosyncratic. It was predictably affected by the certainty with which the belief was held. I addressed each of these findings briefly in turn.

First, I established that the U.S. and EU trade agencies developed beliefs about the trade threat posed by non-market economies during the cold war based on an assessment of the interests, capabilities, and incentives of NMEs. The agencies then designed special anti-dumping laws and procedures to grapple with the perceived extraordinary trade threat. These beliefs became institutionalized in policy practices and frames of reference, which continued to affect the interpretation and implementation of trade cases in the post–cold war period.

The beliefs not only impeded policy change, they also impeded the implementation of policy. Even when the formal rules governing anti-dumping laws changed, there was not a commensurate change in policy implementation. As evidence, I reviewed five cases of formal rule change to the anti-dumping laws as applied to non-market economies: two cases by the U.S. International Trade Administration, and three cases by DG Trade in the European Commission. Each of these formal rule changes was initiated by the trade agency itself, and each agency had sole responsibility for its implementation. Each rule change was circumvented by the trade agency that initiated it; some changes went unimplemented for more than ten years. This rule circumvention was not accidental. I presented an explanation of the trade agencies as disproportionate information processors. New information about the changing interests and incentives of former Communist countries was not completely assimilated by the trade agencies. By discounting new information, beliefs about the threatening nature of trade with non-market economies remained resistant to change. In sum, beliefs discounted contrary information, contributed to the stickiness of decision making, and stymied the implementation of formal rule change.

My theory about institutionalized beliefs was not static. Belief stasis may impede the actual implementation of formal rule change for some time, but not indefinitely. In my model I demonstrated how a series of formal rule changes albeit unimplemented, layered on top of each other, would cause a critical tipping point in policy implementation. There is a fundamental cognitive dissonance that results when a foundation of beliefs, which do not reflect empirical conditions, lies beneath layers of unimplemented formal rule changes, which do reflect empirical conditions. In both the U.S. and EU cases, I demonstrated how the layering of unimplemented formal rule changes on top of a foundation of anachronistic beliefs resulted in fledgling policy change. The policy change was incomplete, and was the least onerous policy options; however, it was significant. The actual policy change created a new standard for implementing the trade rules, which in turn shifted the underlying belief structure.

The second main theoretical finding of this project was a coherent logic to belief change. The certainty with which a belief is held affects the stickiness of the belief. Belief change is a function of changes in information discounted by degree of belief certainty. Beliefs held with more certainty will act as stronger information discounters, minimizing the effects of new information. Beliefs held with less certainty will discount contradictory evidence less dramatically, and will therefore be easier to dislodge. Both United States and European Union reclassification decisions were largely explained by looking at degree of belief certainty as an important independent variable. The order of country reclassifications and the actual implementation of the formal rule changes were predicted by the certainty with which Western trade agencies held antagonistic beliefs about the non-market economy. These findings are contrary to what would have been predicted by economic and political reforms in the NMEs alone, or by other interest based hypotheses.

The introduction of a new variable, belief certainty, is a contribution to the decision making literature Belief certainty, derived from objective material factors, helps to grapple with the measurement problem inherent in most ideational approaches. It is difficult to ascribe much variation to a variable broadly defined as beliefs. However, by measuring differences in the intensity with which a belief is held, one can obtain more explanatory leverage. The preliminary testing of this variable is positive enough to suggest potential future applicability for other decision-making of questions.

Limitations of a Belief Based Theory

There are limitations to a theory based on beliefs. The timing of belief change cannot be predicted, nor can one say that country A will *always* change beliefs about country B before beliefs about country C. A belief based theory cannot explain month to month, or year to year variations in trade protection. However, I started out this project by arguing that belief based theories complement not supplant interest based accounts of trade protection. An important role remains for material factors and interest based accounts of trade protection.

First, material factors are useful to explain lower order questions. What explains yearly variations in number of anti-dumping cases filed, or percentage of total cases against non-market economies in any given year? This lower order question only looks at outcomes, and does not ask about systematic treatment of NMEs over time. For these types of questions, material economic conditions might be helpful in understanding patterns of trade protection. For example, changes in unemployment rates or changes in GDP levels may affect the number of anti-dumping case initiated in any given year. Second, material conditions are helpful to better understand the factors that affect belief change. Changes in empirical reality are necessary in order for beliefs to change. Both institutions and interactions facilitate information flows, which improve the chances for belief change. These are just some of the material factors that might affect the speed and scope of belief change.

In the case of the EU in particular, the explanatory tale would have been impoverished without considering additional material factors. When combined with belief certainty, geographic proximity became a useful variable to understand why the EU might be more concerned about trade relations with NMEs than other developing countries. The EU pre-Association agreements with countries in Central and Eastern Europe were important facilitators of reclassification. Russia and China's bid for WTO membership caused the EU to rethink its trade policies toward these countries, although neither caused a change in EU policy. Without an understanding of the causal role of beliefs, these material factors would be unable to explain NME treatment. However, when combined with a discussion of belief certainty, the material factors enriched the explanation.

Finally, there is the empirical limitation of beliefs. Because beliefs do not covary in a direct way with outcomes, it is always possible to argue that beliefs do not matter. Maybe something else explains U.S. and EU discrimination against NMEs. Since beliefs cannot be directly observed, only inferred from written and verbal evidence, there is always room for doubt. To overcome this "disbelief," one can only refute alternatives and proffer a mountain of circumstantial evidence and a story about the causal role of beliefs. I hope that I have accomplished this.

Theoretical Implications

This project makes two theoretical contributions to the institutionalist literature, potentially expanding the range of this book beyond the scope of trade policy. First, this project directly addressed the relationship between formal and informal institutional constraints on policy outcomes.[3] Other scholars have argued that once ideas and beliefs are institutionalized into formal rules, the formal rules resist change. It might take a crisis or some type of major policy shift to dislodge the ideas and change the formal rules. Even in the area of trade policy, scholars have highlighted how institutionalized beliefs affect issue framing and policy outcomes to impede change (Goldstein 1988, 1993; Milner 1997).

However, I am taking a slightly different approach to these issues. In my project the formal rules are changing, and moreover they are being redesigned by the very trade agencies that are implementing them. I am demonstrating that even if those formal rules do change, the beliefs may continue to impede the intended implementation of the formal rule change. Beliefs not only affect rule formation but also rule implementation. The implementation of the rules is often the neglected side of politics, and this is what I am highlighting in this project.

This has important applications for a range of issue areas in politics, economics, and social relations. Just because one changes the rules, it does not mean the rules will actually affect outcomes. Any developing country that has attempted to legislate appropriate ways of doing business only to have the informal practices trump the formal rules is aware of the problem. The ability of informal institutional constraints, such as beliefs, ideas, values and norms, to undermine the intended consequences of rule changes needs to be addressed.

Beliefs and ideas are oft overlooked factors in institutional analysis because they are not easily measured or operationalized. Or, if they are included in an analysis, they are often used in an ad hoc manner, in the same way that culture is employed as an explanatory variable when other explanations have failed. Or even worse, ideational explanations are only considered credible when one has refuted every possible interest based or institutional explanation. This second best approach to ideational variables impoverishes many discussions in the social sciences. The relationship between formal rules and informal beliefs, norms, and procedures must be considered as a first order question, not viewed as something that matters only if there is an inconsistency between formal rule changes and outcomes. This project has highlighted that that one can come up with very misleading conclusions about formal institutions or formal rules if one ignores the impact of informal institutional constraints on policy implementation.

Second, this project has illustrated a limitation to the purported contract promoting, exchange facilitating, and cooperation enhancing role of institutions and institutional safeguards. Institutions have not proven to be a magic panacea for trade relations between the West and NMEs. Although one can always retort that the institutions just were not structured appropriately, the inability of institutions to promote exchange relations in this context cannot be ignored. International institutional safeguards, such as WTO membership or European trade agreements, have proven insufficient in order to change the manner in which the West treated NMEs. Domestic institutional reforms in NMEs also did not change the way NMEs were treated by the West. And Western institutional changes in the form of formal rule changes to U.S. and EU anti-dumping trade remedy laws have often failed to change policy outcomes.

In essence, institutions played a qualified role. They were important, but not always decisive. While institutions and institutional affiliations might promote more transactions, facilitate information flows, and provide contract safeguards, alone they were insufficient to explain or predict the behavior of the United States and the EU with regard to NMEs and trade. One needs to consider the interaction of institutions and beliefs to understand the process of administering trade laws, and the resulting trade protection. This was an interesting and important finding that should be more rigorously incorporated into the institutionalist research agenda.

In sum, institutionalists in any policy venue or issue area might rethink the way in which they conceptualize informal institutional constraints in their models. Informal institutional constraints, be they beliefs about the other, or norms and practices, or values and culture, should play a more explicit and systematic role in any discussion of institutions and outcomes.

Policy Implications for NMEs

There are many policy implications to be drawn from the Western use of anti-dumping trade remedies against non-market economies: how Western anti-dumping use has affected other countries in the international system; new trade impediments facing reclassified NMEs; and how the ability of NMEs to afford domestic economic reforms and integrate into the international political economy might be affected if they continue to be treated as outsiders.

First, the West's use of anti-dumping laws has set a deleterious precedent in the international system. Other developing countries, especially current and former NMEs, have jumped on the anti-dumping bandwagon. For example, China initiated a host of retaliatory cases against Japan, Korea, the United States, and Germany in response to frequent accusations by these countries of Chinese dumping (Asianinfo Daily China News 2001; European Commission 2002, 2003). Bulgaria against the EU (European Commission 2003), Hungary against Russia, Ukraine, and Moldova imports (Hungarian News Agency 2000), Russia against Ukraine (Interfax News Agency 2001d) and Ukraine against Russia, the EU and Canada (Newsbase Russian Daily Bulletin 1999), are just some of the flagrant tit-for-tat anti-dumping cases. Estonia and Latvia have also developed anti-dumping laws so that they can get into the international trade protection game (Baltic Times 1999a, 1999b; Estonian News Agency 2001). Even blatantly unmerited cases are freely initiated. Hungary launched several anti-dumping cases against Russian pipe in spite of their dubious economic merit arguing that "Russian pipe imports in Hungary are insignificant . . . but the affair is essential because it may entail other inquiries" (Interfax 2000). The harassment effect and concomitant trade deterring effects of even unmerited cases encourage the filing of anti-dumping complaints.

Developed countries are setting a costly example for developing countries. Anti-dumping duties impede trade flows and have substantial negative welfare effects. Developing countries cannot afford such economic costs. Intentionally forgoing cheaper foreign products in order to protect domestic producers simply redistributes the costs of production domestically, so that every one pays more. However, the anti-dumping rules of the game mean developing countries must emulate the actions of the developed world in order to stay economically flush. As such, a negative spiral of anti-dumping tit for tat threatens to impede the economic development of the lowest countries on the international totem pole—developing countries and transitional economies. "Global prosperity depends on international trade which needs liberalization, and its focus has to be on exports from developing countries to advanced economies so that they would become equal players in the world field" (Czech News Agency 2000a).

Second, the continued discriminatory treatment of NME imports by the West in the post-cold war period has implications for the development of NMEs and their ability to integrate into the international political economy in two ways. There is the lingering impact of anti-dumping duties. Once an anti-dumping duty is in place, it tends to be renewed and continues to have trade deterring effects. For example, both the European Union and the United States routinely renew duties in round after round of administrative case reviews. Therefore, the effects of past flagrant anti-dumping abuse against NME imports will continue to impede NME trade development for some time to come.

For example, in the case of bicycles from China, the EU initiated an anti-dumping case against Chinese imports in 1991, and has continued to grant ever higher levels of protection to European bicycle producers since then (COM Reg No. 550/93 1993; European Commission 2000b). The rationale behind continued trade protection was that the EU domestic bicycle market was too small and unprepared for international competition, after almost a decade of trade protection. In 1968, U.S. industries were awarded protection from Soviet titanium sponge imports, and every five years the dumping margins were renewed until 1998 (63 FR 47474 1998). When the USSR broke up, the ITA simply applied the existing margins to the republics. This is 20 years of nonstop trade protection for U.S. producers.

These are not anomalous cases. The European Union has had trade protection in place against imports of Chinese pocket lighters (Council Reg No. 192/1999 1999), potassium permanganate from China (Council Reg No. 299/2001 2001), and silicon carbide from Russia, and Ukraine for ten years running (Council Reg No. 1100/2000 2000). The United States has continued to renew protection against tapered roller bearings from Hungary (64 FR 213 1999) and Romania (62 FR 31075 1997), uranium from Russia (U.S. International Trade Administration 2000a), and urea from Russia, Ukraine, Belarus, Kazakhstan, Tajikistan, Lithuania, Latvia, Estonia, Turkmenistan, Azerbaijan, Armenia, Georgia and Uzbekistan for more than ten years.[4] Once trade protection is in place, it tends to remain in place. As such, the past history of anti-dumping use against NMEs will continue to have an insidious effect on their export capacity for the near future.

In addition, continued Western discrimination against imports from non-market economies directly affects their ability to afford domestic economic and political reforms. Export revenue and the tax money it generates are needed to pay for social safety nets for those disadvantaged by the extensive economic restructuring, and to compensate those left unemployed in the wake of massive bankruptcies of state owned industries. Export oriented growth also has positive spillover effects on the macroeconomy. Industries able to build an export market will source more goods from domestic producers of factor inputs, who will employ more workers, who will want to spend their money on consumer products: essentially releasing a virtuous cycle of economic growth and expansion. Export oriented firms forced to compete in the international market will learn business skills and improve production efficiency. These lessons will be brought back to the domestic market, and have ripple effects as well.

In essence, trade is not simply about revenue generation. Trade is also about learning the rules of the international market. There is a space for NMEs in the international division of labor, if the West allows them to compete.

Third, other trade laws could be applied to non-market economies as they become reclassified and attempt to reenter the international division of labor. Non-market economies have not traditionally been subjected to countervailing duty trade laws (Marcus 1985; United States Senate Committee on Finance 1984, 30). Countervailing duty laws are designed to offset the benefits an industry receives from government subsidization of design, production, or export (Marvel and Ray 1996, 1576). "It is a fundamental distinction than in an NME system the government does not interfere in the market process, but supplants it . . . and therefore the concept of subsidization has no meaning outside of the context of a market economy" (U.S International Trade Administration 2002b, 14–15). Therefore, due to the pervasive nature of subsidies in non-market economies, subsidies could not be singled out in trade cases against NME imports and were therefore not applied.[5]

Once reclassified, the countervailing duty laws would potentially apply to all NME industries. Since many firms in transitional economies receive government assistance, even a reclassified country would most likely continue to have government intervention in many economic sectors. Therefore, the industries in reclassified NMEs would be prime targets for countervailing duty investigations (Cornell 1994, 1312–1314). As a harbinger of what is to come, in the 2003 reclassification of Romania by the United States the ITA concluded with, "In addition, the U.S. countervailing duty law will now apply to Romania" (68 FR 54418 2003).

Recently there has been support in the United States to allow countervailing duties to be used against non-market economies. The Stopping Overseas Subsidies Act (H.R. 1216) would make it possible to apply duties to subsidies provided to state run or state influenced firms in non-market economies (U.S. Fed News 2005b). The bill specifically targeted China, but would be applicable to all NMEs (States News Service 2005). This bill was based on the perception that there were "loopholes" through which NME trade continued to permeate the United States, and these loopholes must be closed in order to protect U.S. economic interests (U.S. Fed News 2005a). Couching the debate in terms of threats and unfair NME loopholes reaffirms beliefs about the antagonistic and threatening nature of trade with NMEs. Whether or not the bill becomes a law is irrelevant. The drafting and debate of a bill about the extraordinary trade threat posed by NMEs reproduces fear of NME incentives and interests, and thereby perpetuates discriminatory treatment by Western trade agencies.

In sum, there are important policy implications resulting from the continued impact of cold war beliefs on the present international political economy. These include domestic as well as international policy ramifications for both the developed world and the developing world. Ameliorating the potential negative policy implications requires direct policy change; it will not happen as a by-product of other trade or development policies. Given the durability of beliefs in the face of direct institutional change, only a direct attempt to change both rules and policies toward NMEs might elicit the desired outcome.

Conclusion

There are no true non-market economies anymore. There are countries in transition who used to be NMEs. Shedding the NME mantle has proven to be more challenging for former Communist countries than anticipated. At a European Bank for Reconstruction and Development sponsored conference on trade, a Russian steel firm summarized the problem it faced integrating into the international political economy. "Russia's problem is that it is not seen as a market economy. We are facing abusive practices in the investigation of our production costs because (those bringing suites against us) say that our costs are not the real costs" (Moscow Times 2001). Beliefs and perceptions affect how one views "real" costs and prices. Until the West can change the way it sees Russia and other NMEs, the implementation of the laws will not change.

During the period of *perestroika* reforms in the Soviet Union, Gorbachev scolded his compatriots that in order to work in harmony with the West they would have to reject their "enemy image" of the United States (Gorbachev 1987, 203). He argued that such an image was unnecessary and would spoil international relations. Gorbachev's sage advice might well be heeded by the West. Enemy images of NMEs have undermined the normalization of trade relations between former Communist countries and the West.

Are NMEs our enemies? According to the words and deeds of Western trade agencies, one might be lead to think so. Beliefs about the extraordinary threat of trade with Communist (and now former

Communist) countries have had a lingering influence on the way Western trade laws were administered. It may take some time and some effort to change the perceptions and beliefs the West held about non-market economies, and visa-versa. However, the mutual gains would surely exceed the costs.

A P P E N D I X   I

Explanation of Variables in Data Analysis

Corruption—Index of corruption values, ordinal scale 0–10 with 0 being most corrupt and 10 being least corrupt.

Compilation of results from 3 to 16 surveys measuring perceptions of corruption.

Democratization—Combination of autocracy and democracy rankings to arrive at a level of democratization or "polity." 20 point ordinal scale from +10 full democracy to −10 full autocracy. 1997 figures used.

Dumping Margin—weighted average dumping margin (percentage). Continuous numeric values. No upward limit.

Economic Freedom—1997 economic freedom rankings based on average freedom scores for eight indicators of economic freedom. Ordinal scale 1–5 with 1 being most free (market oriented) and 5 being least free (extensive government intervention).

Employment—number of workers employed in industry for that year, including both production workers and other workers.

Geographic Proximity—kilometers between national capitals (Brussels, Belgium reference point for the EU, and Washington, DC reference point for the United States).

Gross Domestic Product—U.S. million $ converted from national currency using 1997 period average dollar exchange rates.

GDP per capita—Gross Domestic Product/Population

Gross Domestic Product (U.S.): Implicit Price Deflator—1996 = 100 (for analyses 1–3)

Industry Shipments—(at time t-1) (million \$). Based on net selling values, f.o.b. plant, after discounts and allowances. This includes receipts for contract work and miscellaneous service provided by the plant to others.

Import change—[Imports (million \$)—imports lagged (million \$)]/ imports lagged (million \$)

Import penetration lagged—Imports (t-1, million \$) / Industry shipments (t-1, million \$)

Political Freedom—1997 political freedom ranking based on political and civil liberties. Ordinal scale 1–7 with 1 being most free and 7 being least free (increments of .5).

Population—in millions.

Profitability—proxy for the profitability of the industry at t-1 (Value-added lagged—wages lagged)/industry shipments lagged

Trade Importance—percentage of total U.S. or EU exports going to the country, range 0–100

Type of Government—dependent variable, nominal—0=market economy, 1=non-market economy or former NME (analysis 4)

Value-added per employee—[(Total Value-added by Manufacture (t-1, million \$) / industry employment] /GDP deflator (value-added equals industry shipments + cost materials + change in finished goods and inventories)

Wages lagged (million \$)—production worker wages at t-1

Note: Lagged variables are one year lagged from the year of initiation of the anti-dumping case. T = year case initiated.

Dummy Variables for Country Coding

Non-Market Economy

South America

Big Emerging Markets (aggregate of countries from various groupings)

Other Asian countries

Asia NICs

Japan

Europe

Other (includes countries such as Canada, New Zealand, Saudi Arabia, UAE, Kenya)

Trade Data Codes and Relevant Years

Harmonized Tariff Schedule Commodity Codes (HS) (1987–1997)

North American Industry Classification Standard (NAICS) (1997–present)

Standard Industrial Classification Commodity Codes (SIC)

Standard Industrial Trade Classification Commodity Codes (SITC)

Tariff System of the United States (TSUSA) (1985–1987)

APPENDIX II

U.S. Anti-Dumping Cases Initiated against

Non-Market Economies, 1980–2004

Year	ITA Case Number	Country	Product
2004	A-570-898	China	Chlorinated Isocyanurates
2004	A-570-878	China	Circular Welded Carbon Pipe
2004	A-821-819	Russia	Magnesium Metal
2004	A-570-878	China	Magnesium Metal
2004	A-570-878	China	Crepe Paper Products
2004	A-570-878	China	Tissue Paper Products
2004	A-570-878	China	Frozen and Canned Shrimp
2003	A-570-878	China	Carbazole Violet Pigment 23
2003	A-570-878	China	Wooden Bedroom Furniture
2003	A-570-878	China	Hand Trucks and Parts
2003	A-570-878	China	Electrolytic Manganese Dioxide
2003	A-570-878	China	Metal Top Ironing Tables
2003	A-570-878	China	Tetrahydrofurfuryl Alcohol
2003	A-570-878	China	Polyethylene Carrier Bags
2003	A-570-878	China	Stilbenedisulfonic Acid
2003	A-570-878	China	Color Television Receivers
2002	A-570-878	China	Refined Brown Aluminum Oxide
2002	A-570-878	China	Malleable Iron Pipe Fittings
2002	A-570-878	China	Barium Carbonate
2002	A-570-878	China	Polyvinyl Alcohol
2002	A-570-878	China	Saccharin
2002	A-570-877	China	Lawn and Garden Fence Posts
2002	A-823-812	Ukraine	Urea Ammonium Nitrate

(Continued)

Year	ITA Case Number	Country	Product
2002	A-821-818	Russia	Urea Ammonium Nitrate
2002	A-451-804	Lithuania	Urea Ammonium Nitrate
2002	A-822-805	Belarus	Urea Ammonium Nitrate
2002	A-823-812	Ukraine	Oil Country Tubular Goods
2002	A-485-808	Romania	Oil Country Tubular Goods
2002	A-570-876	China	Oil Country Tubular Goods
2002	A-570-874	China	Ball Bearings and Parts
2002	A-570-875	China	Cast Iron Pipe Fittings
2001	A-570-873	China	Ferrovanadium
2001	A-437-804	Hungary★	Sulfanilic Acid
2001	A-821-815	Russia	Cold Rolled Flat Steel Products
2001	A-570-872	China	Cold Rolled Flat Steel Products
2001	A-823-812	Ukraine	Alloy Steel Wire Rod
2001	A-570-870	China	Carbon Quality Steel Pipe
2001	A-821-814	Russia	Structural Steel Beams
2001	A-570-869	China	Structural Steel Beams
2001	A-570-868	China	Folding Metal Tables and Chairs
2001	A-834-807	Kazakhstan	Silicomanganese
2001	A-570-867	China	Auto Glass Windshields
2001	A-570-866	China	Folding Gift Boxes
2000	A-821-813	Russia	Pure Magnesium
2000	A-570-864	China	Pure Magnesium
2000	A-570-864	China	Pure Magnesium
2000	A-449-804	Latvia	Steel Concrete Reinforcing Bars
2000	A-822-804	Belarus	Steel Concrete Reinforcing Bars
2000	A-570-860	China	Steel Concrete Reinforcing Bars
2000	A-455-803	Poland★	Steel Concrete Reinforcing Bars
2000	A-821-812	Russia	Steel Concrete Reinforcing Bars
2000	A-823-809	Ukraine	Steel Concrete Reinforcing Bars
2000	A-841-804	Moldova	Steel Concrete Reinforcing Bars
2000	A-570-859	China	Steel Wire Rope
2000	A-570-858	China	Citric Acid and Sodium Nitrate
2000	A-570-862	China	Foundry Coke Products
2000	A-570-863	China	Honey
2000	A-570-861	China	Desktop Note Counters/Scanners
2000	A-560-812	Kazakhstan	Hot-Rolled Steel Products
2000	A-823-811	Ukraine	Hot-Rolled Steel Products
2000	A-570-865	China	Hot-Rolled Steel Products
2000	A-485-805	Romania	Hot-Rolled Steel Products
1999	A-823-810	Ukraine	Ammonium Nitrate
1999	A-570-857	China	Paintbrushes
1999	A-821-811	Russia	Ammonium Nitrate
1999	A-570-856	China	Synthetic Indigo
1999	A-851-802	Czech Republic	Line and Pressure Pipe
1999	A-485-805	Romania	Line and Pressure Pipe

(Continued)

Year	ITA Case Number	Country	Product
1999	A-570-855	China	Apple Juice Concentrate
1999	A-570-854	China	Cold-Rolled Steel Products
1999	A-821-810	Russia	Cold-Rolled Steel Products
1999	A-859-801	Slovakia	Cold-Rolled Steel Products
1999	A-570-853	China	Bulk Aspirin
1999	A-851-801	Czech Republic	Steel Plate
1999	A-570-852	China	Creatine
1998	A-821-809	Russia	Hot-Rolled Steel Products
1998	A-570-851	China	Preserved Mushrooms
1996	A-570-850	China	Roofing Nails
1996	A-821-808	Russia	Steel Plate
1996	A-823-808	Ukraine	Steel Plate
1996	A-570-849	China	Steel Plate
1996	A-570-848	China	Crawfish Tail Meat
1996	A-834-805	Kazakhstan	Beryillium Metal and Alloys
1996	A-570-847	China	Persulfates
1996	A-570-845	China	Brake Drums
1996	A-570-846	China	Brake Rotor
1996	A-570-844	China	Melamine Dinnerware
1995	A-570-843	China	Bicycles
1995	A-570-842	China	Polyvinyl Alcohol
1994	A-570-841	China	Manganese Sulfate
1994	A-570-840	China	Manganese Metal
1994	A-570-839	China	Steel Drawer Slides with Rollers
1994	A-570-838	China	Honey
1994	A-570-837	China	Wheel Inserts
1994	A-570-836	China	Glycine
1994	A-570-835	China	Furfuryl Alchol
1994	A-821-807	Russia	Ferrovanadium and Nitrided Vanadium
1994	A-570-833	China	Disposable Lighters
1994	A-821-806	Russia	Magnesium
1994	A-821-805	Ukraine	Magnesium
1994	A-570-832	China	Magnesium
1994	A-570-831	China	Fresh Garlic
1993	A-570-830	China	Coumarin
1993	A-570-829	China	Saccharin
1993	A-823-805	Ukraine	Silicomanganese
1993	A-570-828	China	Silicomanganese
1993	A-570-827	China	Cased Pencils
1993	A-437-803	Hungary	Phthalic Anhydride
1993	A-570-826	China	Paper Clips
1993	A-570-825	China	Sebacic Acid
1993	A-570-824	China	Silicon Carbide
1993	A-570-823	China	Nitromethane

(Continued)

Year	ITA Case Number	Country	Product
1992	A-570-822	China	Spring Lock Washers
1992	A-570-821	China	Hairbrushes
1992	A-570-820	China	Ductile Iron Waterworks Fittings
1992	A-455-802	Poland	Steel Plate
1992	A-485-803	Romania	Steel Plate
1992	A-570-819	China	Ferrosilicon
1992	A-834-804	Kazakhstan	Ferrosilicon
1992	A-821-804	Russia	Ferrosilicon
1992	A-823-804	Ukraine	Ferrosilicon
1992	A-437-802	Hungary	Sulfanilic Acid
1992	A-570-818	China	Sulfur Dyes
1991	C-570-817	China★★★	Chrome Plated Lug Nuts
1991	A-461-801	USSR★★	Uranium
1991	C-570-816	China★★★	Oscillating and Ceiling Fans
1991	A-570-815	China	Sulfanilic Acid
1991	A-485-802	Romania	Non-alloy Steel Pipe
1991	A-570-814	China	Butt Weld Pipe Fittings
1991	A-570-813	China	Refined Antimony Trioxide
1991	A-455-801	Poland	Ball Bearings
1991	A-570-812	China	Ball Bearings
1991	A-437-801	Hungary	Ball Bearings
1991	A-570-810	China	Shopping Carts
1991	A-570-811	China	Tungsten Ore Concentrates
1990	A-570-809	China	Steel Wire Rope
1990	A-570-808	China	Chrome Plated Lug Nuts
1990	A-570-807	China	Oscillating and Ceiling Fans
1990	A-570-806	China	Silicon Metal
1990	A-570-805	China	Certain Sulfur Chemicals
1990	A-570-804	China	Sparkers
1990	A-570-803	China	Forged Hand Tools
1989	A-570-802	China	Industrial Nitrocellulose
1988	A-485-801	Romania	Antifriction Bearings
1988	A-570-801	China	Certain Headwear
1986	A-461-601	USSR★★	Urea
1986	A-437-601	Hungary	Tapered Roller Bearings
1986	A-485-601	Romania	Tapered Roller Bearings
1986	A-570-601	China	Tapered Roller Bearings
1986	A-429-601	East Germany	Urea
1986	A-485-601	Romania	Urea
1985	A-570-506	China	Porcelain on Steel Cooking Ware
1985	A-570-505	China	Small Diameter Standard Pipe
1985	A-570-504	China	Petroleum Wax Candles
1985	A-455-502	Poland	Steel Wire Nails
1985	A-570-503	China	Steel Wire Nails
1985	A-455-501	Poland	Steel Wire Rod

(Continued)

Year	ITA Case Number	Country	Product
1985	A-570-502	China	Iron Construction Castings
1985	A-485-801	Romania	Oil Country Tubular Goods
1985	A-570-501	China	Natural Bristle Paintbrushes
1984	A-435-401	Czechoslovakia	Carbon Steel Products
1984	A-429-404	East Germany	Carbon Steel Products
1984	A-437-401	Hungary	Carbon Steel Products
1984	A-455-402	Poland	Carbon Steel Products
1984	A-485-401	Romania	Carbon Steel Products
1984	A-455-403	Poland	Carbon Steel Structural Shapes
1984	A-429-403	East Germany	Steel Wire Rod
1984	A-455-401	Poland	Barbed Wire
1984	A-461-402	USSR	Muriate of Potash
1984	A-429-402	East Germany	Muriate of Potash
1984	C-461-401	USSR★★★	Muriate of Potash
1984	C-429-401	East Germany★★★	Muriate of Potash
1983	A-455-002	Poland	Steel Wire Rod
1983	C-435-001	Czechoslovakia★★★	Steel Wire Rod
1983	C-455-003	Poland★★★	Steel Wire Rod
1983	A-570-006	China	Barium Carbonate
1983	A-570-007	China	Barium Chloride
1983	A-570-005	China	Textiles and Apparel
1983	A-570-002	China	Chloropicrin
1983	A-570-001	China	Potassium Permanganate
1981	A-485-001	Romania	Carbon Steel Plate
1981	A-437-001	Hungary	Trailer Axles
1981	A-429-001	East Germany	Manual Typewriters
1981	A-455-001	Poland	Electric Golf Carts
1980	A-485-006	Romania	Carbon Steel Products

Notes:

★ In this case Poland and Hungary have been reclassified as market economies.

★★ When the Soviet Union broke into individual republics in 1991, the ITA converted this one case into 15 separate anti-dumping cases.

★★★ Indicates countervailing duty investigations instead of anti-dumping.

Sources: United States International Trade Administration, *Antidumping and Countervailing Duty Cases Initiated since January 1, 1980*; April 3, 2000 <www.ia.ita.doc.gov/stats>; accessed April 3, 2000 and *Federal Register*, 2000–2005, and *Antidumping and Countervailing Duty Investigations: January 2000 to Current*, http://ia/ita.doc.gov/stats/inv-invitations-2000-2004.html, accessed 17/06/04 and 20/12/04.

A P P E N D I X   I I I

European Union Anti-Dumping Cases Initiated
against Non-Market Economies
and Former NMEs, 1980–2004

Year Initiated	Official Journal*	Country	Product
2004	C24, 28/01/04	Belarus	Polyester High Tenacity Filament Yarn
2004	C103, 29/04/04	Vietnam	Bicycles
2004	C103, 29/04/04	China	Hand Pallet Trucks and Essential Parts
2004	C104, 30/04/04	China	Barium Carbonate
2004	C104, 30/04/04	China	Castings
2004	C144, 28/05/04	Russia	Grain-Oriented Electrical Sheets
2004	C144, 28/05/04	Russia	Styrene-Butadience-Styrene
2004	C160, 17/06/04	China	Polyester Filament Apparel Fabrics
2004	C178, 10/07/04	China	Trichloroisocyanuric Acid (TCCA)
2004	C180, 13/07/04	China	Magnesia Bricks
2004	C203, 11/08/04	Vietnam	Tube or Pipe Fittings
2004	C212, 24/08/04	China	Stainless Steel Fasteners
2004	C212, 24/08/04	Vietnam	Stainless Steel Fasteners
2004	C225, 09/09/04	Russia	Granular Polytetrafluoroethylene
2004	C225, 09/09/04	China	Granular Polytetrafluoroethylene
2004	C267, 30/10/04	China	Tartaric Acid
2003	C120, 22/05/03	China	Polyethylene Terephthalate (PET)
2003	C195, 19/08/03	China	Okoume Plywood
2003	C309, 19/12/03	China	Polyester Staple Fibres
2003	L75, 21/03/03	China	Paracresol
2002	C318, 19/12/02	China	Sodium Cyclamate
2002	C249, 16/10/02	Russia	Hollow Sections
2002	C246, 12/10/02	Russia	Silicon Metal
2002	C189, 09/08/02	China	Furfuryl Alcohol

(Continued)

Year Initiated	Official Journal★	Country	Product
2002	C153, 27/06/02	China	Lighters (Disposable Gas)
2002	C111, 08/05/02	Russia	Grain Oriented Electrical Sheets
2002	C111, 08/05/02	Poland★★	Grain Oriented Electrical Sheets
2001	C367, 21/12/01	Russia	Rubber Grade Carbon Blacks
2001	C364, 20/12/01	Lithuania★★	Filament Yarns of Cellulose Acetate
2001	C364, 20/12/01	Slovakia★★	Flat Rolled Products of Iron
2001	C364, 20/12/01	Hungary★★	Flat Rolled Products of Iron
2001	C190, 06/07/01	China	Sulphanilic Acid
2001	C183, 29/06/01	Czech Republic★★	Welded Tubes and Pipes
2001	C183, 29/06/01	Poland★★	Welded Tubes and Pipes
2001	C183, 29/06/01	Ukraine	Welded Tubes and Pipes
2001	C159, 01/06/01	Czech Republic★★	Tube and Pipe Fittings, Iron, or Steel
2001	C159, 01/06/01	Russia	Tube and Pipe Fittings, Iron, or Steel
2001	C159, 01/06/01	Slovakia★★	Tube and Pipe Fittings, Iron, or Steel
2000	C45, 18/02/00	China	Aluminum Foil
2000	C45, 18/02/00	Russia	Aluminum Foil
2000	C127, 05/05/00	Czech Republic★★	Steel Ropes and Cables
2000	C127, 05/05/00	Russia	Steel Ropes and Cables
2000	C134, 13/05/00	China	Paracetamol
2000	C138, 17/05/00	China	Lamps
2000	C301, 21/10/00	Belarus	Urea
2000	C301, 21/10/00	Bulgaria★★	Urea
2000	C301, 21/10/00	Estonia★★	Urea
2000	C301, 21/10/00	Lithuania★★	Urea
2000	C301, 21/10/00	Poland★★	Urea
2000	C301, 21/10/00	Romania★★	Urea
2000	C301, 21/10/00	Ukraine	Urea
2000	C320, 09/11/00	Ukraine	Ferro Molybdenum
2000	C322, 11/11/00	China	Granite Stones
2000	C366, 20/12/00	China	Zinc Oxides
1999	C4, 07/01/99	Bulgaria★★	Flat Rolled Products of Iron or Steel
1999	C10, 14/01/99	China	Yellow Phosphorus
1999	C63, 05/03/99	China	Compact Disc Boxes
1999	C133, 13/05/99	China	Hot Rolled Flat Steel Products
1999	C133, 13/05/99	Romania★★	Hot Rolled Flat Steel Products
1999	C151, 29/05/99	Czech Republic★★	Cast Iron Tube or Pipe Fittings
1999	C151, 29/05/99	China	Cast Iron Tube or Pipe Fittings
1999	C181, 26/06/99	Belarus	Urea and Ammonium Nitrate
1999	C181, 26/06/99	Lithuania★★	Urea and Ammonium Nitrate
1999	C181, 26/06/99	Russia	Urea and Ammonium Nitrate
1999	C181, 26/06/99	Slovakia★★	Urea and Ammonium Nitrate
1999	C181, 26/06/99	Ukraine	Urea and Ammonium Nitrate
1999	C216, 29/07/99	China	Cathode Ray Picture Tubes

(Continued)

Year Initiated	Official Journal*	Country	Product
1999	C216, 29/07/99	Lithuania**	Cathode Ray Picture Tubes
1999	C231, 13/08/99	China	Hairbrushes
1999	C239, 24/08/99	China	Glycine
1999	C262, 16/09/99	China	Electronic Weighing Scales
1999	C262, 16/09/99	China	Coke
1999	C311, 29/10/99	Lithuania**	Ammonium Nitrate
1999	C311, 29/10/99	Poland**	Ammonium Nitrate
1999	C311, 29/10/99	Ukraine	Ammonium Nitrate
1999	C318, 05/11/99	China	Bicycle Forks
1999	C318, 05/11/99	China	Bicycle Frames
1999	C318, 05/11/99	China	Bicycle Wheels
1998	C1, 03/01/98	Poland**	Binder or Baler Twine
1998	C65, 28/02/98	Czech Republic**	Binder or Baler Twine
1998	C65, 28/02/98	Hungary**	Binder or Baler Twine
1998	C155, 20/05/98	China	Steel Ropes and Cables
1998	C155, 20/05/98	Ukraine	Steel Ropes and Cables
1998	C239, 30/07/98	Poland**	Steel Ropes and Cables
1998	C239, 30/07/98	Hungary**	Steel Ropes and Cables
1998	C353, 19/11/98	Ukraine	Seamless Pipes and Tubes
1997	C32, 01/11/98	China	Fax Machines
1997	C130, 26/04/97	Ukraine	Potassium Permanganate
1997	C205, 05/07/97	Vietnam	Monosodium Glutamate
1997	C210, 11/07/97	China	Cotton Fabric Unbleached
1997	C211, 12/07/97	Russia	Narrow Steel Strips
1997	C256, 21/09/97	China	Unwrought Magnesium
1997	C323, 24/10/97	China	Thiourea Dioxide
1997	C324, 25/10/97	China	Laser Optical Reading Systems
1997	C336, 07/11/97	Bulgaria**	Hardboard
1997	C336, 07/11/97	Estonia**	Hardboard
1997	C336, 07/11/97	Latvia**	Hardboard
1997	C336, 07/11/97	Lithuania**	Hardboard
1997	C336, 07/11/97	Poland**	Hardboard
1997	C336, 07/11/97	Russia	Hardboard
1996	C50, 21/02/96	China	Cotton Fabrics Unbleached
1996	C111, 17/04/96	China	Briefcases and Schoolbags
1996	C111, 17/04/96	China	Luggage and Travel Goods
1996	C132, 04/05/96	China	Handbags
1996	C253, 31/08/96	Czech Republic**	Seamless Pipes and Tubes
1996	C253, 31/08/96	Romania**	Seamless Pipes and Tubes
1996	C253, 31/08/96	Russia	Seamless Pipes and Tubes
1996	C253, 31/08/96	Slovakia**	Seamless Pipes and Tubes
1996	C369, 07/12/96	China	Fasteners
1996	C381, 17/12/96	China	Ferrosilicomanganese
1995	C45, 22/02/95	China	Footwear (Textile)

(Continued)

Year Initiated	Official Journal★	Country	Product
1995	C45, 22/02/95	China	Footwear (Leather)
1995	C95, 19/04/95	China	Furfuryl Alcohol
1995	C143, 09/06/95	Kazakhstan	Unwrought Zinc
1995	C143, 09/06/95	Poland★★	Unwrought Zinc
1995	C143, 09/06/95	Russia	Unwrought Zinc
1995	C143, 09/06/95	Ukraine	Unwrought Zinc
1995	C143, 09/06/95	Uzbekistan	Unwrought Zinc
1995	C178, 13/07/95	Poland★★	Wooden Pallets
1995	C180, 14/07/95	Czech Republic★★	Iron or Steel Sections
1995	C180, 14/07/95	Hungary★★	Iron or Steel Sections
1995	C266, 13/10/95	China	Glyphosate
1995	C284, 28/10/95	China	Ring Binders
1994	C11, 15/01/94	Kazakhstan	Unwrought Magnesium
1994	C11, 15/01/94	Russia	Unwrought Magnesium
1994	C11, 15/01/94	Ukraine	Unwrought Magnesium
1994	C11, 20/01/94	China	Cotton Fabric
1994	C35, 23/02/94	China	Pipe or Tube Fittings
1994	C35, 23/02/94	Slovakia★★	Pipe or Tube Fittings
1994	C64, 02/03/94	China	Persulphates
1994	C64, 02/03/94	China	Activated Powdered Carbon
1994	C117, 28/04/94	Poland★★	Portland Cement
1994	C117, 28/04/94	Czech Republic★★	Portland Cement
1994	C117, 28/04/94	Slovakia★★	Portland Cement
1994	C138, 20/05/94	Russia	Electrical Steel Sheets
1994	C138, 20/02/94	China	Coumarin
1994	C139, 21/05/94	Czech Republic★★	Pig-Iron
1994	C158, 09/06/94	Russia	Ammonium Nitrate Fertilizer
1994	C158, 09/06/94	Lithuania	Ammonium Nitrate Fertilizer
1994	C212, 03/08/94	Belarus	Polyester Staple Fiber
1993	C104, 15/04/93	China	Refractory Chamottes
1993	C123, 05/05/93	Bulgaria	Urea Ammonium Nitrate
1993	C123, 05/05/93	Poland★★	Urea Ammonium Nitrate
1993	C208, 31/07/93	China	Furfuraldehyde
1993	C210, 04/08/93	Russia	Ferro-Silico-Manganese
1993	C210, 04/08/93	Ukraine	Ferro-Silico-Manganese
1993	C210, 04/08/93	Georgia	Ferro-Silico-Manganese
1993	C302, 09/11/93	China	Furazolidone
1993	C341, 18/12/93	China	Microwave Ovens
1992	L 298, 20/11/94	China	Potassium Permanganate
1992	L215, 25/08/93	China	Polyolefin Woven Bags
1992	L226, 07/09/93	China	Flourospar
1992	L228, 09/09/93	China	Photo Albums
1992	L237, 22/09/93	China	Ferro-Silicon
1992	L246, 02/10/93	Russia	Isobutanol

(Continued)

Year Initiated	Official Journal★	Country	Product
1992	L58, 11/03/93	China	Bicycles
1992	L80, 02/04/93	Russia	Ferrochrome
1992	L80, 02/04/93	Ukraine	Ferrochrome
1992	L80, 02/04/93	Kazakhstan	Ferrochrome
1992	L95, 21/04/93	China	Microdisks
1992	L120, 15/05/93	Hungary★★★	Seamless Steel Tubes
1992	L120, 15/05/93	Poland★★★	Seamless Steel Tubes
1992	L120, 15/05/93	Czech Republic★★★	Seamless Steel Tubes
1992	L120, 15/05/93	Slovakia★★★	Seamless Steel Tubes
1992	L145, 17/06/93	China	Magnesium Oxide
1992	L306, 11/12/93	China	Dead burned Magnesia
1992	L127, 27/05/93	China	Paintbrushes
1992	L244, 30/09/93	China	Unwrought Manganese
1991	L94, 13/04/93	Russia	Silicon Carbide
1991	L94, 13/04/93	Ukraine	Silicon Carbide
1991	L94, 13/04/93	China	Silicon Carbide
1991	L328, 14/11/92	Poland	Seamless Pipes
1991	L328, 14/11/92	Czechoslovakia	Seamless Pipes
1991	L328, 14/11/92	Hungary	Seamless Pipes
1991	L88, 03/04/92	China	Polyester Yarns
1991	L90, 04/11/91	Albania	High Carbon Ferrochromium
1991	L90, 04/11/91	USSR	High Carbon Ferrochromium
1990	L106, 26/04/91	China	Video Tapes
1990	L187, 13/07/91	China	Dihydrostreptomycin
1990	L110, 28/04/92	Russia	Potash
1990	L110, 28/04/92	Belarus	Potash
1990	L110, 28/04/92	Ukraine	Potash
1990	L183, 03/07/92	Poland	Ferrosilicon
1989	L133, 29/05/91	China	Pocket Lighters
1989	L145, 08/06/90	USSR	Potassium Permanganate
1989	L174, 07/07/90	China	Typewriter Ribbon
1989	L187, 19/07/90	China	Woven Polyolefin sacks
1989	L365, 28/12/90	China	Espadrilles
1989	L80, 27/03/90	China	Silicon Metal
1989	L188, 20/07/90	Hungary	NPK Fertilizers
1989	L188, 20/07/90	Poland	NPK Fertilizers
1989	L188, 20/07/90	Romania	NPK Fertilizers
1989	L202, 31/07/90	Czechoslovakia	Electric Motors
1989	L202, 31/07/90	Bulgaria	Electric Motors
1989	L202, 31/07/90	Romania	Electric Motors
1988	C20, 26/01/88	China	Calcium Metal
1988	C20, 26/01/88	USSR	Calcium Metal
1988	C241, 16/09/88	Romania	Welded Steel Tubes

(Continued)

Year Initiated	Official Journal*	Country	Product
1988	C288, 12/11/88	China	Television Receivers
1988	C308, 03/12/88	China	Barium Chloride
1988	C308, 03/12/88	GDR	Barium Chloride
1988	C322, 15/12/88	China	Ammonium Paratungstate
1988	C322, 15/12/88	China	Tungstic Oxide and Acid
1988	C322, 15/12/88	China	Tungsten Metal Powder
1988	C322, 15/12/88	China	Tungsten Carbide
1988	C322, 15/12/88	Bulgaria	Methenamine
1988	C322, 15/12/88	Czechoslovakia	Methenamine
1988	C322, 15/12/88	Hungary	Methenamine
1988	C322, 15/12/88	Poland	Methenamine
1988	C322, 15/12/88	Romania	Methenamine
1987	C53, 28/02/87	USSR	Mercury
1987	C77, 24/03/87	USSR	Ferro-Silicon
1987	C173, 01/07/87	Romania	Polyester Fiber
1987	C271, 09/10/87	Hungary	Urea
1987	C271, 09/10/87	Romania	Urea
1986	C63, 18/03/86	China	Potassium Permanganate
1986	C63, 18/03/86	Czechoslovakia	Potassium Permanganate
1986	C63, 18/03/86	GDR	Potassium Permanganate
1986	C103, 30/04/86	China	Paintbrushes
1986	C125, 24/05/86	GDR	Polyester Fiber
1986	C125, 24/05/86	Romania	Polyester Fiber
1986	C254, 11/10/86	Czechoslovakia	Urea
1986	C254, 11/10/86	GDR	Urea
1986	C254, 11/10/86	USSR	Urea
1985	C84, 02/04/85	GDR	Portland Cement
1985	C84, 02/04/85	Poland	Portland Cement
1985	C96, 17/04/85	China	Hammers
1985	C159, 29/06/85	Romania	Acrylic Fibers
1985	C200, 08/08/85	Bulgaria	Flat Glass
1985	C200, 08/08/85	Czechoslovakia	Flat Glass
1985	C200, 08/08/85	Hungary	Flat Glass
1985	C200, 08/08/85	Romania	Flat Glass
1985	C319, 11/12/85	USSR	Freezers
1985	C319, 11/12/85	GDR	Freezers
1984	C13, 19/01/84	Hungary	Horticultural Glass
1984	C13, 19/01/84	GDR	Iron or Steel Angles
1984	C55, 28/02/84	Czechoslovakia	Skates
1984	C55, 28/02/84	GDR	Asbestos Cement Sheets
1984	C55, 28/02/84	Czechoslovakia	Asbestos Cement Sheets
1984	C67, 08/03/84	GDR	Oxalic Acid
1984	C90, 31/03/84	Bulgaria	Copper Sulphate
1984	C90, 31/03/84	Hungary	Copper Sulphate

(Continued)

Year Initiated	Official Journal*	Country	Product
1984	C90, 31/03/84	Poland	Copper Sulphate
1984	C201, 31/07/84	Hungary	Artificial Corundum
1984	C201, 31/07/84	Poland	Artificial Corundum
1984	C201, 31/07/84	USSR	Artificial Corundum
1984	C202, 01/08/84	China	Silicon Carbide
1984	C202, 01/08/84	Czechoslovakia	Silicon Carbide
1984	C202, 01/08/84	Poland	Silicon Carbide
1984	C202, 01/08/84	USSR	Silicon Carbide
1984	C204, 03/08/84	Hungary	Skates
1984	C204, 03/08/84	Romania	Skates
1984	C235, 05/09/84	USSR	Roller Chains for Bicycles
1984	C235, 05/09/84	China	Roller Chains for Bicycles
1984	C305, 16/11/84	Bulgaria	Wood Particle Board
1984	C305, 16/11/84	Czechoslovakia	Wood Particle Board
1984	C305, 16/11/84	Poland	Wood Particle Board
1984	C305, 16/11/84	Romania	Wood Particle Board
1984	C305, 16/11/84	USSR	Wood Particle Board
1983	C31, 05/02/83	USSR	Unwrought Nickel
1983	C31, 05/02/83	USSR	Unwrought Aluminum
1983	C87, 29/03/83	Czechoslovakia	Sanitary Fixtures
1983	C87, 29/03/83	Hungary	Sanitary Fixtures
1983	C98, 12/04/83	China	Lithium Hydroxide
1983	C109, 23/04/83	Romania	Iron or Steel Angles
1983	C109, 23/04/83	GDR	Choline Chloride
1983	C109, 23/04/83	Romania	Choline Chloride
1983	C194, 21/07/83	Czechoslovakia	Horticultural Glass
1983	C194, 21/07/83	GDR	Horticultural Glass
1983	C194, 21/07/83	Poland	Horticultural Glass
1983	C194, 21/07/83	Romania	Horticultural Glass
1983	C194, 21/07/83	USSR	Horticultural Glass
1982	C8, 14/01/82	GDR	Aluminum Foil
1982	C8, 14/01/82	Hungary	Aluminum Foil
1982	C79, 31/03/82	GDR	Methylamines
1982	C79, 31/03/82	Romania	Methylamines
1982	C133, 25/05/82	Czechoslovakia	Perchlorethylene
1982	C133, 25/05/82	Romania	Perchlorethylene
1982	C162, 29/06/82	China	Magnesite Caustic Burned
1982	C162, 29/06/82	China	Magnesite Deadburned
1982	C207, 10/08/82	China	Barium Chloride
1982	C207, 10/08/82	GDR	Barium Chloride
1982	C211, 13/08/82	Czechoslovakia	Methenamine
1982	C211, 13/08/82	GDR	Methenamine
1982	C211, 13/08/82	Romania	Methenamine
1982	C211, 13/08/82	USSR	Methenamine

(Continued)

Year Initiated	Official Journal*	Country	Product
1982	C230, 03/09/82	Czechoslovakia	Polyethylene
1982	C230, 03/09/82	GDR	Polyethylene
1982	C230, 03/09/82	Poland	Polyethylene
1982	C230, 03/09/82	USSR	Polyethylene
1982	C276, 19/10/82	China	Canned Pears
1982	C310, 27/11/82	GDR	Glass Textile Fiber
1982	C310, 27/11/82	Czechoslovakia	Glass Textile Fiber
1982	C331, 17/12/82	USSR	Copper Sulphate
1982	C331, 17/12/82	Czechoslovakia	Copper Sulphate
1981	C35, 18/02/81	GDR	Upright Pianos
1981	C35, 18/02/81	Poland	Upright Pianos
1981	C71, 01/04/81	Czechoslovakia	Codeine
1981	C71, 01/04/81	Hungary	Codeine
1981	C71, 01/04/81	Poland	Codeine
1981	C162, 02/07/81	Czechoslovakia	Refrigerators
1981	C162, 02/07/81	GDR	Refrigerators
1981	C162, 02/07/81	Hungary	Refrigerators
1981	C162, 02/07/81	Poland	Refrigerators
1981	C162, 02/07/81	Romania	Refrigerators
1981	C162, 02/07/81	USSR	Refrigerators
1981	C164, 04/07/81	Bulgaria	Fiber Building Board
1981	C164, 04/07/81	Hungary	Fiber Building Board
1981	C181, 23/07/81	Czechoslovakia	Pianos
1981	C181, 23/07/81	USSR	Pianos
1981	C241, 19/09/81	China	Oxalic Acid
1981	C241, 19/09/81	Czechoslovakia	Oxalic Acid
1981	C241, 19/09/81	Hungary	Oxalic Acid
1981	C241, 19/09/81	GDR	Oxalic Acid
1981	C245, 25/09/81	Czechoslovakia	Vacuum Cleaners
1981	C245, 25/09/81	GDR	Vacuum Cleaners
1981	C245, 25/09/81	Poland	Vacuum Cleaners
1981	C271, 23/10/81	USSR	Photographic Enlargers
1981	C271, 23/10/81	Czechoslovakia	Photographic Enlargers
1981	C271, 23/10/81	Poland	Photographic Enlargers
1981	C271, 23/10/81	Czechoslovakia	Trichlorethylene
1981	C271, 23/10/81	GDR	Trichlorethylene
1981	C271, 23/10/81	Poland	Trichlorethylene
1981	C271, 23/10/81	Romania	Trichlorethylene
1981	C299, 18/11/81	Romania	Steel Tubes
1981	C332, 19/12/81	Czechoslovakia	Polyvinylchloride
1981	C332, 19/12/81	GDR	Polyvinylchloride
1981	C332, 19/12/81	Hungary	Polyvinylchloride
1981	C332, 19/12/81	Romania	Polyvinylchloride
1981	C337, 24/12/81	China	Paracetamol

(Continued)

Year Initiated	Official Journal*	Country	Product
1980	C181, 19/07/80	USSR	Mechanical Watches
1980	C219, 27/08/80	China	Furfural
1980	C296, 14/11/80	Hungary	Hermetic Compressors

Notes:

* *Official Journal* citations are for edition C or edition L. Dates are in format: day/month/year, as per the format used in the *Official Journal*.

** Indicates country was reclassified as a market economy, therefore these countries are technically *former* NMEs.

*** Country was reclassified in 1992, the year of the investigation.

Sources: European Commission, 1983–2005. *Annual Report from the Commission to the European Parliament on the Community's Anti-Dumping and Anti-Subsidy Activities.* Brussels: The European Commission; and Commission Regulations and Council Regulations, 1983–2005, *Official Journal.*

N O T E S

<u>Chapter One   Introduction: Transitions and Trade</u>

1. This means that Yugoslavia was never labeled a NME because it was not allied with the Soviet Union. Moreover, Communist regimes in Africa or Latin America were not labeled NMEs. The United States and the EU maintained independent but identical lists. I discuss this political designation in detail in chapters three and four.
2. The title to this project is an actual quote from an interview with U.S. Department of Commerce International Trade Analyst, who said that instead of calling non-market economies by their commonly used acronym NMEs, they are commonly referred to as "enemies." (Phone interview, February 14, 2001.) Note, I assured my interviewee's anonymity, therfore neither their full names nor titles are cited.
3. Article VI, Section 1 of the General Agreement on Tariffs and Trade (GATT) corresponds to Article 2.1 of the WTO (General Agreement on Tariffs and Trade 1970).
4. In interviews, U.S. trade officials acknowledged that in about 99 % of cases, non-market economies were found guilty of dumping. The 1 % not found guilty were cases in which the non-market economy did not produce the goods for export, and therefore had been falsely accused of dumping. In one interview I had to remind the trade official about spurious cases, since he contended that in 100 % of anti-dumping cases non-market economies were found guilty. (Various interviews at International Trade Administration, U.S. Department of Commerce, Washington, DC, February 2001.)
5. For example, Vice Prime Minister Boris Nemtsov of Russia refused to meet Sir Leon Brittan, the vice president of the European Commission and its chief trade negotiator, during Brittan's 1997 visit to Moscow, stranding him on the tarmac in protest over the way Russia was treated in European anti-dumping cases (Agence Europe 1997d; Thornhill 1997).
6. Note, prior to the dissolution of the USSR in 1991, each anti-dumping case against the USSR was counted as one case (not 15 cases or one for each republic). After the breakup in 1991, anti-dumping cases were counted against each country involved in a case. This is in keeping with the accounting used by the European Commission in tabulating anti-dumping cases.
7. For calculations in the following figures I have used relative instead of absolute numbers. As such, I compared percentage total imports to percentage total anti-dumping cases. This was done to smooth out the yearly fluctuations in number of anti-dumping cases filed due to things like staffing, budgeting, or macroeconomic cycles. It also makes the differences between levels of trade protection by country group more comparable.
8. The comparative groupings are U.S. Department of Commerce constructed aggregates (see table 3.2 for complete list).

South America: Argentina, Bolivia, Brazil, Chile, Colombia, Ecuador, Paraguay, Peru, Uruguay, Venezuela

Asian Newly Industrialized Economies (NICs): Hong Kong, Singapore, South Korea, Taiwan

Big Emerging Markets (BEM): Argentina, Brazil, Brunei, Hong Kong, India, Indonesia, Malaysia, Mexico, Philippines, Singapore, South Korea, South Africa, Taiwan, Thailand, Turkey.

Other Asian Countries: Afghanistan, Bangladesh, Bhutan, Brunei, Burma, Cambodia, India, Indonesia, Macao, Malaysia, Maldives, Mongolia, Pakistan, Philippines, Sri Lanka, Thailand

NMEs: Eastern Europe (Albania, Bulgaria, Czech Republic, Hungary, Poland, Romania, Slovakia), the Baltics (Latvia, Lithuania, Estonia), the former Soviet Republics (Russia, Belarus, Ukraine, Armenia, Azerbaijan, Georgia, Kazakhstan, Kyrgyzstan, Moldova, Turkmenistan, Tajikistan, Uzbekistan) China, and Vietnam.

Average Nonmarket Economies Group: average percentage total of anti-dumping cases.

9. For both the United States and EU, data is available only for anti-dumping cases that are actually initiated. While this does pose a selection bias in the data, this is the standard method of measuring trade protection in the literature. The dog that never barks remains uncounted.

Chapter Two   A Logic of Belief Stasis
and Belief Change

1. Beliefs and ideas are used interchangeably in the international relations and comparative politics literature, and for the purposes of this study they will have similar meanings and usage. (See Goldstein 1993; Goldstein and Keohane 1993).
2. See Garrett and Weingast's discussion of focal points in the construction of the European Community's internal market for another example of the combination of principled and causal beliefs and ideas (Garret and Weingast 1993).
3. Goldstein examines how different beliefs can engender different trade rules. Over time those rules can become layered on each other, thereby creating an internally inconsistent package of trade policies.
4. To model every variable that could affect information receptivity is not possible. For example, there are many micro-level factors that affect the ability of individuals to change their beliefs, including the propensity of an individual to be open-minded or self-critical, and the degree to which an individual is responsible for outcomes not processes (Tetlock 1998, 880). Since this study focuses on beliefs held by organizations, I have chosen the organizational level factors that appear most pertinent to this study.
5. The Council for Mutual Economic Assistance was founded in 1949. The original members included: the USSR, Bulgaria, Czechoslovakia, Hungary, Poland, and Romania. Albania, the German Democratic Republic, and Mongolia joined later. China, Cuba, North Korea, North Vietnam, and Yugoslavia had associate memberships (Talbott 1974).
6. Bryan Jones discusses the problems associated with processing information in multidimensional spaces. Because of both information uncertainty and various types of cognitive limitations, decision makers will take multiple attribute issues and narrow the dimensionality in order to render decisions (Jones 1994, 75; Jones 1996). This is the same type of problem that trade agencies faced when trying to ascertain whether to stress the importance of the interests or institutional incentives of NMEs.
7. See Janos for a comparison of the timing and scope of collectivization across Eastern Europe (Janos 2000, 249).
8. Hanson uses the term "true believer" to reflect whether an individual was true to the beliefs of Marxist–Leninism. It is equally applicable in thinking about the degree to which NMEs embraced the dogmas of communism (Hanson 1991).
9. See Janos Kornai's *The Socialist System* (1992) for the quintessential description of all aspects of Communist systems.

Chapter Three   Crawfish, Sparklers, and Rebar: Testing Theories of Trade Protection

1. See the works of Luigi Guiso, Paola Sapienza, and Luigi Zingales, "Cultural Biases in Economic Exchange," as cited in "Why Cultural Biases May Be the Ultimate Trade Barrier," *The Economist*, July 21, 2005, http://www.economist.com/finance/displayStory. cfm?story_id=4199095, accessed July 30, 2005.

2. There is reference category "other" that is not used in the analysis, so there is a case that is not coded as "1" for at least one of the regional dummy variables.

3. There is some disagreement in this literature over the relationship between industry value - added and the level or incidence of trade protection. Low wage industries have been shown to be more likely to get protection than high wage industries (Moore 1992). But Hansen (1990) argues that low value-added industries are less likely to initiate trade protection cases, and Cheh (1976) finds no positive or negative relationship between the variables at all. Findings are still inconclusive.

4. Kreuger and Trefler have separately demonstrated that the degree of protection afforded to an industry is not correlated with lobbying variables such as unionization (Krueger 1996; Trefler 1993). Finger has demonstrated that the size of an industry, not its concentration has an effect on trade protection (Finger 1981; Finger et al. 1982). I use these findings in determining which factors to test in my analysis.

5. There is a sample bias built into the dataset. The sample cannot capture cases that are never filed. Only cases for which an anti-dumping claim is initiated are included. Therefore cases of informally negotiated trade protection or trade protection that is not initiated because it was addressed in another format are not included. Since this is the case with all studies on trade protection, namely an inability to count cases that never transpire, it should not affect its validity relative to the findings of others.

6. For NMEs, Commerce uses the two most recently completed fiscal quarters. For other countries, Commerce uses the four most recently completed fiscal quarters. I have tried to take this into account by looking at one year lagged figures. See Chapter 4 "Questionnaires," in the International Trade Administration, 2005. *Anti-Dumping Manual.* http://ia.ita.doc.gov/admanual/index.html

7. All data conform to the SIC 4-digit level of analysis or its equivalent, and have been converted from the 10-digit Harmonized Tariff Schedule Commodity Codes reported in the anti-dumping cases. From 1985 to1987, the Department of Commerce used the Tariff System of the United States (TSUSA) to designate imports, then 1987–1997 the Harmonized Tariff Schedule Commodity Codes (HS), and finally 1997–2005 the North American Industry Classification Standard (NAICS). Each of these has been converted into a standard code in order to compile comparable industry level data across the 15-year period. (See Appendix I for an explanation of each variable).

8. Moreover, there is inconclusive evidence to support the contention that PACs influence patterns of trade protection. Even when looking at the most likely cases, such as tariff levels, PACs demonstrate statistical significance but lack substantive significance in explaining incidence of trade protection (Baldwin and Magee 2000).

9. This logistic regression model used deviation coding for the categorical variables (Menard 1995). Outliers were not removed due to insufficient theoretical justification.

10. The dependent variable is a continuous numeric value, with a range of 1–100, with the exact dumping margin amount being used for the dependent variable. Therefore there is a full range of potential values.

Chapter Four   The Nuts and
Bolts of Anti-dumping Laws: Actors and Institutions
in the United States and the European Union

1. The GATT/WTO definition of dumping reads: "a product is considered as being dumped, i.e. introduced into the commerce of another country at less than its normal value, if the export price of the product exported from one country to another is less than the comparable price, in the ordinary course of trade, for the like product when destined for consumption in the exporting country" (World Trade Organization 1994).

2. This brief summary is drawn largely from Chapter 2 of the U.S. International Trade Commission report assessing the economic welfare of anti-dumping and countervailing duty laws (U.S. International Trade Commission 1995).

3. The 1984 Act established a special program to monitor persistent dumping and to allow for cumulation of imports in injury determinations. The 1988 Act added provisions to curb circumvention of duty orders, modify material injury determinations, and address concerns about third country dumping. The 1990 Act absolved Caribbean Basin Initiative Countries from cumulation requirements. See U.S. International Trade Commission 1995 for further discussion of cumulative changes to the anti-dumping regulations.

4. Section 702(c)(4)(A) of the Act requires that a firm(s) have standing, that is, be representative of the industry, to petition for an anti-dumping investigation. A petition meets the minimum requirements if the domestic producers or workers who support the petition account for (1) at least 25 % of the total production of the domestic like product and (2) more than 50 % of the production of the domestic-like product produced by that portion of the industry expressing support for, or opposition to, the petition (see *Initiation of Antidumping Duty Investigation: Beryllium Metal and High Beryllium Alloys from Kazakhstan*, (61 FR 15770 1996) and U.S. Department of Commerce International Trade Administration 1998, Chapter 1.

5. For example, a single exporter in Malaysia might not be injuring the domestic competing industry enough to merit an anti-dumping case. But the cumulated effect of imports from Malaysia, China, and Thailand might be causing injury to a domestic firm. By naming all these countries in the anti-dumping case, the domestic industry improves its chances of proving it is being injured by foreign competition and therefore in need of trade protection. The European Union has the same cumulation of injury practice.

6. Dumping margins less than 2 % ad valorem are considered de minimis and are disregarded. If de minimis dumping is found, the case is terminated. See Section 733, 19 U.S.C. 1673a of Title VII of the Tariff Act of 1930.

7. For an example of the European Court of Justice's influence on anti-dumping cases, see "Eugen Noelle v Hauptzollamt Bremen-Freihafen," European Court of Justice 1991. For an example of the oversight provided by the European Court of First Instance, see "Climax Paper Converters Ltd. v Council of the European Union," *Case T-155/94* 18 September 1996.

8. See Bael and Bellis 1990 for a good discussion of the legal delegation of authority between the Council and the Commission, and within the Commission.

9. A Community producer has "standing" to file a complaint if the "collective output constitutes more than 50% of the total production of the like product produced by that portion of the Community industry expressing either support for or opposition to the complaint." No case should be initiated if Community producers involved in the case account for less than 25% of total production (Council Reg No. 384/96 1996, Article 5(4)).

10. Personal interviews revealed that the Commission rejects between 80–90% of dumping petitions, because they do not meet the criteria. Two separate interviews with Trade Officials in Directorate General Trade (then DG I), European Commission, Brussels, Belgium, Fall 1999.

11. For a politically charged exception see Unbleached Cotton (COM Reg No. 773/98 1998).

12. Interview with top ranking Trade Official at the European Commission, DG Trade Brussels, Belgium, Fall 1999.

13. For examples, see Agence Europe 1998, 1999a, and 1999b). This information was collaborated in my personal interviews with Anti-dumping Trade Officials at the European Commission, Directorate General Trade (then DG I and IA)Brussels, Belgium, Fall 1999.

14. Separate Rates criteria were established in Sparklers from China (56 FR 20588 1991) and Silicon Carbide from China (59 FR 22585 1994). See Sebaic Acid From China (59 FR 28053 1994), Roller Bearings from Romania (62 FR 31075 1997), Pressure Pipe from Romania (65 FR 5594 2000), and Fertilizer Grade Ammonium Nitrate from Russia (65 FR 1139 2000) for examples of separate rate determinations.

15. Amendments to Council Reg. No. 1765/82 and 1/66/82 include EEC No. 1243/86, EEC No. 1434/90, EEC No. 3859/91, EC No. 519/94 (combining China and other non-market economies under one statute), and EEC No. 848/92 (dividing up the USSR into its constitutive republics).

Chapter Five   The Institutionalization of Beliefs

1. Information confirmed in interviews with trade analysts in the Office of Anti-Dumping Investigations, U.S. International Trade Administration, at Department of Commerce, Washington, DC, February 2001.

2. The term "comparable" is vague, and could mean a comparable producer of merchandise based on similarities in production factors (physical and non-physical) and/or factor intensities.

3. See *Persulfates from China* (66 FR 42628, 2001) and *Pure Magnesium from Russia* (66 FR 49347, 2001).

4. India does have a seafood processing industry and could have been used as a surrogate. India's GNP per capita was $320, and China's was $530 (U.S. International Trade Administration 1996).

5. In 1993, Poland was the first country to be reclassified as a "market economy" by the United States. Since it is a market economy, its prices can be directly used in anti-dumping cases. The irony is that Polish prices were used in a Russian anti-dumping case, but were not actually used in subsequent Polish cases until 2001 (see 66FR 18752, 2001).

6. Interview with analyst in Office of Anti-Dumping Investigations, U.S. International Trade Administration, at Department of Commerce, Washington, DC, February 2001.

7. For more details, see U.S. Department of Commerce, International Trade Administration, *Non-Market Economy Anti-Dumping Questionnaire.* <www.ita.doc.gov/IAFrameset.html>, accessed December 30, 2004. Note, extensions of a few days are possible, contingent on ITA formal approval.

8. See *Sulfanilic Acid from Hungary (1993)* and *Seamless Pressure Pipe from the Czech Republic(1999)* for examples of cases in which the cost of defending against dumping allegations resulted in the defendants simply halting exports. Information also collaborated in personal interviews with analysts in Office of Anti-Dumping Investigations, U.S. International Trade Administration, at Department of Commerce, Washington, DC, February 2001.

9. Interview with Policy Analyst, Office of Anti-Dumping Investigations, U.S. International Trade Administration, at Department of Commerce, Washington, DC, February 2001.

10. For example, in a recent case against Ukrainian exporters, the Government of Ukraine agreed to restrict sales to the United States, and therefore suspended the AD duty investigation prior to a final determination of dumping. See *Suspension of Anti-Dumping Duty Investigation: Certain Cut to Length Carbon Steel Plate from Ukraine*, 62 Fed. Reg. 61766, November 19, 1997.

11. Section 776 (a) (2) of the Tariff Act of 1930, as amended, provides guidelines for use of BIA:

> If an interested party or any other person (A) withholds information that has been requested by the administering authority; (B) fails to provide such information by the deadlines for the

submission of the information or in the form and manner requested subject to subsections (c) (1) and (e) of section 782; (C) significantly impedes a proceeding under this title; or (D) provides such information but the information cannot be verified as provided in section 782, (I) the administering authority shall, subject to section 782 (d), use the facts otherwise available in reaching the applicable determination under this title. (62 FR 41355 1997)

See also *United States Code Annotated, Title 19 Customs Duties*, 19 § 1677e. Verification of Information, 311.

12. Examples of BIA include but are not limited to: Complete financial statement(s) and footnotes, or interim financial statements and footnotes covering the period of investigation; general ledger and subsidiary ledgers for accounts receivable, accounts payable and expenses; chart of accounts and sub-accounts, translated into English for the period of investigation; and a compete copy of each sales listing for the months of the period of investigation, as reported to the Department of Commerce (U.S. International Trade Administration 2000c).

13. S. Rep. No. 100–71, 100th Cong., 1st Sess., at 108 (1987); Omnibus Trade and Competitiveness Act of 1988, P.L. 100–418, § 1316 (b), and Conf Report No. 100–576, 100th Cong., 2nd Sess. at 591 (1988).

14. Various interviews with trade officials at the European Commission, Directorate General Trade (then DG I) Brussels, Belgium, Fall 1999.

15. Ibid.

16. Note, the United States relies on publicly available information from surrogates in its investigations. The EU relies on confidential industry financial statements, which are much more difficult to obtain. This explains why the United States does not have the same information problems that the EU does in obtaining surrogate information for normal value calculations.

17. Various interviews with high ranking officials in Anti-dumping Investigations, European Commission, DG Trade (then DG I). Brussels, Belgium, Fall 1999.

18. Dumping duties are not always levied because the duties might run counter to the Community's interest, or the dumping might not be causing injury to the domestic injury. Dumping community interest and injury are all required in order to assess a dumping margin. However, the method used by the Commission almost always calculates dumping on the part of NMEs.

19. Information from several interviews with Heads of Units and Directors in Directorate General Trade (then DG I and DG IA), European Commission. Brussels, Belgium, Fall 1999.

20. Moreover, this case was highly contentious because Russia had already been reclassified as a "market economy," and therefore should not have been subjected to the analogue country method at all. This flagrant example of circumvention of formal rule changes is addressed in chapter seven.

21. Interview with Deputy Head of Unit, DG Trade (then DG I) Brussels, Belgium, Fall 1999.

22. Interviews with various Heads of Unit and Directors in the European Commission, Directorate General Trade (then DG I) Brussels, Belgium, Fall 1999.

23. See Appendix 1 for an explanation of the operationalization and data source used for each variable. For the U.S. data, the natural logarithms of GDP/capita and trade importance, the square roots of political freedom, economic freedom, geographic proximity, and the square of democracy are used in order to make the data better approximate a normal distribution. For the EU data, the natural logarithms of geographic proximity, corruption, GDP/capita, the square roots of political freedom, trade importance, economic freedom, and the square of democracy are used in order to meet assumptions of normality.

24. Confirmed in three different interviews with officials in Directorate General Trade (then DG I and DG IA). European Commission: Brussels, Belgium, Fall 1999.

25. Interview with Official in Anti-dumping Investigations, DG Trade (then DG I). European Commission: Brussels, Belgium, Fall 1999. For a discussion of Korea's industrial conglomerates called chaebol, see Haggard 1990, esp. 130–138.

Chapter Six   Rule Change but Outcome Stasis

1. There have been various formal rule changes associated with the reform efforts in NMEs. For instance, Separate Rates/Individual Treatment determinations were also instituted. They are akin to the Individual Treatment test used by the European Commission, and discussed later in this chapter. Only one formal rule change is examined in this section on U.S. policy.

2. At first, the ITA grappled with the issue of what degree of government involvement in an industry would negate the presence of a MOI (See *Sparklers from the People's Republic of China* (56 FR 20588 1991) and *Oscillating Fans from the People's Republic of China* (56 FR 55274, 1991)). Through a series of precedent setting cases, the Department of Commerce clarified its position about what "degree of state control" in the economy would constitute too much control and negate the finding of a MOI (See *Headwear from the People's Republic of China*, 54 FR 11983 1989).

3. Discussion with Analyst in Countervailing Duty Investigations, at the International Trade Administration, U.S. Department of Commerce, May 27, 1993.

4. Discussion with Analyst in Import Investigation, at the International Trade Administration, U.S. Department of Commerce, Washington, DC, 1993, April 7, 1993.

5. Interview with Analyst, Office of Anti-Dumping Investigations, U.S. International Trade Administration, at Department of Commerce, Washington, DC, February 2001.

6. Ibid.

7. These interviews were conducted in the Spring of 1993 with follow-up interviews in Winter 2001. During both the periods, different analysts admitted that the MOI test was interpreted in a way to deny NMEs market access.

8. For example, see COM Reg No. 165/97 1997, COM Reg No. 773/98 1998, and Council Reg No. 119/97 1997.

9. Interview with two trade officials in Anti-dumping Investigations, Directorate General Trade (then DG I), European Commission. Brussels, Belgium, Fall 1999.

10. Ibid.

11. Goldstein uses the term "layering" to describe the imposition of various trade policies on top of each other, despite their contradictory nature. See Goldstein 1993, especially Chapter 1. I am using the term in a slightly different way, suggesting that this layering leads to a change in policy rather than an accumulation of contradictory policies.

12. See Council Reg. No. 92/2002 of January 17, 2002, *Urea from Belarus, Bulgaria, Croatia, Estonia, Libya, Lithuania, Romania, and the Ukraine.* OJL 01/19/2002.

13. Various interviews with trade officials at the European Commission, DG Trade (thenDG I and DG IA). Brussels, Belgium, Fall 1999.

14. This is similar in intent and practice to the Market Oriented Industry Test (MOI Test).

15. The Russian steel ropes ruling is interesting because it came despite an independent Canadian anti-dumping study of the Russian steel industry in 1999 that concluded the Russian steel industry was market oriented, and therefore should have never been subjected to the MES test in the first place (Interfax News Agency 1999).

16. It is interesting to note that the size of the community industry that won protection in this case was one firm employing a total of 50 workers. This strongly suggests that the power of domestic interest groups is not the primary explanation for patterns of trade protection in these cases.

17. For similar Commission reasoning in recent cases, see COM Reg No. 837/2000 2000, COM Reg No. 967/2000 2000, and COM Reg No. 2536/1999 1999.

18. Interview with Head of Unit in DG Trade (then DG I), European Commission. Brussels, Belgium, Fall 1999.

19. Chapter seven explores the topic of country reclassifications, with particular focus on the Russian case.

20. Information confirmed in several interviews with officials in Directorate General Trade (then DG IDG IA), European Commission. Brussels, Belgium, Fall 1999.

21. Information confirmed in several interviews with officials in Directorate General Trade (then DGI and DGIA), European Commission. Brussels, Belgium, Fall 1999.
22. Ibid.
23. Ibid.
24. There is a vast organizational economics literature stressing different ways of creating an organizational culture among its members, including the important role of incentives as well as the leadership role of managers. See Miller 1992 for an institutional approach to such issues.
25. Interview with Analyst in Import Investigation, at the International Trade Administration, U.S. Department of Commerce, Washington, DC, 2001, February 20, 2001.
26. Ibid.

Chapter Seven   Belief Stickiness and
Belief Change

1. See Poland (Commission Decision 522/92/ECSC 1992; Council Reg. No. 518/92 1992; Council Reg. No. 3492/93 1993); Hungary (Commission Decision 523/92/ECSC 1992; Council Reg. No. 519/92 1992; Council Reg. No. 3491/93 1993); Czech and Slovak Republics (Commission Decision 524/92/ECSC 1992; Council Reg. No. 520/92 1992).
2. The Heritage Foundation's Index of Economic Freedoms measures ten different indicators of economic freedom and takes an average across the indicators to minimize the effect of any one factor. Factors include trade policy, fiscal burden, government intervention, monetary policy, foreign investment, banking/finance, wages/prices, property rights, regulations, and black market activities. The freedoms are each ranked on a scale of 1–5 with 1 being the most free and 5 being the least free. See <www.heritage.org/index/ and www.heritage.org/research/features/index/downloads/Pastscores.xls>, accessed 12/30/04.
3. Discussion with Analyst at Import Administration, International Trade Administration, U.S. Department of Commerce, Washington, DC, April 7, 1993.
4. Discussion with Analyst in Countervailing Duty Investigations of the International Trade Administration, U.S. Department of Commerce, Washington, DC, May 27, 1993.
5. Cuba, North Korea, Ethiopia, Libya, or Syria, for example, have never been labeled nonmarket economies or treated as such.
6. For example, Azerbaijan, Armenia, Uzbekistan, and Georgia have all signed Interim Trade Agreements, but have not been reclassified. See Interim Agreements in OJL 129, May 21, 1997; OJL 43, February 14, 1998; and OJL 285, October 22, 1998.
7. Interviews, U.S. International Trade Administration, Department of Commerce, Washington, D, C, February 2001.
8. Jeffrey Sachs and David Lipton, the two primary architects of Poland's "Shock Therapy," reform program detail the nature of the reforms in Lipton and Sachs 1990 and Sachs 1993.
9. Interview with Analyst in Office of Policy, International Trade Administration, Department of Commerce, Washington, DC, Winter 2001, February 23, 2001.
10 See Czestochowa v United States, 890 F. Supp. 1053 (CIT 1995).
11. According to Heritage Foundation's Economic Freedom Scores, 2000. See <www.heritage.org/index/ and www.heritage.org/research/features/index/downloads/Pastscores.xls>, accessed 12/30/04.
12. This issues discussed in (White and Case Law Firm 2000a), and confirmed in personal interview with Analyst in Anti-Dumping Investigations, International Trade Administration, Department of Commerce, Washington, DC, Winter 2001.
13. See Hyundai Electronics Co., Ltd v United States, 55 F. Supp. 2d 1334, 1344 (1999).
14. On a scale of 2–14 of a combined index of economic and political freedoms, with 2 being the most free and 14 being the least free, the countries rank as follows: Lithuania 4.08, Estonia 4.56,

Latvia, 4.89, and Slovakia, 5.75. See Freedom House, *Nations in Transit, Country Reports 2000.* <www.freedomhouse.org/research/nitransit>, accessed April 25, 2001.

15. On a scale of 1–5 with 1 being the most free and 5 being the least economically free, Romania scored 3.3, Indonesia scored 3.5, and Egypt scored 3.5. In terms of economic freedoms, Romania was ranked 94th of 161 and Indonesia and Egypt ranked 110th. The Heritage Foundation, 2000. *The Index of Economic Freedom.* <www.heritage.org/index/>, accessed May 27, 2001. Interviews at International Trade Administration, Department of Commerce, Washington, DC, February 2001.
16. Ibid.
17. This is a bone of contention between the countries. China's attempt to place the topic on the agenda of the September 2005 meeting of Mr. Bush and Mr. Hu was not successful. The Economist, "Special Report: America and China," September 3, 2005, 24–26.
18. For a discussion of the 2005 Orange Revolution in Ukraine, see Karatnychy 2005.
19. Interview with Deputy Head of Unit, DG Trade (then DG I). European Commission: Brussels, Belgium, Fall 1999.
20. To placate Central and Eastern Europe, in 1997 the EU promised to improve and expand the use of price undertakings, or informally negotiated side agreements to anti-dumping cases. This includes informing the countries of impending anti-dumping cases before they reach the press in order to try and resolve issues behind the scenes. (Interview with official in DG Trade [then DG I], European Commission, Brussels. Fall 1999).
21. Interview with Deputy Head of Unit in Directorate General Trade (then DG IA), European Commission: Brussels, Belgium, Fall 1999.
22. See the World Trade Organization's website <http://www.wto.org/english/thewto_e/whatis_e/if_e/org6_e.htm>, accessed December 30, 2004.
23. Interview at Department of Commerce, Washington, DC, February 2001.
24. Interviews at International Trade Administration, Department of Commerce, Washington, DC, February 2001.

Chapter Eight   Integrating Non-Market Economies into the International Trading System

1. The chicken leg quarters are referred to as "Bush's legs," in reference to the first Bush administration's emergency shipments of chicken meat to Russia after the 1991 collapse of the Soviet Union (see Birch 2004).
2. For a similar discussion of the dumping of frozen chicken parts by the United States and European Union on African markets, see Linus Atarah 2005. "Playing Chicken: Ghana vs. the IMF." *Corpwatch.* June 14. <http://www.corpwatch.org/print_article.php?&id=12394>, accessed June 15, 2005.
3. For the definitive work laying out the theory of formal and informal institutional constraints, see Douglass North 1990. *Institutions, Institutional Change and Economic Performance.* Cambridge: Cambridge University Press.
4. See ITA case numbers A-844–801, 823–801, 843–801, 842–801, 821–801, 835–801, 449–801, 451–801, 834–801, 832–801, 822–801, 831–801, and 833–801 for details on the urea cases.
5. Interview with Trade Analyst, U.S. International Trade Administration, Department of Commerce, Washington, DC, February 2001. For examples of countervailing duty cases initiated and terminated against NMEs, see 49 FR 19371 1984 and 56 FR 57616 1991.

BIBLIOGRAPHY

Sources for datasets and regression analyses

Bartelsman, Eric, Randy Becker, and Wayne Gray. 2000. *NBER-CES Manufacturing Industry Database, 1958–1996* Washington, DC: National Bureau of Economic Research, June 2000. <http://www.nber.org/nberces/.> Accessed 10/10/2000.

External and Intra-European Union Trade, Statistical yearbook 1958–1996. 1997. Luxembourg: Office for Official Publications of the European Communities.

Feenstra, Robert. *U.S. Imports and Exports by SIC Category, 1958–1994.* Washington, DC: National Bureau of Economic Research, October 1997. http://www.nber.org/pub/feenstra/

Freedom House. *1997–1998, Annual Survey of Freedom Country Scores.* http://www.freedomhouse.org/ratings/index.htm.

Freedom House. 2001. *Nations in Transit, 2000.* http://www.freedomhouse.org/research/nitransti/2000/table_a.htm.> Accessed 04/25/2001.

Haveman, Jon. *Industry Concordances.* http://www.eiit.org/Trade.Resources/ TradeConcordances. html>. Accessed 12/10/2000.

The Heritage Foundation. 2004. *Heritage Foundation Scores: Economic Freedom.* <http: www. heritage.org/research/features/index/downloads/Pastscores.xls> Accessed 10/06/2005.

The Heritage Foundation with the Wall Street Journal. *2001. Edition Interactive Index of Economic Freedom.* <www.heritage.org/index/>, Accessed 05/27/2001.

International Monetary Fund. 1997. *Balance of Payments Statistics Yearbook.* Country Reports, CD Rom. Washington, DC: International Monetary Fund.

———. 1997. *Direction of Trade Statistics Yearbook.* Washington, DC: International Monetary Fund.

———. 2002. *Annual Report 2001.* http://www.freedomhouse.org/uploads/special_report/10.pdf. Accessed September 2002.

———. 2004. *Annual Report 2003.* http://www.freedomhouse.org/uploads/special_report/20.pdf. Accessed June 2004.

———. 2005. *Annual Report 2004.* http://www.freedomhouse.org/uploads/special_report/23.pdf. Accessed 20/11/2005.

———. 2000. *Direction of Trade Statistics Yearbook.* Washington, DC: International Monetary Fund.

———. 2003. *Direction of Trade Statistics Yearbook.* Washington, DC: International Monetary Fund.

National Bureau of Economic Research. NBER Trade Database, Disk 1, 1958–1994.

National Bureau of Economic Research. U.S. Imports and Exports by 4 digit SIC Industry, 1958–1994. <http://cid.econ.ucdavis.edu/usixd/usixd4sic.html>, Accessed October 2000.

Polity IV Project. 2000. *Policy IV Dataset.* [Computer file; version p4v2000]. College Park, MD: Center for International Development and Conflict Management.

Slater, Courtenay, ed. 1999. *Foreign Trade of the United States: Including State and Metro Area Export Data.* 1999. 1st ed. Washington, DC: Bernan Press.

Transparency International. 2000. *2000 Corruption Perceptions Index.* September 13, 2000. http://www.transparency.org/policy_research/surveys_indices/cpi/previous_cpi__1/2000, Accessed December 2000.

U.S. Census Bureau. 1980–1992. *Annual Survey of Manufactures: Statistics for Industry Groups and Industries.* Washington, DC. 1993–1998. <http://www.census.gov/prod/www/abs/industry.html.>

———. 2000. *Census-Economic Outlook 1997.* <www.census.gov/epcd/ec97sic/E97SUSB>, Accessed 06/29/2000.

———. *Geographic Distance.* <www.indo.com/cgi-bin/dist>, Accessed September 2000.

———. 1992 and 1997. "Mining-Industry Series." *Economic Census.* Washington, DC: Bureau of the Census.

———. 1997. *International DataBase: Total Midyear Population.* <www.census.gov/ipc/www/idbrank.html.>

U.S. Census Bureau. 2000. *Annual Survey of Manufacturers: Statistics for Industry Groups and Industries: 1998 and 1997.* Available on <www.census.gov/prod/www/abs/manu-min.html.>

U.S. Department of Commerce, Bureau of Economic Analysis. 2000. *Gross Domestic Product: Implicit Price Deflator.* <www.stls.frb.org/fred/data/gdp/gdpdef>

———. "Highlights of U.S. Foreign Trade: Top 50 Partners in Total U.S. Trade in Goods, 1988–1994." <http: //www.clark.net/pub/lschank/highlights-trade.txt.> Accessed 11/22/1998.

U.S. Department of Commerce, International Trade Administration. "AD and CVD Investigations Decisions." <http://www.ita.doc.gov/PRFrameset.html> Accessed 12/31/99.

———. *Antidumping and Countervailing Duty Cases Initiated Since January 01, 1980.* <http://www.ia.ita.doc.gov/stats/pet-init.html>

———. Antidumping and Counterfailing Duty Investigations: January 2000 to Current. <http://ita.doc.gov/stats/inv-invitations-2000–2004.html>, Accessed 06/17/2004 and 12/20/2004.

———. *Antidumping and Countervailing Duty Petitions Filed since January 01, 1980.* http://www.ita.doc.gov/import_admin/records/stats/petpub.html. Accessed 11/14/98.

———. 2004. *Antidumping and Countervailing Duty Investigations: January 01, 2000 to current.* <http: // ia.ita.doc.gov/stats/inv-invitations-2000–2004.html.> Accessed 06/17/04, and 12/20/2004.

———. "Economic and Trade Data by Country, 1983–1993," *U.S. Global Trade Outlook, CD-ROM.* Available on <http: //www.clark.net/pub/lschank/trade-data.txt>. Accessed 11/22/1998.

———. *Foreign Trade Highlights: U.S. Trade in Goods, 1972–1999.* www.ita.doc.gov/td/industry/otea/usfth/aggregate/H99t03.txt. Accessed 04/12/2000.

———. *Foreign Trade Highlights in 1999.* <www.ita.doc.gov/td/industry/otea/usfth/aggregate/H99t11.txt>. Accessed 04/12/2000.

———. "Foreign Trade Highlights: Top 50 Suppliers of U.S. Imports in 1999." <http: www.ita.doc.gov/tf/industry/otea/usfth/aggregate/H99t11.txt.> Accessed 04/12/2000.

———. "Import Administration AD and CVD Decisions." 1995–2000. <http://www.ia.ita.doc.gov/frn/frnhome.htm>, Accessed 04/3/2000.

———. "North American Industry Classification Standard (formerly SIC)—1997 NAICS and 1987 SIC Correspondence Tables." <http://www.ita.doc.gov/PRFrameset.html>

U.S. Department of Commerce, International Trade Administration. *U.S. International Trade in Goods and Services Balance of Payments (BOP) Basis.* <http://www.ita.doc.gov/industry/otea/usfth/t01.prn.> Accessed 11/14/1998.

U.S. Department of Commerce. 1985–1999. *STAT-USA. National Trade Data Bank-CD Rom.* Annual Reports.

———. *U.S. Imports for Consumption.* Washington, DC: U.S. Department of Commerce, Bureau of the Census. Annual Reports, 1985–1999.

———, *U.S. Imports: Consumption and General SIC Based Products by World Areas.* Washington, DC: U.S. Department of Commerce, Bureau of the Census. Annual Reports, 1985–1999.

U.S. Department of the Interior, Bureau of Mines. 1987–1997. *Mineral Commodity Summaries.* Washington, DC.

U.S. Department of Labor, Bureau of Labor Statistics. 2000. *Industry Productivity.* 1987–1997 Statistics. Office of Productivity and Technology. <http://stats.bls.gov/news.release/>. Accessed 10/10/2000.

U.S. Government Printing Office. 1980–2000. *Federal Registrar.* 1996–2005. <http://www.access.gpo.gov/su_docs/aces/aces140.html> 1980–1996. <http://web.lexis-nexis.com/universe>

U.S. International Trade Commission. 2000. *Harmonized Tariff Schedule of the United States Annotated.* <http://www.usitc.gov/reports.htm>

Other Sources

1997. "Questions Nos H-0379/97 by Mr. Bertens and H-0380/97 by Mr. Gahrton on EU Policy toward China." *European Foreign Policy Bulletin* 97/317.

1999. "Russia Agrees to Limit Steel Shipments, Avoiding Antidumping Duties by US." *The Wall Street Journal*, February 23, 1.

43 FR 1356. 1978. "Electric Golf Carts from Poland; Antidumping-Preliminary Determination of Sales at Less than Fair Value." *United States Federal Register*, January 9.

46 FR 3258. 1981. "Natural Menthol from the People's Republic of China; Antidumping-Preliminary Determination of Sales at Less than Fair Value and Suspension of Liquidation." *United States Federal Register*, January 14.

49 FR 19371. 1984. "Carbon Steel Wire Rod from Czechoslovakia; Final Negative Countervailing Duty Determination." *United States Federal Register*, May 7.

51 FR 25085. 1986. "Petroleum Wax Candles from the People's Republic of China; Antidumping-Final Determination of Sales at Less than Fair Value and Suspension of Liquidation." *United States Federal Register*, July 10.

53 FR 30385. 1988. "Carbon Black from Mexico." *United States Federal Register*, August 26.

54 FR 11983. 1989. "Final Determination of Sales at Less than Fair Value: Headwear from the People's Republic of China." *United States Federal Register*, March 23.

54 FR 12941. 1989. "Study of the Application of U.S. Trade Laws to Countries Developing Market Oriented Economies; Request for Comments." *United States Federal Register*, March 29.

54 FR 43440. 1990. "Final Affirmative Countervailing Duty Determination: Aluminum Sulfate from Venezuela." *United States Federal Register*, October 25.

56 FR 241. 1991. "Final Determination of Sales at Less than Fair Value: Heavy Forged Handtools from the People's Republic of China." *United States Federal Register*, January 3.

56 FR 19640. 1991. "Final Antidumping Administrative Review: Potassium Permanganate from the People's Republic of China." *United States Federal Register*, April 29.

56 FR 20588. 1991. "Final Determination of Sales at Less than Fair Value: Sparklers from the People's Republic of China." *United States Federal Register*, May 6.

56 FR 46153. 1991. "Final Determination of Sales at Less than Fair Value: Chrome-Plated Lug Nuts from the People's Republic of China." *United States Federal Register*, September 10.

56 FR 55274. 1991. "Final Determination of Sales at Less than Fair Value: Oscillating Fans from the People's Republic of China." *United States Federal Register*, October 25.

56 FR 57616. 1991. "Initiation of Countervailing Duty Investigations: Oscillating Fans and Ceiling Fans from the People's Republic of China." *United States Federal Register,* November 13.

56 FR 60969. 1991. "Final Results of Antidumping Duty Administrative Review: Shop Towels of Cotton from the People's Republic of China." *United States Federal Register*, November 29.

56 FR 66833. 1991. "Preliminary Determination of Sales at Less than Fair Value: Certain Carbon Steel Butt-Weld Pipe Fittings from the People's Republic of China." *United States Federal Register*, December 26.

57 FR 8800 1992. "Preliminary Affirmative Countervailing Duty Determination: Softwood Lumber Products from Canada." *United States Federal Register*, March 12.

57 FR 9409. 1992. "Preliminary Determination of Sales at Less than Fair Value: Sulfanilic Acid from the People's Republic of China." *United States Federal Register*, March 18.

57 FR 15052. 1992. "Amendment to Final Determination of Sales at Less than Fair Value and Amendment to Antidumping Duty Order: Chrome-Plated Lug Nuts from the People's Republic of China." *United States Federal Register*, April 24.

57 FR 24018. 1992. "Final Negative Countervailing Duty Determinations: Oscillating and Ceiling Fans from the People's Republic of China." *United States Federal Register*, June 5.

57 FR 29705. 1992. "Final Determination of Sales at Less than Fair Value: Sulfanilic Acid from the People's Republic of China." *United States Federal Register*, July 6.

57 FR 36070. 1992. "Amendment to Titanium Sponge from the Russian Federation." *United States Federal Register*, August 12.

57 FR 61876. 1992. "Preliminary Determination of Sales at Less than Fair Value: Ferrosilicon from Kazakhstan, the Russian Federation, and Ukraine." *United States Federal Register*, December 29.

58 FR 7539. 1993. "Final Determination of Sales at Less than Fair Value: Sulfur Dyes, Including Sulfur Vat Dyes, from the People's Republic of China." *United States Federal Register*, February 8.

58 FR 29192. 1993. "Final Determination of Sales at Less than Fair Value: Ferrosilicon from Kazakhstan, the Russian Federation, and Ukraine." *United States Federal Register*, May 19.

58 FR 37209. 1993. "Final Determination of Sales at Less than Fair Value: Certain Cut-to-Length Carbon Steel Plate from Romania." *United States Federal Register*, July 9.

58 FR 37315. 1993. "Final Affirmative Countervailing Duty Determinations: Certain Steel Products from Germany." *United States Federal Register*, July 9.

58 FR 44166. 1993. "Antidumping Duty Order and Initiation of Changed Circumstance Antidumping Duty Administrative Review: Certain Cut-to-Length Carbon Steel Plate from Poland." *United States Federal Register*, August 19.

59 FR 22585. 1994. "Notice of Final Determination of Sales at Less than Fair Value: Silicon Carbide from the People's Republic of China." *United States Federal Register* May 2.

59 FR 28053. 1994. "Notice of Final Determination of Sales at Less than Fair Value: Sebacic Acid from the People's Republic of China." *United States Federal Register*, May 31.

59 FR 55625. 1994. "Notice of Final Determination of Sales at Less than Fair Value: Certain Cases Pencils from the Peoples Republic of China." *United States Federal Register*, November 8.

60 FR 16433. 1995. "Notice of Final Determination of Sales at Less than Fair Value: Pure Magnesium from the Ukraine." *United States Federal Register*, March 30.

60 FR 22359. 1995. "Notice of Final Determination of Sales at Less than Fair Value: Disposable Pocket Lighters from the People's Republic of China." *United States Federal Register*, May 5.

60 FR 54472. 1995. "Notice of Final Determination of Sales at Less than Fair Value: Certain Partial-Extension Steel Drawer Slides with Rollers from the People's Republic of China." *United States Federal Register*, October 24.

61 FR 192. 1996. "Tapered Roller Bearings from Romania: Final Results and Rescission in Part of Antidumping Duty Administrative Review." *United States Federal Register*, October 2.

61 FR 15770. 1996. "Initiation of Antidumping Duty Investigation: Beryllium Metal and High Beryllium Alloys from Kazakhstan." *United States Federal Register*, April 9.

61 FR 27049. 1996. "Solid Urea from the Former German Democratic Republic; Initiation of Changed Circumstances Antidumping Review." *United States Federal Register*, May 30.

61 FR 29543. 1996. "Electric Golf Carts from Poland; Amended final Results of Antidumping Duty Administrative Review." *United States Federal Register*, June 11.

61 FR 44212. 1996. "Notice of Preliminary Determination of Sales at Less than Fair Value and Postponement of Final Determination: Beryllium Metal and High Beryllium Alloys from Kazakhstan." *United States* Federal Register, August 28.

61 FR 58514. 1996. "Chrome Plated Lug Nuts from the People's Republic of China: Final Results of Administrative Review." *United States Federal Register*, November 15.

62 FR 4250. 1997. "Porcelain-on-Steel Cooking Ware from the People's Republic of China: Preliminary Results of Antidumping Duty Administrative Review." *United States Federal Register*, January 29.

62 FR 6189. 1997. "Tapered Roller Bearings and Parts Thereof, Finished and Unfinished, from the People's Republic of China: Final Results of Antidumping Duty Administrative Review and Revocation in Part of Antidumping Duty Order." *United States Federal Register*, February 11.

62 FR 31075. 1997. "Tapered Roller Bearings and Parts Thereof, Finished and Unfinished, from Romania: Final Results of Antidumping Duty Administrative Review." *United States Federal Register*, June 6.

62 FR 41355. 1997. "Notice of Final Determination of Sales at Less than Fair Value: Freshwater Crawfish Tail Meat from the People's Republic of China." *United States Federal Register*, August 1.

62 FR 61754. 1997. "Notice of Final Determination of Sales at Less Than Fair Value: Certain Cut-to-Length Steel Plate from Ukraine." *United States Federal Register*, November 19.

62 FR 61766. 1997. "Suspension of Antidumping Duty Investigation: Certain Cut-to-Length Carbon Steel Plate from Ukraine." *United States Federal Register*, November 19.

63 FR 13031. 1998. "Ferrovanadium and Nitrided Vanadium from the Russian Federation: Termination of Antidumping Dutys Administrative Review." *United States Federal Register*, March 17.

63 FR 47474. 1998. "Titanium Sponge from the Russian Federation: Preliminary Results of Antidumping Administrative Review and Partial Revocation." *United States Federal Register*, September 8.

63 FR 72255. 1998. "Notice of Final Determination of Sales at Less than Fair Value: Certain Preserved Mushrooms from the People's Republic of China." *United States Federal Register*, December 31.

64 FR 213. 1999. "Final Results of Expedited Sunset Review: Tapered Roller Bearings from Hungary." *United States Federal Register*, November 4.

64 FR 38626 1999. "Notice of Final Determination of Sales at Less than Fair Value: Hot-Rolled Flat-Rolled Carbon-Quality Steel Products from the Russian Federation." *United States Federal Register*, July 19.

65 FR 1110. 2000. "Notice of Preliminary Determination of Sales at Less than Fair Value and Postponement of Final Determination; Certain Cold-Rolled Flat-Rolled Carbon Quality Steel Products from Slovakia." *United States Federal Register*, January 7.

65 FR 1117. 2000. "Preliminary Determination of Sales at Less than Fair Value and Postponement of Final Determination; Certain Cold-Rolled Flat-Rolled Carbon Quality Steel Products from the People's Republic of China." *United States Federal Register,* January 7.

65 FR 1139. 2000. "Notice of Preliminary Determination of Sales at Less than Fair Value: Solid Fertilizer Grade Ammonium Nitrate from the Russian Federation." *United States Federal Register,* January 7.

65 FR 5594. 2000. "Notice of Preliminary Determination of Sales at Less Than Fair Value and Postponement of Final Determination: Certain Small Diameter Carbon and Alloy Seamless Standard, Line and Pressure Pipe from Romania." *United States Federal Register,* February 4.

65 FR 5599. 2000. "Notice of Preliminary Determination of Sales at Less than Fair Value and Postponement of Final Determination; Certain Small Diameter Carbon and Alloy Seamless Standard, Line, and Pressure Pipe from the Czech Republic." *United States Federal Register,* February 4.

65 FR 18054. 2000. "Cut-to-Length Carbon Steel Plate from Finland, Poland, and Sweden: Final Results of Expedited Sunset Reviews." *United States Federal Register,* April 6.

66 FR 18752, 2001. "Notice of Final Determinations of Sales at Less than Fair Value: Steel Concrete Reinforcing Bars from Indonesia, Poland, and Ukraine." *United States Federal Register,* April 11.

66 FR 33525. 2001. "Notice of Final Determination of Sales at Less than Fair Value: Steel Concrete Reinforcing Bars from Moldova." *United States Federal Register,* June 22.

66 FR 33528, 2001. "Notice of Final Determinations of Sales at Less than Fair Value: Steel Concrete Reinforcing Bars from Belarus." *United States Federal Register,* June 22.

66 FR 33530. 2001. "Notice of Final Determination of Sales at Less than Fair Value: Steel Concrete Reinforcing Bars from Latvia." *United States Federal Register,* June 22.

66 FR 42628. 2001. "Persulfates from the People's Republic of China: Final Results of Antidumping Administrative Review." *United States Federal Register,* August 14.

66 FR 49347. 2001. "Issues and Decision Memorandum for the Antidumping Duty Investigation of Pure Magnesium from the Russian Federation." *United States Federal Register,* September 27.

66 FR 50397. 2001."Isues and Decision Memorandum for the Less than Fair Value Investigation of Hot-Rolled Carbon Steel Flat Products from Kazakhstan." *United States Federal Register,* October 3.

67 FR 15535 2002. "Notice of Final Determination of Sales at Less Than Fair Value: Silicomanganese from Kazakhstan." *United States Federal Register,* April 2.

67 FR 35490. 2002. "Notice of Final Determination of Sales at Less Than Fair Value: Structural Steel Beams from the Russian Federation." *United States Federal Register,* May 20.

67 FR 55790. 2002. "Notice of Final Determination of Sales at Less Than Fair Value: Carbon and Certain Alloy Steel Wire Rod from Moldova." *United States Federal Register,* August 30.

68 FR 6885 2003. "Notice of Final Determination of Sales at Less Than Fair Value: Silicon Metal from the Russian Federation." *United States Federal Register,* February 11.

68 FR 9977 2003. "Notice of Final Determination of Sales at Less Than Fair Value: Urea Ammonium Nitrate Solutions from the Russian Federation." *United States Federal Register,* March 3.

68 12672 2003. "Certain Small Diameter Carbon and Alloy Seamless Standard, Line, and Pressure Pipe from Romania: Final Results of Antidumping Duty Administrative Review." *United States Federal Register,* March 17.

68 FR 35626. 2003. "Certain Cut-to-Length Carbon Steel Plate from Ukraine: Final Results of Administrative Review of the Suspension Agreement and Determination Not to Terminate." *United States Federal Register,* June 16.

68 FR 54418. 2003. "Certain Small Diameter Carbon and Alloy Seamless Standard, Line, and Pressure Pipe from Romania: Final Results of Antidumping Duty Administrative Review." *United States Federal Register*, September 17.

68 FR 55589. 2003. "Notice of Final Determination of Sales at Less Than Fair Value: Refined Brown Aluminum Oxide (Otherwise Know as Refined Brown Artificial Corundum or Brown Fused Alumina) from the People's Republic of China." *United States Federal Register*, September 26.

68 FR 71067. 2003. "Notice of Final Results of Antidumping Duty Administrative Review: Steel Concrete Reinforcing Bars from Latvia." *United States Federal Register*, December 22.

69 FR 20594. 2004. "Notice of Final Determination of Sales at Less than Fair Value and Negative Final Determination of Critical Circumstances: Certain Color Television Receivers from the People's Republic of China." *United States Federal Register*, April 16.

69 FR 60980. 2004. "Notice of Final Determination of Sales at Less than Fair Value: Hand Trucks and Certain Parts Thereof from the People's Republic of China." *United States Federal Register*, October 14.

69 FR 67313. 2004. "Final Determination of Sales at Less than Fair Value: Wooden Bedroom Furniture from the People's Republic of China." *United States Federal Register*, November 17.

69 FR 77722. 2004. "Separate Rates Practices in Antidumping Proceedings Involving Non-Market Economy Countries." *United States Federal Register*, December 28.

AFX News Limited. 2005. "Ukraine President Yuschenko Appeals for U.S. Congress for Economic Aid." *AFX News Limited, AFX.COM*. April 7.

Agence Europe. 1995a. "Commission Contests Existence of Trade Discrimination against Russian Products—Sharp Rise in Exports and Very Favourable Trade Balance for Russia." *Europe Daily Bulletins* 6559.

———. 1995b. "While Introducing Definitive Anti-Dumping Duty on Russian Ammonium Nitrate, the Council Reiterates Its Will to Encourage the Development of Trade with Russia." *Europe Daily Bulletins* 6552.

———. 1996a. "FTA Criticizes Anti-Dumping Proceedings on Handbags and Satchels Originating in China." *Europe Daily Bulletins* 6748.

———. 1996b. "Chinese Exporters Are Not Sufficiently Independent of the State to be Entitled to Demand Individual Treatment in Anti-Dumping Cases." *Europe Daily Bulletins* 6814.

———. 1997a. "Ambassador Song Calls on EU to End Its 'Unjustified' Anti-Dumping Policy Regarding China by Granting It the Status of Market Economy Country." *Europe Daily Bulletins* 7107.

———. 1997b. "Association Council Session Enables Observing Polish Progress in Preparation for Membership and Ironing Out Several Technical Difficulties." *Europe Daily Bulletins* 6967.

———. 1997c. "At Anti-Dumping Seminar, Sir Leon Brittan Announces a New, More Flexible System for Price Undertakings." *Europe Daily Bulletins* 6902.

———. 1997d. "Differences between Member States over Definitive Duties on Imports of Steel Pipes and Tubes—Criticism from Russian Producers, Commission Reaction." *Europe Daily Bulletin* 7063.

———. 1997e. "European Commission Sponsors a High Level Seminar on Anti-Dumping Policy." *Europe Daily Bulletins* 6899.

———. 1997f. "Trade Unions against Any Review of Anti-Dumping Measures on Potash from Russia, Ukraine and Belarus." *Europe Daily Bulletins* 7008.

———. 1998. "Council Refuses to Impose Definitive Anti-Dumping Duties on Steel Bars from India." *Europe Daily Bulletins* 7351.

———. 1999a. "Commission Should Close Proceedings on Import of CD Players for Car Radios Without Imposing Duties." *Europe Daily Bulletins* 7383.

Agence Europe. 1999b. "Council Rejects Definitive Duties on Electrolytic Aluminum Capacitators Originating in the United States and Thailand." *Europe Daily Bulletins* 7422.

Agence France Presse. 2004. "China Says EU Refusal to Give Market Economy Status Unreasonable." *Agence France Presse-English in Lexis-Nexis*, June 29. <http://web.lexis-nexis.com/universe/document?_m = 6a9cc04dbb4315.> Accessed 07/10/2004.

———. 2005. "EU Chief Barosso Says China Not Ready for Market Economy Status." *Agence France Presse-English*, July 14.

Alden, Edward. 2003. "Russian Agreement Eases U.S. Trade Spat." *The Financial Times*, September 30, 13.

Anderson, Keith. 1993. "Agency Discretion or Statutory Direction: Decision Making at the U.S. International Trade Commission." *Journal of Law and Economics* 36:915–935.

Aris, Ben. 2001. "EBRD and Severstal Slam West's Steel Suits." *The Moscow Times*. April 24. <http://web.lexis-nexis.com/univers.> Accessed 05/06/01.

Asianinfo Daily China News. 2001. "Memo of China's Anti-Dumping Cases in 2000." *Financial Times Information*, January 18.

Asia Pulse. 2003. "India Gives Russia Market Economy Status." *Asia Pulse Pte Limited in Lexis-Nexis*, November 12.

———. 2004. "China Firmly Pushing forward to Full Market Economy." *Asian Pulse Pte Limite in Lexis-Nexis*, July 2.

Atarah, Linus. 2005. "Playing Chicken: Ghana vs. the IMF." *Corpwatch*, June 14. <http://www.corpwatch.org/print_article.php?&id = 12394, Accessed 06/15/2005.

Axelrod, Robert. 1984. *The Evolution of Cooperation*. New York: Basics Books.

Axelrod, Robert, and Robert Keohane. 1986. "Achieving Cooperation under Anarchy: Strategies and Institutions." in *Cooperation under Anarchy*, ed. Kenneth Oye. Princeton: Princeton University Press, 226–254.

Bael, Ivo Van, and Jean-Francois Bellis. 1990. *Anti-Dumping and Other Trade Protection Laws of the EEC*. Oxfordshire, UK: CCh Editions Limited.

Bailey, Michael, Judith Goldstein, and Barry Weingast. 1997. "The Institutional Roots of American Trade Policy: Politics, Coalitions, and International Trade." *World Politics* 49:309–398.

Baldwin, David. 1985a. *Economic Statecraft*. Princeton: Princeton University Press.

Baldwin, Robert. 1985b. *The Political Economy of U.S. Import Policy*. Cambridge, MA: MIT Press.

Baldwin, Robert, and Christopher Magee. 2000. *Congressional Trade Votes: From NAFTA Approval to Fast-Track Defeat*. Washington, DC: Institute for International Economics.

Baltic Times. 1999a. "Anti-Dumping Law Reviewed." *Financial Times Information*, September 2.

———. 1999b. "Truth, Lies and the Farmer." *Financial Times Information*, September 2.

Banks, Gary. 1993. "The Antidumping Experience of a GATT Fearing Country." in *Antidumping: How It Works and Who Gets Hurt*, ed. J. Michael Finger. Ann Arbor: University of Michigan Press, 183–201.

Barner-Barry, Carol. 1990. "Political Psychology in the 1980s and the Cognitive Perspective." in *Annual Review of Political Science*, ed. Samuel Long. Norwood, NJ: Ablex Publishing Corporation, 198–220.

Bates, Robert. 1998. "The International Coffee Organization: An International Institution." in *Analytic Narratives*, ed. Robert Bates, Avner Greif, Margaret Levi, Jean-Laurent Rosenthal, and Barry Weingast. Princeton: Princeton University Press, 194–230.

BBC Worldwide Monitoring. 2004. "Ukraine President Slates EU over Market Access." April 28.

Beattie, Alan. 2005. "Mandelson Says China Not Ready for EU's Market Economy Status." *The Financial Times (London Edition)*. July 7, 9.

Bellaby, Mara. 2005. "EU to Give Ukraine Market Economy Status." *Associated Press Financial Wire*, December 1.

Bezlova, Antoaneta. 2004. "Trade: China Wants International Market Economy Status." *IPS-Inter Press Service/Global Information Network*, June 13.

Bhagwati, Jagdish. 1988. *Protectionism*. Cambridge, MA: MIT Press.

Birch, Douglas. 2004. "A New Cold War over Chickenn." *The Seattle Times*, Feburary 11, A 15.

Boltuck, Richard, and Robert Litan (Eds.). 1991. *Down in the Dumps: Administration of the Unfair Laws*. Washington, DC: Brookings Institution.

Brenton, Paul, and Francesca Di Mauro. 1998. "Sensitive Industrial Products between the CEECs and the EU." *World Economy* 21:285–304.

British Broadcasting Corporation. 2004. "Ukraine Wants Stronger Ties with EU, President Says at Summit." *BBC Worldwide Monitoring*, July 8.

Brittan, Sir Leon. 1997a. "Europe, Russia, and the World Trading System." *Directorate General for Trade, Speeches and Articles*, June 17. <htto://europa.eu.int/comm/dg01/sps1b12.html>, Accessed 12/2/1999.

———. 1997b. "Speech at CEEC Anti-Dumping Seminar." *Directorate General for Trade, Speeches and Articles*, January 27. <http://europa.eu.int/comm/dg01/sp270197.html>, Accessed 12/2/ 1999.

Brock, William, and Stephen Magee. 1978. "The Economics of Special Interest Politics: The Case of the Tariff." *American Economic Review* 68:246–250.

Brown, J.F. 1988. *Eastern Europe and Communist Rule*. Durham: Duke University Press.

———. 1991. *Surge to Freedom: The End of Communist Rule in Eastern Europe*. Durham: Duke University Press.

Brown, Stuart. 1989. "Export Uncertainty in Centrally Planned Economies and Administered Protection." *Journal of Comparative Economics* 13:553–565.

Brown, Stuart, and Deborah Haas-Wilson. 1990. "Centrally Planned Economy Vulnerability to Antidumping Protection." *Comparative Economic Studies* 32(4):1–27.

Buckley, Neil. 1998. "Cotton Dumping Dispute May Reignite: European Commission Accused of 'Horse-Trading' in Attempt to Win Backing for Action against Asian Countries." *The Financial Times*.

Bush, President George. 1990. "U.S. Assistance to the Soviet Union, Statement at a White House News Conference, Washington DC December 12, 1990." *U.S. Department of State Dispatch* 1(16):331.

Carey, Sarah, Richard Cunningham, and Michael Abbey. 1993. "Transitional Relief for Russia Under the U.S. Trade Laws: New Policies for Assisting Russia's Entry into U.S. and Global Markets." Washington, DC: Steptoe & Johnson, L.L.P.

Caves, Richard, Jeffrey Frankel, and Ronald Jones. 1990. *World Trade and Payments: An Introduction*. Glenview, IL: Scott, Foresman/Little, Brown Higher Education.

Cheh, John. 1976. "A Note on Tariffs, Nontariff Barriers and Labor Protection in United States Manufacturing Industries." *Journal of Political Economy* 84:389–394.

Cheng, Allen. 2004a. "Economic Progress Not Enough for EU; Market-Economy Status Denied Due to Shortcomings." *South China Morning Post*, June 29, 8.

———. 2004b. "U.S. Will Not Support Market Status-Bid," *South China Morning Post*, June 24, 7.

Chernomyrdin. 1997. "Chernomyrdin Criticizes U.S. Trade Policies: Business Speech before U.S. Executives." *ITAR-TASS*, June 24.

China Daily. 1999. "China: Undue Anti-Dumping Measures Harm Trade." *Financial Times Information*, December 21.

Clark, Don. 1980. "The Protection of Unskilled Labor in the United States Manufacturing Industries: Further Evidence." *Journal of Political Economy* 88:1249–1254.

Clark, Torrey. 2002a. "EU Grants Russia Market Status." *The Moscow Times*, November 11.

———. 2002b. "Market Status Not All It's Cracked Up to Be." *The Moscow Times*, August 23.

Clinton, President William. 1995. "The U.S. and Central and Eastern Europe: Forging New Partnerships: Remarks to Plenary Session of the White House Conference on Trade and

Investment in Central and Eastern Europe, Cleveland, Ohio, January 13, 1995." *U.S. Department of State Dispatch* 6(3):27–31.

Coleman, James. 1988. "Social Capital in the Creation of Human Capital." *American Journal of Sociology* 94:95–120.

COM Reg. No. 550/93. 1993. "Commission Regulation (EEC) no 550/93 of 5 March 1993 Imposing a Provisional Anti-Dumping Duty on Imports of Bicycles Originating in the People' s Republic of China." *Official Journal L* 58.

———. 2376/94. 1994. "Commission Regulation (EC) no 2376/94 of 27 September 1994 Imposing a Provisional Anti-Dumping Duty on Imports of Colour Television Receivers Originating in Malaysia, the People' s Republic of China, the Republic of Korea, Singapore and Thailand." *Official Journal L* 255.

———. 1645/95. 1995. "Commission Regulation (EC) no 1645/95 of 5 July 1995 Imposing a Provisional Anti-Dumping Duty on Imports of Microwave Ovens Originating in the People's Republic of China, the Republic of Korea, Thailand and Malaysia." *Official Journal L* 156.

———. 1984/95. 1995. "Commission Regulation (EC) no 1984/95 of 10 August 1995 Imposing a Provisional Anti-Dumping Duty on Imports of Powdered Activated Carbon Originating in the People's Republic of China." *Official Journal L* 192.

———. 2997/95. 1995. "Commission Regulation (EC) No. 2997/95 of 20 December 1995 Imposing a Provisional Anti-Dumping Duty on Imports of Unwrought Magnesium Originating in Russia and Ukraine." *Official Journal L* 312.

———. 394/1996. 1996. "Commission Regulation (EC) No. 394/96 of 4 March 1996 Imposing a Provisional Anti-Dumping Duty on Imports of Polyester Staple Fibre Originating in Belarus." *Official Journal L* 54.

———. 1465/96. 1996. "Commission Regulation (EC) No. 1465/96 of 25 July 1996 Imposing a Provisional Anti-Dumping Duty on Imports of Certain Ring Binder Mechanisms Originating in Malaysia and the People's Republic of China." *Official Journal L* 187.

———. 2208/96. 1996. "Commission Regulation (EC) No. 2208/96 of 18 November 1996 Imposing a Provisional Anti-Dumping Duty on Imports of Unbleached (Grey) Cotton Fabrics Originating in the People's Republic of China, Egypt, India, Indonesia, Pakistan and Turkey." *Official Journal L* 295.

———. 165/97. 1997. "Commission Regulation (EC) No. 165/97 of 28 January 1997 Imposing a Provisional Anti-Dumping Duty on Imports of Certain Footwear with Textile Uppers Originating in the People's Republic of China and Indonesia." *Official Journal L* 20.

———. 593/97. 1997. "Commission Regulation (EC) No. 593/97 of 25 March 1997 Imposing a Provisional Anti-Dumping Duty on Imports of Unwrought, Unalloyed Zinc Originating in Poland and Russia." *Official Journal L* 89.

———. 981/1997. 1997. "Commission Regulation (EC) No. 981/1997 Imposing Provisional Anti-Dumping Duties on Imports of Certain Seamless Pipes and Tubes of Iron or Non-Alloy Steel Originating in Russia, the Czech Republic, Romania, and the Slovak Republic." *Official Journal L* 141.

——— 1778/97. 1997. "Commission Regulation (EC) No. 1778/97 of 12 September 1997 Imposing a Provisional Anti-Dumping Duty on Imports of Ferro-Silico-Manganese Originating in the People's Republic of China." *Official Journal L* 252.

———. 773/98. 1998. "Commission Regulation (EC) No. 773/98 of 7 April 1998 Imposing a Provisional Anti-Dumping Duty on Imports of Certain Unbleached Cotton Fabrics Originating in the People's Republic of China, Egypt, India, Indonesia, Pakistan, and Turkey." *Official Journal L* 111.

COM Reg. No. 1002/98. 1998. "Commission Regulation (EC) No. 1002/98 of 13 May 1998 Imposing a Provisional Anti-Dumping Duty on Imports of Unwrought Unalloyed Magnesium Originating in the People's Republic of China." *Official Journal L* 142.

———. 362/1999. 1999. "Commission Regulation (EC) No. 362/1999 of 18 February 1999 Imposing a Provisional Anti-Dumping Duty on Imports of Steel Ropes and Cables Originating in the People's Republic of China, India, Mexico, South Africa and the Ukraine and Accepting Undertakings Offered by Certain Exporters in Hungary and Poland." *Official Journal L* 45.

———. 2536/1999. 1999. "Commission Regulation (EC) No. 2536/1999 of 3 December 1999 Imposing a Provisional Anti-Dumping Duty on Imports of Compact Disk Boxes Originating in the People's Republic of China." *Official Journal L* 310.

———. 255/2000. 2000. "Commission Regulation (EC) No. 255/2000 of 7 February 2000 Imposing a Provisional Anti-Dumping Duty on Imports of Integrated Electronic Compact Fluorescent Lamps Originating in the People's Republic of China." *Official Journal L* 38.

———. 617/2000. 2000. "Commission Regulation (EC) No. 671/2001 of 17 March 2000 Imposing Provisional Anti-Dumping Duties on Imports of Solutions Of Urea and Ammonium Nitrate Originating in Algeria, Belarus, Lithuania, Russia and Ukraine and Accepting, on a Provisional Basis, an Undertaking Offered by an Exporting Producer in Algeria." *Official Journal L.* 75, 24/03/2000, 0003–0017.

———. 837/2000. 2000. "Commission Regulation (EC) No. 837/2000 of 19 April 2000 Imposing a Provisional Anti-Dumping Duty on Imports of Certain Cathode Ray Colour Television Picture Tubes Originating in India, Malaysia, the People's Republic of China and the Republic of Korea." *Official Journal L* 102.

———. 967/2000. 2000. "Commission Regulation (EC) No. 967/2000 Imposing a Provisional Anti-Dumping Duty on Imports of Hairbrushes Originating in the People's Republic of China, the Republic of Korea, Taiwan, and Thailand, and Terminating the Proceedings Concerning Imports of Hairbrushes Originating in Hong Kong." *Official Journal L* 111.

———. 1043/2000. 2000. "Commission Regulation (EC) No. 1043/2000 of 10 May 2000 Imposing a Provisional Anti-Dumping Duty on Imports of Glycine Originating in the People's Republic of China." *Official Journal L* 118.

———. 230/2001. 2001. "Commission Regulation (EC) no 230/2001 of 2 February 2001 Imposing a Provisional Anti-Dumping Duty on Certain Iron or Steel Ropes and Cables Originating in the Czech Republic, Russia, Thailand, and Turkey and Accepting Undertakings Offered by Certain Exporters in the Czech Republic and Turkey." *Official Journal L* 34.

———. 255/2001. 2001. "Commission Regulation (EC) No. 255/2001 of 7 February imposing a Provisional Anti-Dumping Duty on Imports of Integrated Electronic Compact Fluorescent Lamps (CFL-i) Originating in the People's Republic of China." *Official Journal L* 38, 08/02/2001, 0008–0021.

———. 1827/2001. 2001. "Commission Regulation (EC) No. 1827/2001 of 17 September 2001 Imposing a Provisional Anti-Dumping Duty on Imports of Certain Zinc Oxides Originating in the People's Republic of China." *Official Journal L* 248, 18/09/2001, 0017–0038.

———. 215/2002. 2002. "Commission Regulation (EC) No. 215/2002 of 28 January 2002 Imposing Definitive Anti-Dumping Duties on Imports of Ferromolybdenum Originating in the People's Republic of China." *Official Journal L* 035, 06/02/2002, 0001–0008.

———. 575/2002. 2002. "Commission Regulation (EC) No. 575/2002 of 3 March 2002 Imposing a Provisional Anti-Dumping Duty on Imports of Sulphanilic Acid Originating in the People's Republic of China and in India." *Official Journal L* 087, 04/04/2002, 0028–0044.

———. 658/2002. 2002. "Commission Regulation (EC) No. 658/2002 of 15 April 2002 Imposing a Definitive Anti-Dumping Duty on Imports of Ammonium Nitrate Originating in Russia." *Official Journal L* 102, 18/04/2002, 0001–0011.

————. No. 1799/2002. 2002. "Commission Regulation (EC) No. 1799/2002 of 8 October 2002 Imposing a Definitive Anti-Dumping Duty on Imports of Polyester Staple Fibers Originating in Belarus." *Official Journal L* 274, 11/10/2002, 0001–0016.

————. 151/2003. 2003. "Commission Regulation (EC) No. 151/2003 of 27 January 2003 Imposing a Definitive Anti-Dumping Duty on Imports of Certain Grain Oriented Electrical Sheets Originating in Russia." *Official Journal L* 025, 30/01/2003, 0007–0020.

————. 1235/2003. 2003. "Commission Regulation (EC) No. 1235/2003 of 10 July 2003 Imposing a Provisional Anti-Dumping Duty on Imports of Silicon Originating in Russia." *Official Journal L* 173, 11/07/2003, 0014–0034.

————. 1627/2003. 2003. "Commission Regulation (EC) No. 1627/2003 of 17 September 2003 Imposing a Provisional Anti-Dumping Duty on Imports of Sodium Cyclamate Originating in the People's Republic of China and Indonesia." *Official Journal L* 232, 18/09/2003, 0012–0028.

————. 988/2004. 2004. "Commission Regulations (EC) No. 988/2004 of 17 May 2004 Imposing Provisional Anti-Dumping Duties on Imports of Okoumé Plywood Originating in the People's Republic of China." *Official Journal L* 181, 17/05/04, 5–23.

————. 145/2005. 2005. "Commission Regulation (EC) no. 145/2005 of 28 January 2005 Imposing a Provisional Anti-Dumping Duty on Imports of Barium Carbonate Originating in the People's Republic of Chin." *Official Journal L* 27, 28/01/05, 4–21.

————. 426/2005. 2005. "Commission Regulation (EC) No. 426/2005 of 15 March 2005 on Imposing a Provisional Anti-Dumping Duty on Imports of Certain Finished Polyester Filament Apparel Fabrics Originating in the People's Republic of China." *Official Journal L* 69, 15/03/05, 6–28.

————. 552/2005. 2005. "Commission Regulation (EC) No. 552/2005 of 11 April 2005 Imposing a Provisional Anti-Dumping Duty on Imports of Certain Magnesia Bricks Originating in the People's Republic of China." *Official Journal L* 93, 11/04/05, 6–19.

————. 862/2005. 2005. "Commission Regulation (EC) No. 862/2005 of 7 June 2005 Imposing Provisional Anti-Dumping Duties on Imports of Granular Ploytetrafluoroethylene (PTFE) Originating in Russia and the People's Republic of China." *Official Journal L* 144, 08/06/05, 0011–0037.

Commission Decision 85/143/EEC. 1985. "Commission Decision of 18 February 1985 Terminating the Anti-Dumping Proceeding Concerning Imports of Certain Boots with Fitted Ice Skates Originating in Czechoslovakia, Yugoslavia, Romania and Hungary." *Official Journal L* 52.

———— 522/92/ECSC. 1992. "Commission Decision no 522/92/ECSC of 28 February 1992 on Certain Modalities for the Application of the Interim Agreement on Trade and Trade Related Matters between the European Economic Community and the European Coal and Steel Community of the One Part and the Republic of Poland of the Other Part." *Official Journal L* 56.

———— 523/92/ECSC. 1992. "Commission Decision no 523/92/ECSC of 28 February 1992 on Certain Modalities for the Application of the Interim Agreement on Trade and Trade Related Matters between the European Economic Community and the European Coal and Steel Community of the One Part and the Republic of Hungary of the Other Part." *Official Journal L* 56.

———— 524/92/ECSC. 1992. "Commission Decision no 524/92/ECSC of 28 February 1992 on Certain Modalities for the Application of the Interim Agreement on Trade and Trade Related Matters between the European Economic Community and the European Coal and Steel Community of the One Part and the Czech and Slovak Federal Republic of the Other Part." *Official Journal L* 56.

———— 93/377/EEC. 1993. "93/377/EEC: Commission Decision of 22 June 1993 Terminating the Proceeding to Review Anti-Dumping Measures Applicable to Certain Imports of

Gas-Fuelled, Non-Refillable Pocket Flint Lighters Originating in the People's Republic of China." *Official Journal L* 158.

———— 1238/2000/ECSC. 2000. "Commission Decision 1238/2000/ECSC of 14 June 2000 Imposing a Provisional Anti-Dumping Duty on Imports of Coke or Coal in Pieces with a Diameter of More than 80 mm Originating in the People's Republic of China." *Official Journal L* 141.

———— 1758/2000/ECSC. 2000. "Commission Decision 1758/2000/ECSC of 9 August 2000 Imposing a Definitive Anti-Dumping Duty on Imports of Certain Hot Rolled Flat Products of Non-Alloy Steel Originating in the People's Republic of China, India, and Romania, Accepting an Undertaking with Regards, to India and Romania and Collecting Definitively the Provisional Duties Imposed." *Official Journal L* 202.

———— 2730/2000/ECSC. 2000. "Commission Decision 2730/2000/ECSC of 14 December 2000 Imposing A Definitive Anti-Dumping Duty on Imports of Coke or Coal in Pieces with a Diameter of More than 80 mm Originating in the People's Republic of China and Definitively Collecting the Provisional Duty Imposed." *Official Journal L* 316.

Comtex News Network. 2005. "Iceland Becomes 1st European Country to Open Free Trade Talks with China." *Comtex News Network in LexisNexis*, May 18.

Converse, Philip. 1964. "The Nature of Belief Systems in Mass Publics." in *Ideology and Discontent*, ed. David Apter. New York: Free Press, 206–261.

Cooper, Richard. 1973. "Trade Policy Is Foreign Policy." *Foreign Policy* 9:18–36.

————. 1987. "Trade Policy as Foreign Policy." in *U.S. Trade Policies in a Changing World Economy*, ed. Robert Stern. Cambridge, MA: MIT Press, 291–322.

Cornell, David Da Silva. 1994. "Maybe You Can Take It with You, after All: Subsidies and Privatization under U.S. Countervailing Duty Laws." *Law and Policy in International Business* 25:1309–1334.

Council of the European Union. 2004. "265th Council Meeting: Competitiveness (Internal Market, Industry, and Research." *Press Release*, 12487/04 (Presse 269). Brussels: Belgium, September 24.

Council Reg. No. 288/82. 1982. "Council Regulation (EEC) No. 288/82 of 5 February 1982 on Common Rules for Imports." *Official Journal L* 35.

————. 1765/82. 1982. "Council Regulation (EEC) No. 1765/82 of 30 June 1982 on Common Rules for Imports from State-Trading Countries." *Official Journal L* 195.

————. 1766/82. 1982. "Council Regulation (EEC) No. 1766/82 of 30 June 1982 on Common Rules for Imports from the People's Republic of China." *Official Journal L* 195.

————. 2684/90. 1990. "Council Regulation (EEC) No. 2684/90 of 17 September 1990 on Interim Measures Applicable after the Unification of Germany, in Anticipation of the Adoption of Transitional Measures by the Council Either in Cooperation with, or after Consultation of, the European Parliament." *Official Journal L* 263.

————. 2093/91. 1991. "Council Regulation (EEC) No. 2093/91 of 15 July 1991 Imposing a Definitive Anti-Dumping Duty on Imports of Small-Screen Colour Television Receivers Originating in Hong Kong and the People's Republic of China and Collecting Definitively the Provisional Duty." *Official Journal L* 195.

————. 517/92. 1992. "Council Regulation (EC) No. 517/92 of 27 February 1992 Amending the Autonomous Import Arrangements for Products Originating in Hungary, Poland and the Czech and Slovak Federal Republic (CSFR)." *Official Journal L* 56.

————. 518/92. 1992. "Council Regulation (EEC) No. 518/92 of 27 February 1992 on Certain Procedures for Applying the Interim Agreement on Trade and Trade-Related Matters between the European Economic Community and the European Coal and Steel Community, of the One Part, and the Republic of Poland, of the Other Part." *Official Journal L* 56.

———. No. 519/92. 1992. "Council Regulation (EEC) No. 519/92 of 27 February 1992 on Certain Procedures for Applying the Interim Agreement on Trade and Trade-Related Matters between the European Economic Community and the European Coal and Steel Community, of the One Part, and the Republic of Hungary, of the Other Part." *Official Journal L* 56.

———. 520/92. 1992. "Council Regulation (EEC) No. 520/92 of 27 February 1992 on Certain Procedures for Applying the Interim Agreement on Trade and Trade-Related Matters between the European Economic Community and the European Coal and Steel Community, of the One Part, and the Czech and Slovak Federal, of the Other Part." *Official Journal L* 56.

———. 3491/93. 1993. "Council Regulation (EC) No. 3491/93 of 13 December 1993 on Certain Procedures for Applying the Europe Agreement Establishing an Association between the European Communities and Their Member States, of the One Part, and the Republic of Hungary, of the Other Part." *Official Journal L* 319.

———. 3492/93. 1993. "Council Regulation (EC) No. 3492/93 of 13 December 1993 on Certain Procedures for Applying the Europe Agreement Establishing an Association between the European Communities and Their Member States, of the One Part, and the Republic of Poland, of the Other Part." *Official Journal L* 319.

———. 519/94. 1994. "Council Regulation (EEC) No. 519/94 of 7 March 1994 on Common Rules for Imports from Certain Third Countries and Repealing Regulations (EEC) Nos. 1765/82, 1766/82 and 3420/83." *Official Journal L* 67.

———. 3382/94. 1994. "Council Regulation (EC) no 3382/94 of 19 December 1994 on Certain Procedures for Applying the Europe Agreement Establishing an Association between the European Communities and Their Member States, of the One Part, and Romania, of the Other Part." *Official Journal L* 368.

———. 3383/94. 1994. "Council Regulation (EC) no 3383/94 of 19 December 1994 on Certain Procedures for Applying the Europe Agreement Establishing an Association Between the European Communities and Their Member States, of the one part, and the Republic of Bulgaria, of the other part." *Official Journal L* 368.

———. 710/95. 1995. "Council Regulation (EC) no 710/95 of 27 March 1995 Imposing a Definitive Anti-dumping Duty on Imports of Colour Television Receivers Originating in Malaysia, the People's Republic of China, the Republic of Korea, Singapore and Thailand and Collecting Definitively the Provisional Duty Imposed." *Official Journal L* 73.

———. 1006/95. 1995. "Council Regulation (EC) no 1006/95 of 3 May 1995 Amending Regulation (EEC) no 3433/91 in so far as it Imposes a Definitive Anti-dumping Duty on Imports of Gas-fuelled, Non-refillable Pocket Flint Lighters Originating in the People's Republic of China." *Official Journal L* 101.

———. 2022/95. 1995. "Council Regulation (EC) no 2022/95 of 16 August 1995 Imposing a Definitive Anti-dumping Duty on Imports of Ammonium Nitrate Originating in Russia." *Official Journal L* 198.

———. 1347/96. 1996. "Council Regulation (EC) No. 1347/96 of 2 July 1996 Imposing Definitive Anti-dumping Duties on Imports of Unwrought Magnesium Originating in Russia and Ukraine and Collecting Definitively the Provisional Duty Imposed." *Official Journal L* 174.

———. 384/96. 1996. "Council Regulation (EEC) No. 384/96 of 22 December 1995 on Protection Against Dumped Imports from Countries not Members of the European Community." *Official Journal L* 56.

———. 119/97. 1997. "Council Regulation (EC) No. 119/97 of 20 January 1997 Imposing Definitive Anti-dumping Duties on Imports of Certain Ring Binder Mechanisms Originating in Malaysia and the People's Republic of China and Collecting Definitively the Provisional Duties Imposed." *Official Journal L* 22.

Council Reg. No. 85/143/EEC. 1567/97. 1997. "Council Regulation (EC) No. 1567/97 of 1 August 1997 Imposing a Definitive Anti-dumping Duty on Imports of Leather Handbags Originating in the People's Republic of China and Terminating the Proceedings Concerning Imports of Plastic and Textile Handbags Originating in the People's Republic of China." *Official Journal L* 208.

———. 1786/97. 1997. "Council Regulation (EC) No. 1786/97 of 15 September 1997 Amending Regulation (EC) No. 821/94 Imposing a Definitive Anti-dumping Duty on Imports of Silicon Carbide Originating, inter alia, in the Ukraine." *Official Journal L* 254.

———. 2320/97. 1997. "Council Regulation (EEC) No. 2320/97 of 17 November 1997 Imposing Definitive Anti-dumping Duties on Imports of Certain Seamless Pipes and Tubes of Iron or Non-alloy Steel Originating in Hungary, Poland, Russia, the Czech Republic, Romania and the Slovak Republic, repealing Regulation (EEC) No. 1189/93 and Terminating the Proceeding in Respect of such Imports Originating in the Republic of Croatia." *Official Journal L* 322.

———. 449/98. 1998. "Council Regulation (EC) No. 449/98 of 23 February 1998 Amending Regulation (EEC) No. 3068/92 in Respect of Definitive Anti-dumping Duties on Imports of Potassium Chloride Originating in Belarus, Russia and Ukraine." *Official Journal L* 58.

———. 467/98. 1998. "Council Regulation (EC) No. 467/98 of 23 February 1998 Imposing a Definitive Anti-dumping Duty on Imports of Certain Footwear with Uppers of Leather or Plastics Originating in the People's Republic of China, Indonesia, and Thailand." *Official Journal L* 60.

———. 495/98. 1998. "Council Regulation (EC) No. 495/98 of 23 February 1998 Imposing a Definitive Anti-dumping Duty on Imports of Ferro-Silico-Manganese Originating in the People's Republic of China, Amending Regulation (EC) No. 2413/95 in Respect of Anti-dumping Measures Concerning Imports of Ferro-silico-manganese originating in Ukraine and Terminating the Proceeding in Respect of Imports of Ferro-Silico-Manganese Originating in Brazil, South Africa and Russia." *Official Journal L* 62.

———. 904/98. 1998. "Council Regulation (EC) No. 904/98 of 27 April 1998 Imposing Definitive Anti-dumping Duties on Imports into the Community of Personal Fax Machines Originating in the People's Republic of China, Japan, the Republic of Korea, Malaysia, Singapore, Taiwan, and Thailand." *Official Journal L* 128.

———. 905/98. 1998. "Council Regulation (EC) No. 905/98 of 27 April 1998 Amending Regulation (EC) No. 384/96 on Protection Against Dumped Imports from Countries not Members of the European Community." *Official Journal L* 128.

———. 2402/98. 1998. "Council Regulation (EEC) No. 2402/98 of 3 November 1998 Imposing a Definitive Anti-Dumping Duty on Imports of Unwrought Unalloyed Magnesium Originating in the People's Republic of China and Definitively Collecting the Provisional Duty Imposed." *Official Journal L* 298.

———. 192/1999. 1999. "Council Regulation (EC) No. 192/1999 of 25 January 1999 Extending the Definitive Anti-Dumping Duty, Imposed by Regulation (EC) No. 3433/911 on Imports of Gas Fuelled, Non-Refillable Pocket Flint Lighters Originating in the People's Republic of China." *Official Journal L* 22.

———. 194/1999. 1999. "Council Regulation (EC) No. 194/1999 of 25 January 1999 Imposing Definitive Anti-Dumping Duties on Imports of Hardboard Originating in Bulgaria, Estonia, Latvia, Lithuania, Poland and Russia and Definitively Collecting the Provisional Duties Imposed." *Official Journal L* 22.

———. 603/1999. 1999. "Council Regulation (EC) No. 603/1999 of 15 March 1999 Imposing a Definitive Anti-Dumping Duty on Imports of Polypropylene Binder or Baler Twine Originating in Poland, the Czech Republic and Hungary, and Collecting Definitively the Provisional Duty Imposed." *Official Journal L* 075.

————. 1334/1999. 1999. "Council Regulation (EC) No. 1334/1999 of 21 June 1999 Imposing a Definitive Anti-Dumping Duty on Imports of Magnesium Oxide Originating in the People's Republic of China." *Official Journal L* 159.

————. 1100/2000. 2000. "Council Regulation (EC) No. 1100/2000 of 22 May 2000 Imposing Definitive Anti-Dumping Duties on Imports of Silicon Carbide Originating in the People's Republic of China, the Russian Federation, and the Ukraine and Prolonging the Undertakings Accepted by the Commission 94/202/EC." *Official Journal L* 125.

————. 2011/2000. 2000. "Council Regulation (EEC) No. 2011/2000 of 18 September 2000 Imposing a Definitive Anti-Dumping Duty on Imports of Flurospar Originating in the People's Republic of China." *Official Journal L* 241.

————. 2238/2000. 2000. "Council Regulation (EEC) No. 2238/2000 of 9 October 2000 Amending Regulation (EC) No. 384/96 on Protection against Dumped Imports from Countries Not Members of the European Community." *Official Journal L* 257.

————. 2570/2000. 2000. "Council Regulation (EEC) No. 2570/2000 of 20 November 2000 Amending Regulation (EC) No. 393/98 Imposing a Definitive Anti-Dumping Duty on Imports of Stainless Steel Fasteners and Parts Thereof Originating, Inter Alia, in the People's Republic of China." *Official Journal L* 297.

————. 2605/2000. 2000. "Council Regulation (EEC) No. 2605/2000 of 27 November 2000 Imposing Definitive Anti-Dumping Duties on Imports of Certain Electronic Weighing Scales (REWS) Originating in the People's Republic of China, the Republic of Korea, and Taiwan." *Official Journal L* 301.

————. 299/2001. 2001. "Council Regulation (EEC) No. 299/2001 of 12 February 2001 Imposing a Definitive Anti-Dumping Duty on Imports of Potassium Permanganate Originating in the People's Republic of China." *Official Journal L* 44.

————. 950/2001. 2001. "Council Regulation (EEC) No. 950/2001 of 14 May 2001 Imposing a Definitive Anti-Dumping Duty on Imports of Certain Aluminum Foil Originating in the People's Republic of China and Russia." *Official Journal L* 134, 17/05/01, 0001–0017.

————. 92/2002. 2002. "Council Regulation (EEC) No. 92/2002 of 17 January 2002 Imposing Definitive Anti-Dumping Duty and Collecting Definitively the Provisional Anti-Dumping Duty on Imports of Urea Originating in Belarus, Bulgaria, Croatia, Estonia, Libya, Lithuania, Romania, and the Ukraine." *Official Journal L* 17 19/01/2002, 0001–0017.

————. 215/2002. 2002. "Council Regulation (EEC) No. 215/2002 of 28 January 2002 Imposing Definitive Anti-Dumping Duties on Imports of Ferromolybdenum Originating in the People's Republic of China." *Official Journal L* 35 06/02/2002, 0001–0008.

————. 658/2002. 2002. "Council Regulation (EEC) No. 658/2002 of 15 April 2002 Imposing a Definitive Anti-Dumping Duty on Imports of Ammonium Nitrate Originating in Russia." *Official Journal L* 102 18/04/2002, 0001–0011.

————. 1531/2002. 2002. "Council Regulation (EC) No. 1531/2002 of 14 August 2002 Imposing Definitive Anti-Dumping Duty on Imports of Colour Television Receivers Originating in the People's Republic of China, the Republic of Korea, Malaysia and Thailand and Terminating the Proceeding Regarding Imports of Colour Television Receivers Originating in Singapore." *Official Journal L* 231, 29/08/2002, 0001–0028.

————. 1972/2002. 2002. "Council Regulation (EC) No. 1972/2002 of 5 November 2002 Amending Regulation (EC) No. 384/96 on the Protection against Dumped Imports from Countries Not Members of the European Community." *Official Journal L* 305, 07/11/02.

————. 151/2003. 2003. "Council Regulation (EEC) No. 151/2003 of 27 January 2003 Imposing a Definitive Anti-Dumping Duty on Imports of Certain Grain Oriented Electrical Sheets Originating in Russia." *Official Journal L* 25, 30/01/2003, 0007–0020.

Council Reg. No. 2229/2003. 2003. "Council Regulation (EEC) No. 2229/2003 of 22 December 2003 Imposing a Definitive Anti-Dumping Duty and Collecting Definitively the Provisional Duty on Imports of Silicon Originating in Russia." *Official Journal* L 339, 24/12/2003, 0003–0013.

———. 398/2004. 2004. "Council Regulation (EEC) No. 398/2004 of 2 March 2004 Imposing a Definitive Anti-Dumping Duty on Imports of Silicon Originating in the People's Republic of China." *Official Journal* L 66, 04/03/2004, 0015–0030.

———. 1095/2005. 2005. "Council Regulation (EC) No. 1095/2005 of 12 July 2005 Imposing a Definitive Anti-Dumping Duty on Imports of Bicycles Originating in Vietnam, and Amending Regulation (EC) No. 1524/2000 Imposing a Definitive Anti-Dumping Duty on Imports of Bicycles Originating in the People's Republic of China." *Official Journal* L 183, 12/07/05, 1–36.

———. 1891/2005. 2005. "Council Regulation (EC) No. 1891/2001 of 14 November 2005 Amending Regulation (EEC) No. 3068/92 Imposing a Definitive Anti-Dumping Duty on Imports of Potassium Chloride Originating in Belarus, Russia or Ukraine." *Official Journal* L S, 19/11/2005, 0014–0021.

Czech News Agency. 2000a. "Developing Countries Can't Adopt Advanced Norms at Once." *Financial Times Information*, September 22.

———. 2000b. "Ministry Imposes 13% Anti-Dumping Duty on German Salt Imports." *Financial Times Information*, October 20.

Deardorff, Alan. 1995. "The General Validity of the Law of Comparative Advantage." in *International Trade*, ed. J. Neary. Aldershot, UK: Edward Elgar Publishing, 114–130.

Delovoi Peterburg. 2003. "Russia Still Main Buyer of American Poultry," *Ria Oreanda/Economic Press Review in Lexis-Nexis*. November 6.

Department of Treasury. 1977a. "Memorandum to Lynn Barden, Department of Treasury, from Ted Hume, RE: Consideration of Sales Below Cost in State-Controlled Economy Anti-dumping Case." Washington, DC.

———, 1977b. "Memorandum to Robert Mundheim, from Peter Suchman, Department of the Treasury, Office of the General Counsel, Re: Appraisement of Polish Golf Carts." Washington, DC.

———. 1978. "Petition Pursuant to 516 (a) of the Tariff Act of 1930 and Request for Procedural Relief, Filed Before the Commissioner of Customs, U.S. Department of Treasury." Washington, DC.

Duncan, Raymond, and Carolyn McGiffert Ekedahl. 1990. *Moscow and the Third World Under Gorbachev*. Boulder: Westview Press.

Economist. 1999. "Unfair Protection: Protectionism Is on the Rise in a New Guise: Antidumping Cases Are Multiplying in America, Europe and Around the World." *The Economist*. November 7, 75.

———. 2000. "Finance and Economics: For the Byrds." *The Economist*. October 19, 88.

———. 2005a. "Special Report: America and Change." *The Economist*. September 3, 24–26.

———. 2005b. "Why Cultural Biases May Be the Ultimate Trade Barrier." *The Economist*, July 21, <http://www.economist.com/finance/displayStory.cfm?story_id=4199095>Accessed 07/30/ 2005.

Ehrenhaft, Peter, Brian Veron Hindley, Constantine Michalopoulos, and L. Alan Winters. 1997. *Policies on Imports from Economies in Transition: Two Case Studies*. Washington, DC: World Bank.

Eichengreen, Barry, and Richard Kohl. 1998. "The External Sector, the State, and Development in Eastern Europe." in *Enlarging Europe: The Industrial Foundations of a New Political Reality*, ed. John Zysman and Andrew Schwartz. Berkeley: University of California Press, 169–201.

Estonian News Agency. 2001. "Government Approves Anti-Dumping Laws." *Financial Times Information*, April 10.

Europe Information Service. 2000a. "EU/Japan/Taiwan/Russia/China: Special Market Status in Anti-Dumping Cases Confirmed for Russia and China." *European Report*, Section No. 2534.

———. 2000b. "EU/Russia/China: Just One in 10 Companies Benefit from New Dumping Rules." *European Report*, Section No. 2513.

———. 2000c. "Trade Policy: Report Concedes Burst in Anti-Dumping and Anti-Subsidy Measures." *European Report*, April 19.

———. 2005. "Commission Rebuffs British Push for Chinese Market-Economy Status." *European Report*, July 16.

European Coal and Steel Committee. 1991. "Resolution of the European Coal and Steel Committee Consultative Committee on the Association Agreements with Countries of Central and Eastern Europe (Adopted Unanimously at the 292nd Session Held on 7 June 1991)." *Official Journal C* 197.

European Commission. 1983. *First annual report of the Commission to the European Communities on the Community's anti-dumping and anti-subsidy activities (submitted to the Council and the European Parliament by the Commission)*. COM(83) 519 Final. Brussels.

———. 1984. *Second annual report of the Commission of the European Communities to the European Parliament on the Community's anti-dumping and anti-subsidy activities*. COM(84) 721 Final. Brussels.

———. 1986. *Third annual report of the Commission to the European Parliament on the Community's anti-dumping and anti-subsidy activities*. COM(86) 308 Final. Brussels.

———. 1987. *Fourth annual report of the Commission to the European Parliament on the Community's anti-dumping and anti-subsidy activities*. COM (87) 178 Final. Brussels.

———. 1989. *Sixth annual report of the Commission on the Community's anti-dumping and anti-subsidy activities*. COM(89) 106 Final. Brussels.

———. 1990. *Seventh annual report of the Commission on the Community's anti-dumping and anti-subsidy activities*. COM(90) 229 Final. Brussels.

———. 1995. *Twelfth annual report from the Commission to the European Parliament on the Community's anti-dumping and anti-subsidy activities(1993)*. COM(95) 16 Final. Brussels.

———. 1996. *Fifteenth Annual Report from the Commission to the European Parliament on the Community's Anti-Dumping and Anti-Subsidy Activities*. Brussels. <http:trade-infor.ece.eu.int/doclib/cfm/doclib-results.cfm>, Accessed 06/6/2006.

———. 1997a. "Communication from the Commission to the Council and the European Parliament on the Treatment of Former Non-Market Economies in Anti-dumping Proceedings and a Proposal for a Council Regulation Amending Council Regulation (EC) No 384/96." Brussels.

———. 1997b. *Sixteenth Annual Report from the Commission to the European Parliament on the Community's Anti-dumping and Anti-subsidy Activities*. Brussels.

———. 1998a. "Building a Comprehensive Partnership with China." *Communication from the Commission*. March 25, 1998, COM (1998) 181 Final. Brussels: Directorate General for Trade.

———. 1998b. *Seventeenth Annual Report from the Commission to the European Parliament on The Community's Anti-Dumping and Anti-Subsidy Activities*. Brussels: European Union.

———. 1999. *Eighteenth Annual Report from the Commission to the European Parliament on the Community's Anti-dumping and Anti-subsidy Activities*. Brussels.

———. 2000a. "Proposal for a Council Regulation amending Regulation (EC) No. 368/98 imposing a definitive anti-dumping Duty on imports of glyphosate originating in the People's Republic of China." *COM (2000) 269 Final*. Brussels.

———. 2000b. "Proposal for a Council Regulation Imposing a Definitive Anti-Dumping Duty on Imports of Bicycles Originating in the People's Republic of China." *COM (2000) 405 Final*. Brussels.

European Commission. 2000c. "Proposal for a Council Regulation imposing a Definitive Anti-Dumping Duty on Imports of Potassium Chloride Originating in Belarus, Russia, and Ukraine." *COM (2000) 249 Final*. Brussels.

———. 2000d. "Proposal for a Council Regulation Imposing a Definitive Duty and Collecting Definitively the Provisional Duties Imposed on Imports of Certain Malleable Cast Iron Tube or Pipe Fittings Originating in Brazil, the Czech Republic, Japan, the People's Republic of China, the Republic of Korea and Thailand." *COM (2000) 453 Final*. Brussels.

———. 2001a. *Anti-Dumping and Anti-Subsidy Statistics Covering the Year 2000*. Brussels.

———. 2001b. "EC Regional Trade Agreements." Brussels.

———. 2001c. "Proposal for a Council Regulation Imposing Definitive Anti-Dumping Duties on Imports of Urea Ammonium Nitrate Solutions Originating in Poland." *COM (2001) 203 Final*. Brussels.

———. 2001d. *Report from the Commission: Nineteenth Annual Report from the Commission to the European Parliament on the Community's Anti-Dumping and Anti-Subsidy Activities: Overview of the Monitoring of Third Country Anti-Dumping, Anti-Subsidy and Safeguard* Cases. COM (2001) 571 Final/2, 12.10.2001. Brussels.

———. 2002. *Report from the Commission: Twentieth Annual Report from the Commission to the European Parliament on the Community's Anti-Dumping and Anti-Subsidy Activities: Overview of the Monitoring of Third Country Anti-dumping, Anti-Subsidy and Safeguard* Cases. COM (2002) 484 Final/2, 27.09.2002. Brussels.

———. 2003. *Twenty-First Annual Report from the Commission to the European Parliament on the Community's Anti-Dumping, Anti-Subsidy and Safeguard Activities: Overview of the Monitoring of Third Country Anti-Dumping, Anti-Subsidy and Safeguard* Cases. COM (2003) 481 Final, 07.08.2003. Brussels.

———. 2004a. *Annex to the 22nd Annual Report from the Commission to the European Parliament on the Community's Anti-dumping, Anti-Subsidy and Safeguard Activities (2003)*. COM (2004) 828 Final, 27.12.2004. Brussels.

———. 2004b. "External Trade: Anti-dumping Measures." <http: //www.europa.eu/int/ scadplus/leg/en/lvb/r11005.htm.> Accessed 12/07/2004.

———. 2004c. "EU–Ukraine Relations." in *External Relations*. <http: www.europa.eu.int/ comm/external_relations/ukraine/intro/index.html.> Accessed 20/12/04.

European Commission. 2004. *Annex to the 22nd Annual Report from the Commission to the European Parliament on the Community's Anti-dumping, Anti-Subsidy and Safeguard Activities (2003)*. COM (2004) 828 Final, 27.12.2004. Brussels.

———. 2005. *Annex to the 23rd Annual Report from the Commission to the European Parliament on the Community's Anti-dumping, Anti-Subsidy and Safeguard Activities (2003)*. COM (2005) 360 Final, 03.08.2005. Brussels.

European Commission's Delegation to Albania. 2005. "EU Agreements with Albania." *The European Commission*. <http://www.delalb.cec.eu.int/en/eu_and_albania/introduction.htm.> Accessed 09/09/2005.

European Community. 1998a. "98/98/EC, ECSC, Euratom: Decision of the Council and the Commission of 19 December 1997 on the Conclusion of the Europe Agreement Establishing an Association between the European Communities and Their Member States, of the One Part, and the Republic of Latvia, of the Other Part." *Official Journal L 26*.

———. 1998b. "98/150/EC, ECSC, Euratom: Decision of the Council and the Commission of 19 December 1997 on the Conclusion of the Europe Agreement Establishing an Association between the European Communities and Their Member States, of the One Part, and the Republic of Lithuania, of the Other Part." *Official Journal L 51*.

———. 1998c. "98/180/EC, ECSC, Euratom: Decision of the Council and the Commission of 19 December 1997 on the Conclusion of the Europe Agreement Establishing an Association between the European Communities and Their Member States, of the One Part, and the Republic of Estonia, of the Other Part." *Official Journal L* 68.

European Council. 1999. "Conclusions of the European Council Meeting in Cologne, held on 3 and 4 June 1999: Annex II: Common Strategy of the European Union on Russia." *European Foreign Policy Bulletin* 04, June 99.

European Court of First Instance. 1996. "Climax Paper Converters Ltd. v Council of the European Union." *Case T-155/94* 18, September 1996.

European Court of Justice. 1991. "Eugen Noelle v Hauptzollamt Bremen-Freihafen."

European Information Service. 2004. "EU/UKRAINE: Lack of Market Economy Anti-Dumping Status Still Rankles." *European Report*, May 20.

European Parliament. 1996. "Written Question P-2790/96 by Pierluigi Castagnetti (PPE) to the Commission, Subject: Anti-Dumping Duties on Imports under Council Regulation (EEC) No. 3068/92." Brussels.

European Union. 1995. "White Paper: Preparation of the Associated Countries of Central and Eastern Europe for Integration into the Internal Market of the Union." Brussels: Belgium: European Commission.

Fairbanks, John King. 1986. *The Great Chinese Revolution: 1800–1985*. New York: Harper & Row.

Financial Times Information. 2004a. "Market Economy Status on Agenda." *Global News Wire/Business Daily Update*, April 21.

———. 2006. "Ukrainian Foreign Minister Welcomes Market-Economy Status," *BBC Monitoring International Reports*. February 17.

———. 2004b. "Russian Minister Says U.S. Chickens Not Up to Scratch." *Global News Wire/BBC Monitoring International Reports*, November 13.

Findlay, Ronald and Stanislaw Wellisz. 1982. "Endogenous Tariffs, the Political Economy of Trade Rrestrictions." in *Import Competition and Response*, ed. Jagdish Bhagwati. Chicago: University of Chicago Press, 223–244.

Fine, Frank. 1988. "EEC Antidumping: The Problem of Imports from State-Trading Countries." *Law and Policy in International Business* 20:91–107.

Finger, J. Michael. 1981. "The Industry-Country Incidence of 'Less than Fair Value' Cases in US Import Trade." *Quarterly Review of Economics and Business* 21:260–279.

———. 1991. "The Meaning of 'Unfair' in U.S. Import Policy." *Policy, Research, and External Affairs Working Papers: The World Bank*, August.

———. (Ed.). 1993. *Antidumping: How It Works and Who Gets Hurt*. Ann Arbor, MI: University of Michigan Press.

Finger, J.M., H. Keith Hall, and Douglas Nelson. 1982. "The Political Economy of Administered Protection." *The American Economic Review* 72:452–466.

Finger, J.M. and Tracy Murray. 1990. "Policing Unfair Imports: The United States Example." *Journal of World Trade* 24:39–54.

Frieden, Jeffrey. 1988. "Sectoral Conflict and Foreign Economic Policy." *International Organization*.

Gaddis, John Lewis. 1972. *The United States and the Origins of the Cold War, 1941–1947*. New York: Colombia University Press.

———. 1982. *Strategies of Containment: A Critical Appraisal of Postwar American National Security Policy*. Oxford: Oxford University Press.

Gambetta, Diego (Ed.). 1988. *Trust: Making and Breaking Cooperative Relations*. New York: Basil Blackwell.

Garret, Geoffrey, and Barry Weingast. 1993. "Ideas, Institutions and Interests: Constructing the European Community's International Market." in *Ideas and Foreign Policy: Beliefs, Institutions and Political Change*, ed. Judith Goldstein and Robert Keohane. Ithaca: Cornell University Press, 173–206.

General Agreement on Tariffs and Trade. 1970. "*Antidumping Legislation.*" Article VI.

———. 1994. "Council of Representatives of the GATT, December 1993-Resolution No. C/M/268."

George, Alexander. 1983. "The Causal Nexus between Cognitive Beliefs and Decision-Making Behavior." in *Psychological Models in International Relations*, ed. Falkowski. Boulder: Westview, 95–124.

Gerber, Alan, and Donald Green. 1999. "Misperceptions about Perceptual Bias." *Annual Review of Political Science* 2:189–210.

Gilpin, Robert. 1987. *The Political Economy of International Relations*. Princeton: Princeton University Press.

Goldgeier, J.M., and P.E. Tetlock. 2001. "Psychology and International Relations Theory." *Annual Review of Political Science* 4:67–92.

Goldstein, Judith. 1988. "Ideas, Institutions, and American Trade Policy." *International Organization* 42 (1):179–217.

———. 1993. *Ideas, Interests, and American Trade Policy*. Ithaca: Cornell University Press.

Goldstein, Judith, and Robert Keohane (Eds.). 1993. *Ideas and Foreign Policy: Beliefs, Institutions, and Political Change*. Ithaca: Cornell University Press.

Gorbachev, Mikhail. 1987. *Perestroika: New Thinking for Our Country and the World*. New York: Harper and Row Publishers.

Gore, Albert. 1995. "The United States and Russia: A Vision for the Future: Remarks at the U.S. Military Academy West Point, October 17, 1995." *U.S. Department of State Dispatch* 30 (6): 782–786.

Gourevitch, Peter. 1986. *Politics in Hard Times*. Ithaca: Cornell University Press.

Gowa, Joanne. 1994. *Allies, Adversaries, and International Trade*. Princeton: Princeton University Press.

Granik, Irina. 2002. "This Won't Do!" *Kommersant*, August 14.

Graziani, Giovanni. 1990. *Gorbachev's Economic Strategy in the Third World*. New York and Washington, DC: Praeger and the Center for Strategic and International Studies.

Gregory, Paul, and Robert Stuart. 1990. *Soviet Economic Structure and Performance*. New York: Harper Collins Publishers.

Greif, Avner. 1998. "Self-Enforcing Political Systems and Economic Growth: Late Medieval Genoa." in *Analytic Narratives*, ed. Robert Bates, Avner Greif, Margaret Levi, Jean-Laurent Rosenthal, and Barry Weingast. Princeton: Princeton University Press, 23–63.

Grieco, Joseph. 1993. "Anarchy and the Limits of Cooperation: A Realist Critique of the Newest Liberal Institutionalism." in *Neorealism and Neoliberalism: The Contemporary Debate*, ed. David Baldwin. New York: Columbia University Press, 301–338.

Haggard, Stephen. 1990. *Pathways from the Periphery*. Ithaca: Cornell University Press.

Haggard, Stephen, and Robert Kaufman. 1995. *The Political Economy of Democratic Transitions*. Princeton: Princeton University Press.

Hall, John. 1993. "Ideas and the Social Sciences." in *Ideas and Foreign Policy: Beliefs, Institutions, and Political Change*, ed. Judith Goldstein and Robert Keohane. Ithaca: Cornell University Press, 31–56.

Hall, Peter (Ed.). 1989. *The Political Power of Economic Ideas*. Princeton: Princeton University Press.

Hansen, Wendy. 1990. "The International Trade Commission and the Politics of Protectionism." *American Political Science Review* 84:21–46.

Hansen, Wendy, and Thomas Prusa. 1996. "Cumulation and ITC Decision-Making: The Sum of the Parts is Greater than the Whole." *Economic Inquiry* 34:746–769.

Hanson, Stephen. 1991. "Gorbachev: The Last True Leninist Believer?" in *The Crisis of Leninism and the Decline of the Left: The Revolutions of 1989*, ed. Daniel Chirot. Seattle: University of Seattle Press, 33–59.

Hardin, Russell. 1998. "Trust in Government." in *Trust in Governance*, ed. Valerie Braithwaite and Margaret Levi. New York: Russell Sage Foundation, 9–27.

Harris, Robert. 1993. "Goin' Down the Road Feeling Bad: U.S. Trade Laws' Discriminatory Treatment of the East European Economies in Transition to Capitalism." *Columbia Journal of Transnational Law* 31:403–446.

Haus, Leah. 1991. "The East European Countries and GATT: The Role of Realism, Mercantilism, and Regime Theory in Explaining East-West Trade Negotiations." *International Organization* 45:163–182.

Herzfeld and Rubin, P.C. 1992. "Letter to the Honorable Barbara Franklin, Secretary of Commerce, Re: Anti-Dumping Investigation of Cut-to-Length Carbon Steel Plate from Poland; Application for Classification of Poland as a Market Economy Country." Washington, DC: Department of Commerce, unpublished letter.

Hirschman, Albert. 1945. *National Power and the Structure of Foreign Trade*. Berkeley: University of California Press

Holmes, Peter, and Jeremy Kempton. 1996. "EU Anti-Dumping Policy: A Regulatory Perspective." *Journal of European Public Policy* 3:647–664.

Holzman, Franklyn. 1987a. "A Comparative View of Foreign Trade Behavior: Market versus Centrally Planned Economies." in *The Economics of Soviet Bloc Trade and Finance*. Boulder, CO: Westview Press, 91–112.

———. 1987b. "Dumping by Centrally Planned Economies: The Polish Golf Cart Case." in *The Economics of Soviet Bloc Trade and Finance*. Boulder: Westview Press, 121–136.

Hosking, Geoffrey. 1990. *The First Socialist Society: A History of the Soviet Union from Within*. Cambridge: Harvard University Press.

Hungarian News Agency. 2000. "Hungarian Cement Firms Initiate Anti-Dumping Procedures against CIS." *Financial Times Information*, September 8.

Ikenberry, John, David Lake, and Michael Mastanduno (Eds.). 1988. *The State and American Foreign Economic Policy*. Ithaca: Cornell University Press.

Ilina, N., A. Reut, A. Skogoreva. 2002. "We are Recognized." in *Gazeta*, as reproduced in *Lexis-Nexis*, August 22.

Inama, Stefano, and Edwin Vermulst. 1999. *Customs and Trade Laws of the European Community*. The Hague: Kluwer Law International.

Institute of Baltic Studies: Arts and Humanities. 2001. "The Baltics: Nationalities and Other Problems." <www.ibs.ee/ibs/history/baltics.html.> Accessed 06/20/2001.

Interfax News Agency. 1999. "Moscow Welcomes Canadian Decision on Russian Steel." *Interfax Russian News* August 5.

———. 2000. "Hungary Launches Anti-Dumping Inquiry in Relation to Russian Pipe." *Financial Times Information*, December 14.

———. 2001a. "Anti-Dumping Costs Russian Steel Makers." *Financial Times Information*, February 27.

———. 2001b. "Canada Slams Duty of 36% on Ukrainian Armature." *Financial Times Information*, February 5.

———. 2001c. "Russia Could Launch Anti-Dumping Investigation into U.S. Poultry." April 11.

———. 2001d. "Russian Government Using Protectionism to Support Domestic Market." April 22.

Interfax-Ukraine. 2005. "U.S. Trade Secretary Backs Market Economy Status for Ukraine." *BBC Worldwide Monitoring*, April 6.

International Trade Administration. 2005. "Questionnaire." in *Anti-dumping Manual*. Chapter 4. Washington, DC: U.S. Department of Commerce. <http://ia.ita.doc.gov/admanual/index.html.> Accessed 30/07/2005.

ITAR-TASS. 2000. "Russia to Discuss Its 'Non-Market' Status at Summit with EU." October 28.

Jackson, John. 1997. *The World Trading System*. Cambridge, MA: MIT Press.

Janos, Andrew. 2000. *East Central Europe in the Modern World*. Stanford: Stanford University Press.

Jervis, Robert. 1976. *Perception and Misperception in International Politics*. Princeton: Princeton University Press.

Jones, Bryan. 1994. *Reconceiving Decision-Making in Democratic Politics*. Chicago: University of Chicago Press.

————. 1996. "Attributes, Alternatives, and the Flow of Ideas: Information Processing in Politics." Seattle, University of Washington: Center for American Politics and Public Policy, unpublished manuscript.

————. 2001. *Politics and the Architecture of Choice: Bounded Rationality and Governance*. Chicago: University of Chicago Press.

Karatnycky, Adrian. 2005. "Ukraine's Orange Revolution," *Foreign Affairs* 84 (2):35–52.

Kennan, George. 1947. "The Sources of Soviet Conduct." *Foreign Affairs* 25:566–582.

Keohane, Robert. 1984. *After Hegemony: Cooperation and Discord in the World Political Economy*. Princeton: Princeton University Press.

Kindleberger, Charles. 1981. "Dominance and Leadership in the International Economy." *International Studies Quarterly* 25 (2):242–254.

Kornai, Janos. 1992. *The Socialist System: The Political Economy of Communism*. Princeton: Princeton University Press.

Krasner, Stephen. 1976. "State Power and the Structure of International Trade." *World Politics* 28:317–347.

Krueger, Anne (Ed.). 1996. *The Political Economy of American Trade Policy*. Chicago: University of Chicago Press.

Krugman, Paul, and Richard Baldwin. 1990. "Market Access and International Competition: A Simulation Study of 16K Random Access Memories." in *Rethinking International Trade*, ed. Paul Krugman. Cambridge, MA: MIT Press, 199–225.

Lake, David. 1988a. *Power, Protection, and Free Trade*. Ithaca: Cornell University Press.

————. 1988b. "The State and American Trade Strategy in the Pre-Hegemonic Era." in *The State and American Foreign Economic Policy*, ed. Ikenberry, Lake, and Mastanduno. Ithaca: Cornell University Press, 33–58.

Larson, Deborah Welch. 1985. *Origins of Containment: A Psychological Explanation*. Princeton: Princeton University Press.

————. 1997. *Anatomy of Mistrust*. Ithaca: Cornell University Press.

Laurent, Patrick. 1996. "Anti-Dumping Policies in a Globalizing World." Stockholm: European Commission: Directorate General for Trade. <http://europa.eu.int/comm/dg01/splaur01.html>, Accessed 12/3/1999.

Lenin, V.I. 1932. *State and Revolution*. New York: International Publishers.

————. 1939. *Imperialism: The Highest Stage of Capitalism*. New York: International Publishers.

Levi, Margaret. 1997. *Consent, Dissent, and Patriotism*. Cambridge: Cambridge University Press.

————. 1998. "A State of Trust." in *Trust and Governance*, ed. Valerie Braithwaite and Margaret Levi. New York: Russell Sage Foundation, 77–101.

Lipset, Seymour Martin. 1994. "The Social Requisites of Democracy Revisited: 1993 Presidential Address." *American Sociological Review* 59:1–22.

Lipton, David, and Jeffrey Sachs. 1990. "Creating a Market Economy in Eastern Europe: The Case of Poland." *Brookings Papers on Economic Activity* 1:75–133.

Lott, John Jr. 1995. "Are Government or Private Enterprises More Likely to Engage in Dumping? Some International Evidence." *Managerial and Decision Economics* 16:185–204.

Magee, Steven, William Brock, and Leslie Young. 1989. *Black Hole Tariffs and Endogenous Policy Theory*. Cambridge: Cambridge University Press.

Magelby, David, and Candice Nelson. 1990. *The Money Chase: Congressional Campaign Finance Reform*. Washington, DC: Brookings Institution.

Marcus, Randall. 1985. "An Argument for Freer Trade: The Nonmarket Economy Problem Under the U.S. Countervailing Duty Law." *International Law and Politics* 17:407–451.

Marer, Paul. 1984. "United States Market Disruption Procedures Involving Romanian and Other CPE Products, With Policy Recommendations." in *New Horizons in East-West Economic and Business Relations*, ed. Marvin Jackson and James Woodson. New York: Columbia University Press, 129–148.

Marvel, Howard, and Edward John Ray. 1996. "Countervailing Duties." *The Economic Journal* 105:1576–1593.

Marx, Karl, and Friedrich Engels. 1848/1978. "The Manifesto of the Communist Party." in *The Marx-Engels Reader*, ed. Robert Tucker. New York: W.W. Norton and Co., 469–500.

Mastanduno, Michael. 1992. *Economic Containment: CoCom and the Politics of East-West Trade*. Ithaca: Cornell University Press.

Mastanduno, Michael. 1993. "Do Relative Gains Matter? America's Response to Japanese Industrial Policy." in *Neorealism and Neoliberalism: The Contemporary Debate*, ed. David Baldwin. New York: Columbia University Press, 250–266.

McGregor, Richard, and Raphael Minder. 2005. "China to Lead Exports by 2010 Says OECD." *The Financial Times (London Edition)*, September 17, 6.

Meller, Paul. 2004. "EU Ruling Damages Beijing's Trade Status." *International Herald Tribune*, June 29, 15.

Menard, Scott. 1995. *Applied Logistic Regression Analysis*. Thousand Oaks, CA: Sage Publications.

Messerlin, Patrick. 1981. "The Political Economy of Protectionism: The Bureaucratic Case." *Weltwirtschaftliches Archiv* 117:469–496.

———. 2001. *Measuring the Costs of Economic Protection in Europe*. Washington, DC: Institute for International Economics.

Miller, Gary. 1992. *Managerial Dilemmas: The Political Economy of Hierarchy*. Cambridge: Cambridge University Press.

Milner, Helen. 1987. "Resisting the Protectionist Temptation: Industry and the Making of Trade Policy in France and the United States." *International Organization* 41(4) (Autumn):639–665..

———. 1997. *Interests, Institutions, and Information: Domestic Politics and International Relations*. Princeton: Princeton University Press.

Miranda, Jorge. 1996. "Should Antidumping Laws Be Dumped?" *Law & Policy in International Business* 28:255–288.

Moore, Michael. 1992. "Rules or Politics? An Empirical Analysis of ITC Anti-Dumping Decisions." *Economic Inquiry* 30:449–466.

Moscow Times. 2001. "EBRD and Severstal Slam West's Steel Suits." April 24.

Murrell, Peter. 1990. *The Nature of Socialist Economies: Lessons from Eastern European Foreign Trade*. Princeton, NJ: Princeton University Press.

Neeley, Jeffrey. 1989. "Nonmarket Economy Import Regulation: From Bad to Worse." *Law & Policy in International Business* 20:529–554.

Neuberger, Egon, and Juan Lara. 1977. *The Foreign Trade Practices of Centrally Planned Economies and Their Effects on U.S. International Competitiveness*. Washington, DC: National Planning Association.

Newsbase Russian Daily Bulletin. 1999. "Foreign Economic Affairs." *Financial Times Information*, October 12.

Nisbett, Richard, and Lee Ross. 1980. *Human Inference: Strategies and Shortcomings in Social Judgment.* Englewood Cliffs, NJ: Prentice Hall.

North, Douglass. 1990. *Institutions, Institutional Change, and Economic Performance.* Cambridge: Cambridge University Press.

———. 2005. *Understanding the Process of Economic Change.* Princeton: Princeton University Press.

Organisation for Economic Co-operation and Development. 1994. *Barriers to Trade with Economies in Transition.* Paris, France: OECD.

———. 1996. *Trade Policy and the Transition Process.* Paris: OECD Publications.

O'Grady, Mary Anastasia. 2004. "Antidumping Abuses Threaten the Gains in Global Free Trade." in Marc Miles, Kim Holmes. Mary Anastasia O'Grady, Ana Isabel Eiras, and Anthony Kim (Eds.). *2005 Index of Economic Freedom*: Washington, DC: The Heritage Foundation, 49–57.

O'Halloran, Sharyn. 1994. *Politics, Process, and American Trade Policy.* Ann Arbor, MI: University of Michigan Press.

Olechowski, Andrzej. 1990. "Chemicals from Poland: A Tempest in a Teacup." Washington, DC: World Bank.

Olson, Mancur. 1965. *The Logic of Collective Action.* Cambridge: Harvard University Press.

Ostrom, Elinor. 1990. *Governing the Commons.* Cambridge: Cambridge University Press.

Paterson, Thomas. 1973. *Soviet-American Confrontation: Postwar Reconstruction and the Origins of the Cold War.* Baltimore: Johns Hopkins University Press.

Plakans, Andrejs. 1995. *The Latvians.* Stanford: Hoover Institution Press.

Prestowitz, Clyde Jr. 1990. *Trading Places: How We Are Giving Our Future to Japan and How to Reclaim It.* New York: Basic Books.

Prusa, Thomas. 1992. "Why Are So Many Antidumping Petitions Withdrawn?" *Journal of International Economics* 33:1–20.

Przeworski, Adam. 1985. *Capitalism and Social Democracy.* Cambridge: Cambridge University Press.

———. 1991. *Democracy and the Market.* Cambridge: Cambridge University Press.

Ramet, Sabrina Petra. 1995. *Social Currents in Eastern Europe.* Durham: Duke University Press.

Raun, Toivo. 1991. *Estonia and the Estonians.* Stanford: Hoover Institution Press.

Rees, David. 1967. *The Age of Containment: The Cold War, 1945–1968.* London: St. Martin's Press.

RIA Novosti. 2006. "U. S. Granting of Market Status to Ukraine Symbolic." *RIA Novosti from Lexis-Nexis.* February 17.

Rogowski, Ronald. 1989. *Commerce and Coalitions.* Princeton: Princeton University Press.

Rueschmeyer, Dietrich, Evelyn Huber Stephens, and John Stephens. 1992. *Capitalist Development and Democracy.* Chicago: University of Chicago Press.

Russian Economic News. 1999a. "Anti-Dumping Measures Must be Abolished, Russians Say." *Financial Times Information*, September 22.

———. 1999b. "Tough Anti-dumping Limitations." *Financial Times Information* July 29.

Sachs, Jeffrey. 1993. *Poland's Jump to the Market Economy.* Cambridge, MA: MIT Press.

Sanger, David. 1998. "Clinton Warns U.S. Will Fight Cheap Imports." *The New York Times,* A1 and C4, November 11.

Santos, Leonard, and Thomas Vakerics. 1994. "Chinese Imports Face Tough Antidumping Rules." *The National Law Journal* 19:13.

Schattschneider, E.E. 1935. *Politics, Pressure, and the Tariff: A Study of Free Private Enterprise in Pressure Politics, as Shown in the 1929–1930 Revision of the Tariff.* Hamden, CT: Archon Book.

Schlesinger, Arthur. 1967. "Origins of the Cold War." *Foreign Affairs* 46:22–52.

Sheldon and Mark, L.L.P. 1992. "Letter to the Honorable William Daley, Secretary of Commerce, from Sheldon and Mark, L.L.P: Re: Anti-Dumping Investigation of Freshwater Crawfish Tail Meat from the People's Republic of China." Washington, DC: Department of Commerce, unpublished letter.

Sheldon and Mark Attorneys at Law. 1997. "Letter to the Honorable Michael Kantor, Secretary of Commerce Re: Anti-dumping Investigation of Freshwater Crawfish Tail Meat from the People's Republic of China." Washington, DC: Department of Commerce, unpublished letter, unpublished letter.

Shepsle, Kenneth, and Barry Weingast. 1987. "The Institutional Foundations of Committee Power." *American Political Science Review* 81 (1):85–104.

Simon, Herbert. 1955. "A Behavioral Model of Rational Choice." *The Quarterly Journal of Economics* 69:99–118.

Simon, Herbert. 1978. "Rationality as Process and as Product of Thought." *The American Economic Review* 68 (2):1–16.

———. 1985. "Human Nature in Politics: The Dialogue of Psychology with Political Science." *The American Political Science Review* 79:293–304.

Simons, Thomas. 1991. *Eastern Europe in the Postwar World*. New York: St Martin's Press.

Snidal, Duncan. 1993. "Relative Gains and the Pattern of International Cooperation." in *Neorealism and Neoliberalism: The Contemporary Debate*, ed. David Baldwin. New York: Columbia University Press, 170–208.

Sokolova, Veronika. 2001. "Why All This Mud-Slinging against Russia?" *Moscow News*. March 21.

Staiger, Robert. 1995. "A Theory of Gradual Trade Liberalization." in *New Directions in Trade Theory*, ed. Jim Levisohn, Alan Deardorff, and Robert Stern. Ann Arbor, MI: University of Michigan, 249–284.

Staiger, Robert, and Frank Wolak. 1994a. "Measuring Industry-Specific Protection: Antidumping in the United States." in *Brookings Papers: Microeconomics*. Washington, DC: Brookings Institution.

———. 1994b. "The Trade Effects of Antidumping Investigations: Theory and Evidence." in *Analytical and Negotiating Issues in the Global Trading System*, ed. Alan Deardorff and Robert Stern. Ann Arbor, MI: University of Michigan Press,: 231–259.

States News Service. 2005. "Congressman Davis Reacts to Thomas/English Compromise." *States News Service in Lexis-Nexis*, July 15.

———. 2006. "Graduation of Ukraine to Market Economy Status," *States News Service in Lexis-Nexis*. February 19.

Stern, Robert (Ed.). 1987. *U.S. Trade Policies in a Changing World Economy*. Cambridge, MA: MIT Press.

Stewart, T. 1991. "Administration of the Anti-Dumping Law: A Different Perspective." in *Down in the Dumps: Administration of the Unfair Trade Laws*, ed. Richard Boltuck and Robert Litan. Washington, DC: Brookings Institution, 288–330.

Stigler, George. 1971. "The Theory of Economic Regulation." *Bell Journal of Economics and Management Science* 2:3–21.

Stone, William, and Paul Schaffner. 1988. *The Psychology of Politics*. New York: Springer-Verlag.

Stratmann, Thomas. 1991. "What Do Campaign Contributions Buy? Deciphering Causal Effects of Money and Votes." *Southern Economic Journal* 57:606–620.

Talbott, Strobe (Ed.). 1974. *Khrushchev Remembers: The Last Testament*. Boston: Little, Brown and Company.

Tetlock, Philip. 1998. "Social Psychology and World Politics." in *Handbook of Social Psychology*, Daniel Gilbert, Susan Fiske, and Gardner Lindzey (Eds.). New York: Oxford University Press, 868–912.

———. 1999. "Theory-Driven Reasoning about Possible Pasts and Probably Futures: Are We Prisoners of Our Preconceptions?" *American Journal of Political Science* 43:335–366.

Tharakan, P.K.M. 1999. "Is Anti-Dumping Here to Stay?" *World Economy* 22:179–206.

Tharakan, P.K.M, David Greenaway, and Joe Tharakan. 1998. "Cumulation and Injury Determination of the European Community in Antidumping Cases." *Weltwirtschaftliches Archiv* 134:320–339.

Thornhill, John. 1997. "Russia Snubs EU Over Trade Discrimination." *The Financial Times*, June 18, 28.

Trefler, Daniel. 1993. "Trade liberalization and the Theory of Endogenous Protection: An Econometric Study of U.S. Import Policy." *Journal of Political Economy* 101:138–160.

Treisman, Daniel. 2000. "Blaming Russia First." *Foreign Affairs* 79(6):46–155.

Tversky, Amos, and Daniel Kahneman. 1974. "Judgment under Uncertainty: Heuristics and Biases." *Science* 185:1124–1131.

Ukrayinska Pravda. 2005. "Ukraine Hopes for UK Role in Obtaining Market Economy Status." *BBC Monitoring International Reports*, May 26.

U.S. Department of Commerce. 1998. Omnibus Trade and Competitiveness Act, 1998. Pub. L 100–418, 1316 (b), 102 Stat. 1107, 1187.

———. 2000a. "Statement of Policy Governing U.S. Department of Commerce Overseas Trade Missions." <http://osecnt13.osec.doc.gov/public.nsf/doc/trade-missions-policy.> Accessed 09/20/2000.

———. 2000b. "U.S. Commercial Relations with Russia and the NIS: The Road Traveled; The Road Ahead." *Remarks by Jan Kalicki, Counselor to the U.S. Department of Commerce before the World Affairs Council of Northern California*, June 20.

U.S. Department of Commerce International Trade Administration. 1991. *Summary of Procedures for Antidumping Fair Value Investigations under Title VII of the Tariff Act of 1930, As Amended.* Washington, DC: Department of Commerce.

———. 1998. *Anti-Dumping Manual.* Washington, DC: Department of Commerce. <http://ia.ita.doc.gov/admanual/index.html>, Accessed 11/8/1998 and 06/12/2006.

———. 2001. *An Introduction to U.S. Trade Remedies.* Washington, DC: Department of Commerce.

U.S. Fed News. 2005a. "Bill Toughens Trade Law with China, Rep. Camp Says," *U.S. Fed News*, July 28.

———. 2005b. "Rep. McHugh Fights for Manufacturers," *U.S. Fed News*, April 5.

U.S. International Trade Administration. 1996. "Memorandum for Edward Yang, Director AD/CVD Enforcement from David Mueller, Director Office of Policy, Re: Surrogate Country Selection: Freshwater Crawfish Tail Meat from the People's Republic of China." Washington, DC: Department of Commerce, unpublished internal memorandum.

———. 1997a. "Concurrence Memorandum Final: Anti-dumping Investigation of Freshwater Crawfish Tail Meat from the People's Republic of China." Washington, DC: Department of Commerce, unpublished internal memorandum.

———. 1997b. "Letter from Embassy of Ukraine to the Honorable William Haley, Secretary of Commerce, Re: Certain Cut-to-Length Carbon Steel Plate from Ukraine-Status Change." Washington, DC: Department of Commerce, unpublished letter.

———. 1997c. "Memorandum to Jacqueline Arrowsmith, International Trade Analyst, To Maureen Flannery, Program Manager AD/CVD Enforcement Re: Verification of Sales for Yancheng Foreign Trade Corporation in the Review of Freshwater Crawfish Tail Meat from the PRC." Washington, DC: Department of Commerce, unpublished internal memorandum.

———. 1997d. "Memorandum to the File from Elisabeth Urfer Case Analyst, Re: Telephone Conversation with the Commercial Department of the Embassy of Spain: Re: Crawfish Tail Meat from China." Washington, DC: Department of Commerce, unpublished internal memorandum.

———. 1998a. "Index of Factor Values for Other Non-Market Economy Countries." January 1998. <www.ita.doc.gov/IAFrameset.html.> Accessed 2001.

———. 1998b. "Memorandum to Robert S. LaRussa, Assistant Secretary for Import Administration from Joseph Spetrini, Deputy Assistant Secretary for Enforcement, Subject: Issues and Decision Memo for the Administrative Review of Sulfanilic Acid from the

People's Republic of China; Final Results." Washington, DC: Department of Commerce, unpublished internal memorandum.

————. 1999a. "Decision Memorandum from Bernard Carreau, Deputy Assistant Secretary AD/CVD Enforcement, to Robert S. LaRussa, Assistant Secretary Import Administration, Subject: Anti-dumping Duty Determinations on Cold-Rolled Carbon-Quality Steel Products from the Slovak Republic—Market vs. Non-market Economy Analysis." Washington, DC: Department of Commerce, unpublished internal memorandum.

————. 1999b. "Decision Memorandum from John Brinkman, Program Manager to Robert S. LaRussa, Assistant Secretary Import Administration, Subject: Anti-Dumping Investigation of Certain Small Diameter Carbon and Alloy Seamless Standard Line and Pressure Pipe from the Czech Republic: Non Market Economy Country Status." Washington, DC: Department of Commerce, unpublished internal memorandum.

————. 1999c. "Memorandum to David Mueller, Director AD/CVD Enforcement from Jeff May, Director Office of Policy, Re: Certain Small Diameter Pipe from the Czech Republic: NME Country Status and Surrogate Country Selection." Washington, DC: Department of Commerce, unpublished internal memorandum.

————. 1999d. "Memorandum to Rick Johnson, Director AD/CVD Enforcement from Jeff May, Director Office of Policy, Re: Solid Fertilizer Grade Ammonium from the Russian Federation: Nonmarket Economy Status and Surrogate Country Selection." Washington, DC: Department of Commerce, unpublished internal memorandum.

————. 1999e. "Memorandum to Troy Cribb, Acting Assistant Secretary for Import Administration, from: Richard W. Moreland Deputy Assistant Secretary for Import Administration, Subject: Issues and Decision Memorandum for the Investigation of Sales at Less than Fair Value of Synthetic Indigo from the People's Republic of China." Washington, DC: Department of Commerce, unpublished internal memorandum.

————. 2000a. "Decision Memorandum from Jeffrey May, Director Office of Policy, to Robert S. LaRussa, Assistant Secretary for Import Administration, on Issues and Decision Memo for the Sunset Review of Uranium from Russia; Preliminary Results." Washington, DC: Department of Commerce, unpublished internal memorandum.

————. 2000b. "Decision Memorandum from Joseph A. Spetrini to Robert S. LaRussa on Market vs. Non-Market Economy Analysis of the Republic of Hungary." Washington, DC: Department of Commerce, unpublished internal memorandum.

————. 2000c. "Letter to White and Case L.L.P. on behalf of their client Nova Hut Requesting Information, Re: Certain Small Diameter Carbon and Alloy Seamless Standard, Line and Pressure Pipe from the Czech Republic." Washington, DC: Department of Commerce, unpublished internal memorandum.

————. 2000d. "Memorandum to Gary Taverman, Director AD/CVD Enforcement from Jeff May, Director Office of Policy, Re: Anti-dumping Duty Investigation of Steel Concrete Reinforcing Bars from the People's Republic of China: Nonmarket Economy Status and Surrogate Country Selection." Washington, DC: Department of Commerce, unpublished internal memorandum.

————. 2000e. "Memorandum to Holly Kuga, Acting Deputy Assistant Secretary AD/CVD Enforcement, from Magd Zalok, Import Compliance Specialist, Re: Anti-Dumping Duty Investigation of Certain Small Diameter Carbon and Alloy Seamless Standard, Line and Pressure Pipe from Romania, Whether the Seamless Pipe Industry in Romania Should be Treated as a Market-Oriented Industry." Washington, DC: Department of Commerce, unpublished internal memorandum.

———— 2000f. "Memorandum to Robert S. LaRussa, Assistant Secretary for Import Administration from Jeffrey May, Director Office of Policy, Subject: Issues and Decision Memo for the Sunset Review of Uranium from Russia; Preliminary Results." Washington, DC: Department of Commerce, unpublished internal memorandum.

———. 2000g. "Memorandum to Troy Cribb, Acting Assistant Secretary for Import Administration from: Holly Kuga Acting Deputy Assistant Secretary for Import Administration, Subject: Anti-dumping Investigation of Certain Small Diameter Carbon and Alloy Seamless Standard, Line, and Pressure Pipe from the Czech Republic; Respondent's Request for Rescission of Initiation." Washington, DC: Department of Commerce, unpublished internal memorandum.

———. 2000h. "Memorandum to Troy Cribb, Acting Assistant Secretary for Import Administration from: Holly Kuga Acting Deputy Assistant Secretary for Import Administration, Subject: Issues and Decision Memorandum for the Anti-Dumping Investigation of Cold-Rolled Flat-Rolled Carbon Quality Steel Products from Slovakia." Washington, DC: Department of Commerce, unpublished internal memorandum.

———. 2001. "Memorandum to Louis Apple, Director AD/CVD Enforcement from Jeff May, Director Office of Policy, Re: Anti-Dumping Duty Investigation on Pure Magnesium from the Russian Federation: NME Country Status and Surrogate Country Selection." Washington, DC: Department of Commerce, unpublished internal memorandum.

———. 2002a. "Memorandum to Faryar Shirzad, Assistant Secretary for Import Administration from Joseph Spetrini, Deputy Assistant Secretary Import Administration, Subject: Issues and Decision Memorandum for the Antidumping Investigation of Carbon and Certain Alloy Steel Wire Rod from Moldova: Moldova Steel Works (MSW)." A-841–805, August 23, 2002. Washington, DC: Department of Commerce, unpublished internal memorandum.

———. 2002b. "Memorandum to Faryar Shirzad, Assistant Secretary for Import Administration from Richard Moreland, Deputy Assistant Secretary Import Administration, Subject: Issues and Decision Memorandum for the Final Determination in the Countervailing Duty Investigation of Sulfanilic Acid from Hungary." C-437–805, September 18, 2002. Washington, DC: Department of Commerce, unpublished internal memorandum.

———. 2003a. "Expected Wages of Selected Non-Market Economy Countries, 2001 Income Data, Revised September 2003." Updated February 10, 2004. <http://ia.ita.doc.gov/wages/01wages/01wages.html.> Accessed 12/30/04.

———. 2003b. "Market or Non-Market Economy Country Designations." *Import Administration Policy Bulletin*, 03.1. February 28, 2003.

———. 2003c. "Memorandum to Faryar Shirzad, Assistant Secretary for Import Administration from Joseph Spetrini, Deputy Assistant Secretary Import Administration, Subject: Issues and Decision Memorandum for the Less-than-Fair-Value Investigation of Silicon Metal from the Russian Federation." A-821–817, February 3, 2003. Washington, DC: Department of Commerce, unpublished internal memorandum.

———. 2004a. "Memorandum to James Jochum, Assistant Secretary for Import Administration from Jeffrey May, Deputy Assistant Secretary Import Administration, Subject: Issues and Decision Memorandum for the Less-than-Fair-Value Investigation of Bedroom Furniture from the People's Republic of China." A-570–890, November 17, 2004. Washington, DC: Department of Commerce, unpublished internal memorandum.

———. 2004b. "Non-Market Economy Surrogate Selection Process." *Import Administration Policy Bulletin*, No. 04.1: March 1, 2004. <http://ia.ita.doc.gov/policy/bull04–1.html.> Accessed 30/12/04.

U.S. International Trade Commission. 1995. "The Economic Effects of Anti-Dumping and Countervailing Duty Orders and Suspension Agreements." Washington, DC: U.S. International Trade Commission.

———. 2000. *U.S. Anti-Dumping and Countervailing Duty Data: Current through December 31, 1999.* Washington, DC: U.S. International Trade Commission.

Union des Confederations de l'industrie et Employeurs d'Europe. 1996. "Position on the Commission's (DG I) Proposals Regarding Implementation of the Anti-Dumping Regulation vis-a-vis State Trading Countries and CEECs." *UNICE Presse*, November 21.

United States Senate Committee on Finance, Subcommittee on International Trade. 1984. *Non-Market Economy Imports Legislation.* Washington, DC: U.S. Government Printing Office.

Vandenbussche, Hylke. 1996. "Is European Antidumping Protection against Central Europe Too High?" *Weltwirtschaftliches Archiv* 132:116–138.

Viner, Jacob. 1923. *Dumping: A Problem in International Trade.* Chicago: University of Chicago Press.

VNA News Agency. 2005 "Vietnam Europe Trade, Investment Working Group Meets in Hanoi." *BBC Worldwide Monitoring*, April 24.

Wares, William. 1977. *The Theory of Dumping and American Commercial Policy.* Lexington, MA: D.C. Heath and Company.

Weingast, Barry, and Mark Moran. 1983. "Bureaucratic Discretion of Congressional Control? Regulatory Policymaking by the Federal Trade Commission." *Journal of Political Economy* 91:765–800.

White and Case Law Firm. 2000a. "Letter to the Honorable William Daley, Secretary of Commerce, Re: Certain Small Diameter Carbon and Alloy Seamless Standard, Line and Pressure Pipe from the Czech Republic." Washington, DC: U.S. Department of Commerce, International Trade Administration, unpublished letter.

———. 2000b. "Rebuttal Brief of JSC Nevinnomyssky Azot and Transammonia, Inc., Re: Solid Fertilizer Grade Ammonium Nitrate from the Russian Federation." Washington, DC: U.S. Department of Commerce, International Trade Administration, unpublished letter.

Wilczynski, Jozef. 1969. *The Economics and Politics of East-West Trade.* New York: Frederick Praeger.

Willkie, Wendell L. 1990. "The 1988–89 Department of Commerce Study on the People's Republic of China and Its Implications for Economies 'In Transition.' " Washington, DC: Practising Law Institute.

Winters, Alan, Marc Rubin, and Andrew Bond. 1998. "Antidumping Action on American Imports from Russia." *Post-Soviet Geography and Economics* 39:183–224.

World Trade Organization. 1994. *WTO Anti-Dumping Agreement: Agreement on Implementation of Article VI of the General Agreement on Tariffs and Trade 1994.* Geneva: WTO.

———. 2004. "WTO Membership." <http://www.wto.org/english/thewto_e/whatis_e/if_e/org6_e.htm.> Accessed 30/12/04.

Xinhua News Agency. 2005. "OECD Official Acknowledges China's Market Economy Status." *Xinhua General News Service*, September 16.

INDEX